Second Edition

The Accidental Systems Librarian

Second Edition

The
Accidental
Systems
Librarian

Nicole C. Engard
With Rachel Singer Gordon

Information Today, Inc.
Medford, New Jersey

First Printing, 2012

The Accidental Systems Librarian, **Second Edition**

Library of Congress Cataloging-in-Publication Data

Engard, Nicole C., 1979-
    The accidental systems librarian / Nicole C. Engard with Rachel Singer
Gordon. -- 2nd ed.
      p. cm.
    Includes index.
    ISBN 978-1-57387-453-3
    1. Systems librarians. I. Gordon, Rachel Singer. II. Title.
  Z682.4.S94E54 2012
  025.00285--dc23

                                                            2012027930

Printed and bound in the United States of America

President and CEO: Thomas H. Hogan, Sr.
Editor-in-Chief and Publisher: John B. Bryans
VP Graphics and Production: M. Heide Dengler
Managing Editor: Amy M. Reeve
Editorial Assistant: Brandi Scardilli
Cover Designer: Ashlee Caruolo
Copyeditor: Barbara Brynko
Proofreader: Beverly Michaels
Indexer: Kathleen Rocheleau

www.infotoday.com

For my husband,
the best man I know

Contents

Acknowledgments

As with systems librarianship, writing a book is a less-than-solitary endeavor. I would like to thank the many library professionals who took time from their busy schedules to answer survey questions and to participate in interviews, sharing their expertise and experiences with fellow systems librarians. Thanks also to the readers of the first edition of this book for making it a success and facilitating the need for a second edition.

I would also like to extend my gratitude to Rachel Singer Gordon for having the faith in my abilities to update this work for the next generation of systems librarians. Without Rachel's constant encouragement, I would have never thought to take on such a task.

About the Website

tasl.web2learning.net

As a systems librarian, you know that your job—and the resources you use to carry out your duties successfully—are constantly changing. While this book references a number of useful websites for systems personnel in all types of libraries, the nature of the web means that pages move, sites change, and new and helpful resources are constantly emerging.

The website, available to you as a valued reader of *The Accidental Systems Librarian*, will keep you apprised of these changes, updating links and adding new resources and articles of interest to systems librarians. Please feel free to email your comments, changes, or additions to nengard@gmail.com.

Disclaimer

Neither the publisher nor the author make any claim as to the results that may be obtained through the use of this website or of any of the internet resources it references or links to. Neither publisher nor author will be held liable for any results, or lack thereof, obtained by the use of this site or any of its links; for any third-party charges; or for any hardware, software, or other problems that may occur as the result of using it. This website is subject to change or discontinuation without notice at the discretion of the publisher and author.

Foreword

I was very excited to be asked to write the foreword for this book. As a systems librarian myself, I find that resources like this one can be very helpful. I found the book to be a useful, insightful, and well-written guide for people responsible for computer technology in library settings.

Are you an accidental systems librarian? Have you seen your career gravitate toward the management of computers in libraries? I certainly have, and if you have too, then you are a systems librarian. If you just seemed to fall into this position, then you may very well be an accidental systems librarian. Either way, congratulations! This book is for you because you have just become a member of a newer, up-and-coming specialty of the profession—a speciality that is only going to increase in importance and not going to go away anytime soon. Welcome to the club!

In this book, Engard and Gordon describe the competencies of this subdiscipline as well as the various characteristics of a fully qualified systems librarian. This is very important because most of the skills they describe are not taught in the current library school curriculum. Everything you need to know is included: what software to master, techniques for learning new skills, how to network with colleagues, and of course, communication, communication, and more communication. Along the way are very useful and very insightful quotes from people in the field, short interviews, and pointers to websites all supporting and elaborating on the text.

After reading—and understanding—this book, you too will discover that systems librarianship is less about computers and more about librarianship. The skills and competencies of systems librarians are very similar to the skills and competencies of librarians in general. I believe the use of the reference interview is an excellent case in point. The difference between systems librarians and other types of librarians is often more a matter of the intended audiences for services and those tools in which services become a reality.

That said, it is important to understand that systems librarianship is not limited to providing support to other people who work in libraries. No, I think its definition—as Engard and Gordon point out—extends to local collection building and the provision of services to library readers (I no longer use the word *users*). For example, as a systems librarian, I have personally amassed a collection of more than 14,000 public domain full-text books in the areas of American and English literature as well as Western philosophy. I call this digital library the Alex Catalogue of Electronic Texts. Not only does its index support full-text searching, but each and every item in the collection is associated with concordancing functions enabling people who use the catalogue to do distant reading against the content. The catalogue has been online since 1994 and receives thousands upon thousands of hits every day. In this way, I am providing real library services to a global audience, and it is all because of my systems librarianship skills.

Depending on how one counts, librarianship has existed for hundreds if not thousands of years. For much of that time, the principles and processes of librarianship have remained rather constant. I believe they include the collection, organization, preservation, dissemination, and sometimes evaluation of data, information, and knowledge. These processes are the "what's" of librarianship. They don't change very much. On the other hand, the "how's" of librarianship evolve as technology evolves. The evolution of the venerable library catalog is an excellent example. Think first about the knowledge of collections inside a librarian's mind. Then think scrolls, books, card catalogs, online public access catalogs grounded in database applications, and current index-based "discovery" systems—all tools used to help the reader find and access materials in a library, and all examples of evolutions in technology. *The Accidental Systems Librarian* is a book about the most recent "how's" of librarianship, specifically the management and use of computers in libraries. It provides a thorough and excellent introduction to the field.

Read this book. Follow its instructions. Absorb what it has to offer. I sincerely believe the end result will be a more satisfying and purposeful career for you in systems librarianship.

—Eric Morgan, digital projects librarian,
Hesburgh Libraries, University of Notre Dame

Introduction

*Systems work in libraries presents a unique mix of
frustrations, challenges, and triumphs. One
guarantee: You'll never be bored.*
                                —Rachel Singer Gordon[1]

I first started in libraries as a web developer and was not originally
looking to become a librarian. One of the first professional development titles I read while starting out was *The Accidental Systems
Librarian.* While I was being thrown into a systems role among
librarians at the time of the first edition of *The Accidental Systems
Librarian,* so were many other librarians. Today, in the age of
Facebook, Twitter, web-based integrated library systems, and separate discovery layers, it's easier to plan to become a systems
librarian, yet many still say they fell into the job "accidentally."

The *how* behind falling into this new role is different for each of
us. Sometimes accidental systems librarians offered to help on a
technology project, sometimes their superiors assumed that they
knew more about computers than their colleagues, and sometimes they were just in the right place at the right time. Given the
variety of ways a person can become a systems librarian, we come
to the role with different combinations of skill sets, knowledge, and
comfort with technology. In many cases, this may mean we've had
to learn on the job.

In late 2010 through early 2011, 192 systems librarians
responded to an online survey about their experiences. (The survey questions are reproduced at the end of the book as Appendix
A.) Their responses are quoted throughout the book to help provide insight into the lives of working systems personnel in
libraries. Many of the survey respondents emphasize the "accidental" nature of their careers. Typical comments include:

- "I came into the field in the late '90s when it was fairly new and technically-oriented people were desperately needed. My current employer recognized that I had a knack for it, so encouraged me to pursue it."

- "I applied for a job as an adult service librarian with a technological focus, particularly Web 2.0 technology. As we became more interested in evaluating other forms of technology, whether it be ebooks and audiobooks, upgrading our library ILS system, or new website functionality, the administration realized that we need someone to take this role full time."

- "I had a small technical background and interest from my help center jobs, took systems courses in library school, and then got a library manager position where a substantial chunk of my time is spent on the ILS and websites."

- "I started as a parapro cataloger and loved making things fit. Since I work in community college, being a cataloger often means being the systems person as well."

- "It was not *at all* what I envisioned myself doing but rather it happened more by default. I was more interested and more knowledgeable about library technology than anyone else in the library."

- "In the right place at the right time: [I] was the only one in technical services with computer experience when we started delving into automation."

- "I created our systems department. As computers and technology made further demands on the library and its staff, I stepped forward and solved problems. I was often ahead of the university computer center (e.g., use of and development of open source software, database-backed active web pages)."

- "Fell into it … the small public library where I worked needed one and no one else wanted to do it. I had been the backup systems administrator for the ILS because I was the technical services librarian. It was easy to slide into being *the* sys admin."

- "It was accidental. My first job out of library school started getting more and more focused on computers and online systems, and there was no one who wanted or knew how to work on them. I stepped in, and it became my whole job."

Another common theme among survey respondents was that formal training was not offered to them as part of their library school education. Until relatively recently, many MLS programs did not offer systems-related courses. When I tell people that I was required to take one systems class in my LIS program, they are often surprised. However, I found it to be one of the more interesting classes offered—a sign that I had chosen the right focus in libraries. While this systems class was not among my classmates' favorites, it did a good job of showing librarians how systems are organized, a skill that all systems librarians need to foster.

The fact that so many librarians came into systems accidentally can probably be traced back to the fact that librarians love to solve problems. Many of us ended up in our current roles simply because we were on a committee working on a new technology project and volunteered to manage something or had a creative way to solve a problem. As Rachel noted in the first edition of this book, "[O]ne truism of library work is this: If you do something once, it becomes yours forever."[2]

Even today, a decade after the first edition of this book was published, we find that literature on how to manage as a systems librarian is sparse. Search for professional development titles on how to catalog or conduct a reference interview, and you'll have your pick of many titles, but general guides on the roles of systems librarians just aren't written. What we do find are books on technology-related topics and books that will walk you through setting up a network or managing an integrated library system. While these titles are useful, they aren't always written with systems librarians as the intended audience. It is for that reason that we offer you this updated edition of *The Accidental Systems Librarian*.

Throughout this book, you will find advice and information to help you manage and interact with computer technology in your institution, whatever your level of systems responsibility. Chapters 1 through 4 provide a background in systems librarianship and outline the skills you will most likely need on the job. Chapters 5 through 7 explain how to take what you learned in library school or in roles prior to becoming a systems librarian, such as research, communication, and organization of knowledge, and translate them into a successful career managing systems. Chapters 8 and 9 cover continuing education, both for yourself and for your colleagues, including teaching adults how to use new technologies and where to find training for yourself.

Chapter 10 addresses staff management and other administrative tasks, while Chapter 11 covers integrated library system migration. Chapter 12 provides insights on how to find a job in the field (if you are looking for a second career or are interested in becoming a systems librarian) and how to deal with the stresses that will inevitably come with your new role. The conclusion and appendices round out your whirlwind course of instruction, providing resources for further reading and study. While tips, suggestions, and descriptions of technologies are included throughout, this is not a "how-to" guide outlining every aspect of your library's web presence or integrated library systems. Instead, the goal here is to start you off with a good foundation and give you a toolbox of resources to help you move forward.

As I stated earlier, I have worked as a systems librarian, although not completely accidentally, in a special library. Many of the recommendations in this book are based on my own experiences and those of Rachel Singer Gordon, as well as on conversations with colleagues in a variety of library environments. I hope that you find systems librarianship as exciting and dynamic a field as we have, and that these suggestions, resources, and stories prove helpful in your career. Please feel free to contact me with your comments and reactions.

Nicole C. Engard
nengard@gmail.com
tasl.web2learning.net

Endnotes

1. Rachel Singer Gordon. *The Accidental Systems Librarian* (Medford, NJ: Information Today, Inc., 2003), 219.
2. Ibid., 4.

Chapter 1

Systems Librarianship 101: Defining Systems Librarianship

> *The systems librarian is a unique breed. The position requires someone who not only understands libraries and computers but someone who can put both fields into context.*
> —Patricia Ingersoll and John Culshaw[1]

Coming up with a standard definition for systems librarianship is like lumping all technology together into the same category. Fitting the wide variety of tasks systems librarians engage in into one coherent schema is difficult. Depending on the size, type, funding, needs, and philosophy of their institutions, systems librarians may have duties as diverse as:

- Computer hardware selection, installation, purchasing, and troubleshooting
- Software selection, installation, purchasing, and support
- Local and/or wide area network administration and security responsibilities
- Internet support, including router, wireless, proxy server, and firewall configuration
- Security and stability of the public computing environment
- Webpage and/or intranet design and maintenance

- Managing the library's social network presence
- General help desk functions
- Database vendor liaison
- Overseeing the library's technology commons
- Electronic resource selection and implementation
- Original computer programming
- Digitizing, archiving, and cataloging document, audio, and video collections
- Staff and patron technology training
- Integrated library system (ILS) maintenance and automation migration, upgrades, and training
- Database development and programming
- Project management
- Creating technical documentation
- Acting as a liaison between library staff and computer services staff
- Writing/reviewing requests for proposals and required system specifications for vendors

Systems librarians may be responsible for any or all of these functions, for additional functions, or for an entirely different (or as yet unimagined) set of duties. In addition to the specific technological tasks in the previous list, they may also have budgetary and management accountability, as well as responsibility for more traditional library functions such as reference and cataloging.

To add to the confusion, systems librarians may or may not have earned a Master of Library Science (MLS).[2] Systems-related tasks may be a part of their jobs or comprise their full set of responsibilities. Librarians may work as part of an information technology

(IT) department, manage a systems department, serve as a liaison to such a department, assume half-time systems duties, or exist as a department of one (or solo librarian), their library's sole source of automation support. Their library may be part of larger systems or institutions that assume part of the burden of supporting technology in the library, or it may be a stand-alone library with no outside technical support (with the exception of some systems vendors). Each systems librarian position, therefore, comes with a unique blend of responsibilities.

Job titles of those who work with computer technology in libraries also vary tremendously from library to library. A random sampling of titles from the systems librarian survey results in labels as diverse as:

- Information systems librarian
- Library webmaster
- Digital services librarian
- Manager of library systems
- Lead library systems analyst
- Eservices librarian
- Head of information technology
- Instruction and liaison librarian
- Library systems and digital collections administrator
- Virtual branch and innovative tech manager
- Metadata librarian
- Assistant director of technical services for library systems
- Systems manager
- Informatics librarian
- Web services librarian

- Integrated digital systems librarian

- Head of application development and management

- Systems manager/reference librarian

- Library systems liaison officer

There are countless other variations on the theme. However, some librarians with automation responsibilities, especially solo librarians or those in smaller institutions, will have no terms in their title indicating they have taken on such responsibilities.

As librarians, we tend to feel a certain level of discomfort with that which we cannot easily categorize. However, this variety in background, title, and tasks is confusing only if we allow ourselves to be blinded by the technological aspect. More traditional library positions also vary tremendously in scope and duties by type of library. No one could possibly suggest that reference librarians in a largely electronic news library; in a small, largely nonautomated, rural library; or in a sizable research institution are not clearly serving as reference staff—even though the types of questions they receive, the specific tools they use, and their daily tasks may look quite different. What matters is that these librarians are using their reference background to assist library patrons in answering questions and researching topics of interest.

Note also that a number of the job titles in the previous list reflect systems librarians' dual roles in systems and reference or in systems and technical services. Another difficulty in defining systems librarianship occurs because librarians have historically taken on systems duties in addition to their existing responsibilities rather than stepping immediately into a full-fledged systems role. This assumption of technological duties often happens gradually so that systems work becomes identified in an institution as belonging under an existing department rather than as a specialty in its own right. Further, technology becomes so intertwined with all aspects of library operations that it seems difficult to define systems librarianship as a specific subfield; systems librarians have a hand in running each department. As library technology becomes more complex and demanding, however, many librarians who previously held one of these dual roles find the balance of their duties shifting toward systems work. Given this inevitable shift, it may be useful again to think of systems responsibilities in the same way we think of reference or technical services responsibilities. Even in smaller institutions where one person tends to fill dual (or multiple) roles, departments and responsibilities are clearly identifiable as belonging to specific subfields of librarianship.

Another difficulty in definition stems from the tendency to define systems work even now as outside the purview of librarianship and as falling in the realm of the IT department or as the responsibility of computer technicians. This view is shortsighted, reflecting nostalgia for a precomputerized era, a false separation of computer and other technologies, and a lack of understanding that librarians have been involved with the development of technologies that met library needs from the very inception of such tools. (The development of the MARC standard is a preeminent example of such involvement.) We should also remember the libraries' involvement with and use of technologies from the typewriter to microfilm, each of which was used and supported in— and served to transform—our institutions long before the computer age.

We cannot abandon such an integral aspect of library operations to nonlibrarians, since the ways in which we implement and support technology in our libraries affect all of our departments and services. Supporting computer technology does not make you a technician; it makes you a librarian with systems responsibilities. Michael Porter sums it up best, saying, "Today, technology is a powerful driver of change in libraries, and it will stay that way for the rest of your career."[3] Librarianship and systems responsibilities go hand-in-hand, and their skill sets are both complementary and required for any computer services librarian.

Eric Lease Morgan, librarian at University Libraries of Notre Dame, notes: "I consider myself to be a librarian first and a computer user second. My professional goal is to discover new ways to use computers to improve library and knowledge services. Therein lies the essence of systems librarianship. *Systems librarianship is the art and science of combining the principles of librarianship with the abilities of computing technology* [emphasis in original]."[4] Because of this, non-MLS systems personnel can discover that they have as much learning to do on the library side as librarians who assume systems duties have to do on the technology side. The successful systems librarian blends both outlooks and skill sets in finding the appropriate balance for her institution.

Library Skills and Communication

A library background is crucial to effective systems work in libraries. One reason librarians tend to complain about institutionwide systems departments staffed with non-MLS computer science personnel is because this leads to gaps in communication and outlook between IT and the library. MLS systems librarians working in institutions with separate IT departments often find themselves bridging these gaps, which highlights the necessity of communicating equally well with technical staff, librarians, the library administration, and patrons. One of the most important roles of any systems librarian in a larger institution is that of liaison between librarians and the IT department, and, in smaller institutions, that of liaison among patrons, librarians, and the technology itself. Communication and people skills are paramount for any technology librarian, as is the ability to view systems issues from both a library and an IT perspective.

Many survey respondents emphasize the importance of bridging such communication gaps, and I found that I was often used as a translator between IT and the librarians when I was working as a web developer at a library. Sandra Gisela Martín, library director at Universidad Católica de Córdoba, expressed her opinion that "the systems librarian must [have] fundamentally good communication skills." One library supervisor stressed the role of a systems librarian as a people person: "Although you'll work with systems, the people running them are key. Work to establish and maintain excellent working relationships with personnel in all departments." And Eileen Lutzow, systems librarian at Charleston Southern University, finds that in some libraries "you most likely will be the only one doing anything related to technology, and your biggest asset will be an ability to translate techno-speak to library-speak."

As you advance in your career, and the more you learn on both the library and the technical sides, the more effectively you will be able to communicate with all these constituencies. Your library background will give you credibility with staff and patrons, while your technology knowledge provides a way into the world of IT. I found that my computer programming degree went a long way toward helping me work with my IT department. Librarians who work in institutions with a separate IT department must gain familiarity with technology in order to build their credibility and work effectively with an IT staff. Your familiarity will also help you see things from the perspective of IT staff members and understand the reasoning behind their actions.

It is precisely because technology is interwoven into library operations that systems librarians are essential in ensuring that technology always serves the needs of the institution. If a library lacks systems support or lacks librarians who are able to interface with its IT department, technology may either fail to meet institutional needs or it will just plain fail. One reason why library skills are so useful in managing library technology is that systems librarians use their core principles of librarianship to communicate with all library constituents and determine how technology can be used most effectively. This includes communication to bridge the gap between techies and nontechies; communication with library patrons to ensure that their needs are being met by the current technological environment; communication with library staff and patrons when training, providing technical support, or creating documentation; communication with the library's administration to ensure they understand the importance of funding technology and training; and communication with software and hardware vendors to convey the library's unique needs and existing technological environment.

Despite the popular image of librarians as asocial individuals locked away in rooms filled with dusty books, we have always recognized the importance of interacting with others. This is doubly necessary in a systems environment where miscommunication is all too easy. As one systems librarian said, "Learn people skills! Even though you're working with technology, you need to be able to explain to the reference librarian or administrator why things are being done the way they are."

While systems librarians coming from a library background must work to extend their technology skills and vocabulary to communicate effectively with IT departments and vendors, systems personnel in libraries who come from an IT background have the opposite problem in this liaison role. They have the technology skills, but they may lack the background to use them effectively in a library environment or to communicate effectively with library staff and users. IT personnel tend to be heavy on jargon and may emphasize library systems over the people who use them. IT people who find themselves in library roles need to acquaint themselves with the unique requirements of libraries and with the user-centered foundations of the profession. One library systems administrator answering the survey recommended that "[e]ven if it's only for 2 weeks each, work for or shadow a circulation staff member, a reference librarian, an instruction librarian, and a tech services staff member to really get a feel for their needs." IT people (and this also extends to systems librarians) must also realize the importance of keeping the lines of communication open when there is a problem with computing equipment or services. While nontechnical library staff will understandably be frustrated when a service or machine is "down," they will be more understanding if they are kept informed about the progress of the situation.

Realize also that there is no one right way to communicate with others in your institution. One of your goals, for example, will be to communicate to nonsystems staff members how they can use technology effectively in their day-to-day activities. There are a number of ways to do this, ranging from informal one-on-one conversations ("Did you know …") to formal training classes to providing printed and online documentation. You might create a regular newsletter or blog of technology tips that you can post to your staff intranet, send via email, or distribute in print—whichever will reach your colleagues most effectively. You can create tip sheets and brochures describing various aspects of the library's computer technology that public services staff can hand out to patrons and refer to when assisting library visitors. You can archive tip sheets in a subject-divided binder at public services desks or create a section for this information on your library website or intranet for easy searching, so that staff can quickly find half-remembered information. You can create a "what's new in computers" slideshow or screencast that staff members can run on their own PCs. You can also send out tips and reminders explaining how to accomplish occasional tasks, since people are likely to forget if they do not use a feature often. Finally, you can create a regular podcast or videocast that answers frequently asked questions for your colleagues on how to perform specific tasks.

Think of creative ways to get people to use technology more effectively and efficiently in your own environment. When creating these resources, however, keep your audience in mind. Do not inflict excessive jargon on nontechnical library staff, and do not overload them with extraneous information. Keep tips and instructions straightforward, to the point, and useful. Your job is to help staff members use technology to do their jobs more effectively.

If your library is large or tends to have heavy turnover, consider creating a computer procedures manual for public services staff that explains common uses of technology in the library. You can use this while training new staff members, and newer individuals can use this as a resource when they are alone at the desk and no systems support is available. The manual should outline basics such as the process for turning on and logging in machines each morning, lists of available software on the public workstations, basic troubleshooting steps for common problems, and so on. Consider creating equivalent manuals for other departments as your institution's needs dictate; work with department heads to see what specific processes their staff might need to have outlined for them. Publish these guides online and make sure that they are searchable. This way they will help both the new and existing staff in finding answers.

Lastly, understand the necessity of effective communication with your library's administration. You will need to help administrators understand the importance of funding technology projects, staffing technology departments, and allotting sufficient time and resources to your efforts. If members of your administration are less technologically savvy, they may have difficulty seeing why such time, funding, and personnel should be allocated to technology when other departments and projects are also clamoring for funding and attention. You will need to work with your administration on grants, technology plans, and large-scale projects, which requires you to outline the benefits of your proposals and to describe ideas in nontechnical language. (See more on this in Chapter 10.) You will also need to help your administration understand the reasons why technology and related expenses such as staffing and training need to be ongoing. Too often, institutions have funded technology as a one-time allocation on an ad hoc, as-needed basis; you will need to convince them about the necessity of consistent funding.

Yes, You Are a Systems Librarian

Any library, no matter how small, needs to find someone who is willing and able to take responsibility for its technology. As soon as one computer is set up on a desk, one ebook reader purchased, or one tablet computer handed out, somebody needs to support that technology—whether or not that library has a formal IT department and whether or not anyone is formally prepared to assume that role. If you have found yourself in one of these accidental roles and your job title and compensation have not changed to match your new duties, do not hesitate to bring up the topic with your library's administration. (See more on negotiating promotions in Chapter 12.) Take the initiative to try and clarify the boundaries of your own position, and offer to help draft a new job description that reflects your systems as well as your nonsystems responsibilities. Most administrations recognize how important smoothly running technology is in today's library and will be willing to work with you on these points.

Although some librarians' technological skills obviously become more specialized to fit their institutions' needs, all librarians now need a basic facility with technology. The more you know, the more effectively you can use technology to serve your staff and patron needs, instead of the other way around. You may not have defined yourself as a systems librarian, but if you have any responsibilities for supporting and implementing technology, you have responsibilities that fall under the cloak of systems librarianship—in the same way that a children's librarian who works at the adult reference desk once a week can be credited with having reference responsibilities. In some sense, this makes us all systems librarians. As Mayo and Nelson note: "Everyone working in libraries today is part of the technological revolution whether they want to be or not."[5]

It's worth taking the time to learn the skills to work effectively in your position. The more you learn to use your library background to help you discharge your systems responsibilities, the more effectively you can carry out this part of your job. As one systems/reference librarian wrote in her survey response, "I think librarians are so well-versed in teasing out any applicable knowledge from a problem. Systems can often be like patrons, with their vague messages and insufficiently communicated demands, that teasing out the information failure of a system versus a patron often involves the same skill set. A good reference interview, between myself and the system, or sometimes just myself, will often lead to a solution."

Of course, systems librarians with full-time responsibilities for technology in their libraries will devote more of their time and education to their specialty. But realizing that we all share similar responsibilities helps bridge the perceived gap between systems librarianship and other subfields of the profession. This realization also encourages nonsystems librarians to take responsibility for familiarizing themselves with technology and not depending on the systems librarian for day-to-day tasks such as changing the printer toner and minor technical troubleshooting. All librarians today require technological literacy to carry out their duties effectively. Nonsystems staff members need to be comfortable with modern technologies such as ebook readers, tablet computers, and mobile phones (among others) to effectively assist patrons in using such technology. Public services personnel are also fielding more technical questions from their patrons who expect librarians to be knowledgeable about technological issues. Eric Lease Morgan says it best when asking: "In today's world, why would anybody trust a librarian, whose profession is about information and knowledge, who hadn't mastered a computer?"[6] You may have some difficulty convincing your fellow staff members of this truth, but librarians today must come to realize that computers are integral to both library functions and their own jobs.

Writing in *American Libraries*, Joyce Latham points out that "True functional literacy in a library organization begins when frontline staff start to accept responsibility for how their technical installations function and explore just how much they can do with them. Another important moment in the development of institutional literacy occurs when administrators begin to explore ways to crisscross these service areas, involving librarians in technical problem solving and technical staff in public program design. Creating avenues for communication and partnership between these two groups is key to developing the inherent potential of technology."[7] Literacy today includes technological literacy, and as librarians, we cannot pass such literacy on to our patrons if we do not first obtain basic technological skills of our own.

Another part of your responsibility as a systems librarian will be to help transfer appropriate technological skills and a comfort with technology to other library staff—and to your administration. Find more on training staff and patrons in Chapter 8, but for now, realize the importance of communication skills in inculcating technological literacy and the importance of having technologically literate staff. This is as true in the smallest public library as it is in the largest research institution.

Establishing Competencies

If you are in a larger institution with staff from varying backgrounds and with varying levels of computer competence, it will be useful to establish basic technological competencies for all staff. Of course, official computer services staff will be expected to attain a higher degree of competency with library systems than will nonsystems personnel, but you can identify and require the necessary minimum requirements for all staff so the technology in your library runs smoothly. Competencies define the basic computer/technology skills expected of library staff, so they must be observable, measurable, and improvable. Establishing computer competencies for everyone recognizes that technology is integral in all departments, allows staff to use technology effectively to meet institutional needs, and lets systems librarians concentrate their efforts on more complex issues rather than continually helping other staff members with the basics.

Your library's technology competencies should reflect the specific skills that are necessary for staff to carry out their daily duties effectively. To determine individuals' existing levels of competency with your institution's systems and software, it's useful to create a checklist of desired skills and then to let staff members evaluate their own levels of comfort with completing those skills. Emphasize that this is not a test and that no one's job performance will be graded on these sheets. The goal is for staffers to answer honestly so that you can evaluate the areas in which you need to shore up staff skills and provide targeted training, cheat sheets, and other resources to help people use technology to do their jobs well.

Staff Competencies

Nearly every library position, whether professional or paraprofessional, now requires a computer, and more and more are requiring the use of mobile devices such as tablets and smartphones. For the sake of library productivity and staff sanity, employees need to learn the skills to use these devices in their daily work. When developing your competencies, target them to the tasks that the staff will do in their daily activities. In a larger institution, it will be useful to create competencies for each job description or classification; in a smaller library, competencies by department may suffice. For help with developing competencies for your librarians, review Technology Competencies and Training for Libraries by Sarah Houghton-Jan.[8] For an example of thorough staff technology competencies, see the State Library of North Carolina's list of competencies (www.statelibrary.ncdcr.gov/ce/images/Competencies. pdf) for librarians in the state. The University of Minnesota–Duluth has posted a more general set of the technical competencies (www.d.umn.edu/itss/policies/techplan/staff.html) recommended for its staff. These competencies include items such as the ability to "create a secure password" and "access and use general library resources (e.g., catalog, databases, and electronic journals)." Looking at these more general competencies may be useful as a starting point for creating your own set, which can be customized as necessary for your institution's computing environment. One last useful example is Maryland's Eastern Shore Regional Library's set of core competencies (www.esrl.org/Core_ Competencies.pdf), which includes a number of resources for self-study and review.

If your library's environment includes a number of different software packages, electronic databases, and hardware configurations, you might consider dividing these core competencies by subject area. Create a competency checklist (or one basic and one advanced checklist) for operating system usage, each office program, internet usage, email software, basic hardware knowledge, Web 2.0, mobile devices, your ILS, and so on. Be sure to update these lists whenever the library upgrades or changes software packages; keep them current so that they are always usable tools. Remember to never assume that everyone must know how to perform a specific task. It never hurts to list all of the software and hardware in use in your library.

After staff members have been tested (or have self-tested) on these technological basics, use the results to determine whether training is needed to get staff to appropriate levels of technical knowledge. (See more on creating and implementing a staff training program in Chapter 8.) Formal training for the staff can be supplemented with online tutorials, cheat sheets, and other self-study materials. Once staff members have completed training, let them retest their skills on your competency checklists.

If your library's environment includes a number of different software packages, electronic databases, and hardware configurations, you might consider dividing these core competencies by subject area. Create a competency checklist (or one basic and one advanced checklist) for operating system usage, each office program, internet usage, email software, basic desktop hardware knowledge, handheld hardware knowledge, Web 2.0, your ILS, and so on. Be sure to update these lists whenever the library upgrades or changes software packages; keep them current so that they are always usable tools.

Systems Competencies

After mastering the basic competencies required of all staff members, systems personnel should then acquire the additional competencies necessary to run the library technology smoothly. While basic staff competencies will tend to be similar for personnel in most libraries (who mainly use standard browser software, ILS modules, office software, and so on), the specific competencies required of systems personnel will look radically different in different institutions. These competencies need to match the duties assumed by each systems librarian and the software and hardware environment in their institutions.

Sample Questions for a Firefox Competency Self-Assessment Test

Please rate your comfort level on a scale of 1 to 3 with completing the following tasks, with 3 being "very comfortable" and 1 being "not at all comfortable."

I am able to type an internet address into the address bar to visit a particular webpage.

1   2   3

I am able to use Print Preview to select certain pages of a document for printing.

1   2   3

I can use the Find function to locate a word or phrase within a particular webpage.

1   2   3

I can copy and paste a web address from my email or other application into Firefox.

1   2   3

I know how to use toolbar buttons to move back and forward, and to go to the homepage.

1   2   3

I know how to clear the history in Firefox.

1   2   3

I know how to install a plug-in in Firefox.

1   2   3

The Federal Library and Information Center Committee of the Library of Congress has posted a general list of "Knowledge, Skills, and Abilities" for systems librarians (www.loc.gov/flicc/wg/ksa-sys.html). Note that these are not all strictly "technical" skills and that this is a list intended for use in drafting job ads for systems personnel. Still, this gives you a useful starting point for drafting systems competencies for your institution, adapting and adding more specific skills as necessary. Each of these general areas can be divided into specific tasks or competencies and made more specific in terms of the technology used in your institution.

If you have a systems staff, consider creating competencies for each position within your department that will reflect an individual's specific duties. This will help you to see if the skills of current staff members need upgrading and to evaluate new hires for specific skills needed. It will also enable you to balance workload and duties among staff according to their areas of expertise. If you do not have a staff, you may be in the awkward position of creating competencies for yourself, which is especially difficult if you are just starting or working your way into a systems position and do not necessarily know what you need to know. To create competencies in this situation, it will be useful to start by making an inventory of the software and hardware used in the library. Evaluate what you are responsible for supporting and begin to think about how you would like to improve the library's future technological environment. This will give you a base for creating competencies for yourself and finding out what you may need to learn.

Systems Librarians As Change Agents

Beyond the specific responsibilities that systems librarians hold in common to operate library technology smoothly, they hold similar personal responsibilities for maintaining a flexible outlook and fostering the capacity to accept and facilitate technological change within their institutions. While the previous sections have focused on defining systems librarianship in terms of common skills and tasks, focusing on a common outlook is equally important. Just as librarians as a group share a common foundation of principles and philosophy, systems librarians do, too.

In the not-too-recent past, librarianship was seen as an extremely stable profession. We had a fairly clear concept of what a library was supposed to look like (thanks to Carnegie), what it contained (books), and what a librarian's job entailed (selecting, looking up information in, and maintaining the order of those books). From such concepts, stereotypes are made, and libraries of all types and sizes, and librarians of all descriptions, have always flourished. Yet historically, many have been drawn to this profession largely because of its perceived stability and from a love for the permanence of the written word and the books housed in our institutions.

The principles of our profession have not changed, but the containers of information and the methods we use to access such information have. What is most distressing to many is the rapidity of such change; an organization may have moved from providing print-only collections to adding one stand-alone CD-ROM station and setting up a bank of internet terminals with access to subscription databases, to canceling print journals in favor of digital subscriptions and negotiating borrowing rights for ebooks—all within a few short years. As systems librarians, however, we can afford neither to be blinded by appearances nor stunned by change. We must concentrate on the ways we can best facilitate access to all parts of our collection today. We must also be open to new technologies and new methods of information storage and retrieval tomorrow. In fact, we should welcome and work to develop such technologies if they offer advantages to the users of our library's resources. This is not to say that any technological change is automatically desirable merely because it is possible. Our primary goal is to facilitate those changes that help our institution carry out its mission. A secondary role is to help our fellow librarians adapt to these inevitable changes.

We should always view the prospect of technological change first as librarians and second as technologists. IT staff may wish to implement a technology because it is new, cool, and different, but, as librarians, we understand that technology serves the institution rather than vice versa. As systems people, we should be comfortable with and appreciate the power of computing technology, and as librarians, we should appreciate that technology is merely a tool. Mark Stover explains the process: "As librarians gain more power and responsibilities in the arena of information technology, we must not lose sight of our core values as a profession. We have a special imperative to shape the new age of computing with the traditions and values of those who came before us in the information professions."[9] As change agents, we again find ourselves in the role of liaison between technological possibility and institutional goals.

Endnotes

1. Patricia Ingersoll and John Culshaw, *Managing Information Technology: A Handbook for Systems Librarians* (Westport, CT: Libraries Unlimited, 2004), 25.
2. Of the 93.23 percent of respondents who answered this question on the survey, 76.56 percent had an MLS and 16.67 percent did not.
3. Michael Porter and David Lee King, "101 Resources and Things to Know (RTK)," Library 101, 2009, accessed May 21, 2012, www.library man.com/blog/101rtk.
4. Eric Lease Morgan, "On Being a Systems Librarian," Infomotions, November 16, 2004, accessed May 21, 2012, www.infomotions.com/musings/systems-librarianship.
5. Diane Mayo, Sandra S. Nelson, and Public Library Association. *Wired for the Future: Developing Your Library Technology Plan* (Chicago: American Library Association, 1999), 49.

6.   Eric Lease Morgan, "Computer Literacy for Librarians," *Computers in Libraries* 18, no. 1 (January 1998): 39–40.

7.   Joyce Latham, "The World Online: IT Skills for the Practical Professional," *American Libraries* (March 2000): 41.

8.   Sarah Houghton-Jan, *Technology Competencies and Training for Libraries*. Vol. 43. Library Technology Reports 2 (Chicago: ALA TechSource, 2007).

9.   Mark Stover, *Leading the Wired Organization: The Information Professional's Guide to Managing Technological Change* (New York: Neal-Schuman, 1999).

Chapter 2

Systems Librarianship 102: Desktop Software You May Need to Master

*Scratch an expert and you'll often find someone
who's muddling through—just at a higher level.*
—Steve Krug[1]

The body of knowledge that a successful systems librarian needs is a constantly shifting target. The rapid pace of technological change, coupled with the wide range of library environments and technologies, ensures that you will have something, and usually many things, to learn when taking on any systems-related position. What is important to remember is that specific technical skills can always be acquired; don't let an explicit list of technical requirements scare you out of applying for a position or taking on a project. You can learn to work with any program, operating system (OS), automation system, or hardware configuration as needed. (This is why crash courses exist! See more on extending your technological skills in Chapter 9.) Specific technical skills are secondary; what matters most to your success as a systems librarian is your openness to learning, your capacity to embrace and facilitate change, and your foundation in the principles of librarianship.

Any lists of what systems librarians "need to know" are inherently suspect. What these lists generally embody is either a rundown of the competencies for working in a particular institution or the ideals, background, and philosophy of a particular systems manager. While nonsystems librarians may have difficulty understanding that systems librarianship is still a field of librarianship, systems people sometimes get caught up in an idealized view of what work with technology in libraries "should" be. This is especially true among more technically advanced systems personnel in larger libraries, where there is a certain tendency to assume that all systems librarians should possess the same competencies and to spend time arguing over what constitutes true systems librarianship. This is unnecessarily divisive and does little to boost the confidence of many accidental technology librarians who may lack expertise in one of these "true" systems areas but are still quite effective in their positions.

What you as a systems librarian need to know (or to learn) is determined by factors such as the technological environment in your library, the goals of your institution, the needs of your staff and patrons, and the support you receive from your larger institution or library system/consortium. Do not waste time or energy worrying about what you should or could know, or what other systems librarians in other institutions might know. (You need to deal with plenty of other issues.) Instead, learn what you need to know for your particular set of circumstances. In essence, try to acquire the knowledge necessary for the effective support of technology in your library and to extend that knowledge with the goal of improving patron and staff interactions with technology. Always remain open to acquiring new knowledge and learning about new technologies. This openness and willingness to learn will also help if you choose to seek a systems position later in another library, whose environment is likely to differ from yours.

There are, however, a number of similar tasks shared by systems librarians in different institutions. Technology in libraries can take only so many forms, so the following sections will take you on a whirlwind tour of typically broad areas of expertise for technology librarians. Your institutional environment may require familiarity with one, none, or all of these areas, or with more specific technologies and methods not covered here. Note that this isn't a comprehensive list; it is included to give you an idea of the technologies that systems librarians may need to familiarize themselves with and to provide suggestions about setting up systems in an effective way. While library technology encompasses items from photocopiers to microfilm, we are talking just about computer technology in libraries. Be forewarned, however: Administrators and staff members tend to assume that computer expertise translates into a general familiarity with all machines. Be ready to fend off requests to take on duties such as repairing photocopiers and poking into the innards of recalcitrant cash registers.

Do not panic if you are less than an expert in one or more of these topics. Descriptions are designed for background purposes only to offer an overview of current common technologies that require systems librarian support. Reading these sections will not endow you with instant expertise, but it will provide you with a foundation and ideas for learning on your own. A number of resources are listed in each section; use these as a starting point for further reading. The preponderance of these resources pertains either to newer technologies that you may not be familiar with or to heavily used technologies with an existing broad base of support.

Realize also that this list would have looked very different 10 years ago and that it will change again in the next 10—or less. The evolutionary nature of systems librarianship and the limited funding available for upgrading technology in many libraries also means that you may be responsible for simultaneously supporting multiple types or generations of technology: Macs and PCs, or laptops and desktops, or ebook readers and tablets, for example.

Open Source Software

Open source software (OSS) is gaining a stronger following in the library community as pricing, security, and philosophical considerations provide an impetus for considering alternatives to Microsoft's dominance. Systems librarians will need to consider using OSS alongside and/or as a replacement for proprietary alternatives. Cindy Murdock Ames, the IT services director at Meadville Public Library and Crawford County Federated Library System, stated emphatically in her survey response that aspiring systems librarians should "Learn about open source!"

The open source movement shares a great deal with the philosophy of librarianship, most notably an emphasis on sharing information and enabling users to find resources and resolve problems on their own. Eric Lease Morgan notes: "In general, librarianship is an honorable profession and people are drawn to the profession because of a sense of purpose, a desire to provide service to the community. While many OSS developers create applications to solve local, real-world problems, their efforts are shared because they desire to give back to the community. Do you remember the internet saying from about 10 years ago? 'Give back to the 'Net.' That saying lives on in OSS and is manifested in the principles of librarianship."[2] Librarians and open source proponents both sense the value of community and the importance of sharing resources, which seems to make them natural partners.

So, what defines OSS? Most software from traditional vendors is completely proprietary, down to its source code (which is closely guarded and unable to be modified). Open source alternatives allow free and open access to the source code, under the assumption that the wider programming community can improve and adapt the software faster than any conventional programming team. A famous quote from the essay "The Cathedral and the Bazaar," by Eric Raymond, states that "[g]iven enough eyeballs all bugs are shallow."[3] This result is a process similar to peer review, in which unusable projects sink under the weight of community criticism and useful examples shine—and benefit from others' input. Examples of major and popular open source applications include the Apache web server, LibreOffice, Perl, Firefox, and Linux. Much OSS is released under the GNU General Public License (GPL),[4] which provides terms for using, distributing, and freely modifying software.[5]

Useful resources and background material for library OSS proponents include:

- The FOSS4LIB website (www.foss4lib.org) is an open website where library staff can share information on open source software specific to libraries. There is also a series of articles to assist in decision-making when it comes to choosing an open source solution.

- The Open Source Initiative (www.opensource.org), which defines open source, lists various open source licenses, and posts open source–related news

- Eric S. Raymond's book *The Cathedral and the Bazaar: Musings on Linux and Open Source by an Accidental Revolutionary* (O'Reilly & Associates, rev. ed., 2001) or the freely available essay that inspired the book (www.catb.org/~esr/writings/cathedral-bazaar/cathedral-bazaar)

- Another book by the author, *Practical Open Source Software for Libraries* (Chandos Publishing, 2010, opensource.web2learning.net)

- The author's open source bibliography (www.zotero.org/nengard/items/collection/MB5S62ZP) and the Free/Libre and Open Source Software and Libraries Bibliography group (www.zotero.org/groups/freelibre_and_open_source_software_and_libraries_bibliography), which are both available on Zotero and have many open source resources to review

Some open source proponents emphasize the potential cost savings of using free and open source software (FOSS). Keep in mind, however, that the "free" in that statement refers to "freedom" and not necessarily to cost. You will need to factor in the total cost of ownership, which may include a higher learning curve (resulting in the need for additional training), the potential lack of formal or centralized support and documentation, and the necessity for your library to hire someone with the knowledge to maintain these systems when you leave—or with the willingness to acquire such knowledge.

These factors may be balanced by the absence of prohibitive licensing schemes and the ability to rely less on large outside vendors, but this is an informed decision you will need to make in conjunction with your library's administration. (For more on OSS and library automation, see Chapter 11.) If you choose to use open source products, be prepared to participate in community discussions and decisions, since that's the only way to ensure that the software continues to move in the direction you need it to go.

When researching OSS, consider the following:

- Open source alternatives, although sometimes free or at least at a lower cost than proprietary solutions, are not necessarily without cost.

- Open source may require a greater commitment from you and/or your department in terms of staff training and support.

- Always look for an open source product with an active community behind it. Some open source projects, especially those that stem largely from a single developer, run the risk of the developers losing interest (or funding) and ceasing to support or develop an application.

These warnings are not meant to scare you away from using open source alternatives, but rather so you can implement open source in your library with an awareness of the potential pitfalls. You may choose to add and test open source tools to increase the functionality of existing applications or to use them in conjunction with existing proprietary software before diving into a fully open source environment. (Find a number of such tools on Open Source Living at www.osliving.com.)

Blake Carver's Modifications of Ranganathan's Rules[6]

1. Software is for use.
2. Every computer its users.
3. Every reader his source code.
4. Save the time of the user.
5. A system is a growing organism.

Also keep in mind that the low cost and low system requirements for much of OSS provide extra room for experimentation and learning. You might use a soon-to-be-discarded older machine to install and experiment with Linux, for example. You might choose to use an open source blogging tool such as WordPress (www.wordpress.org) to let library staff share comments and news on your institution's intranet. You may choose to install Apache (www.apache.org) as your web server software rather than relying on alternatives from Microsoft and other vendors. You may investigate open source content management systems such as Drupal (www.drupal.org) to add personalization features to your website. You may also look into using Mozilla's Firefox for your public internet stations and LibreOffice (www.libreoffice.org) on your public office machines. Also note that a number of commonly used library-specific tools are open source, such as the Koha (www.koha-community.org) and Evergreen (www.open-ils.org) integrated library systems, LibraryFind (www.libraryfind.org) federated search tool, and the Greenstone Digital Library Software (www.greenstone.org).

The widespread adoption of such tools by libraries provides you with a built-in community of colleagues to help with any implementation or usage issues. If you create a locally used software add-on, script, or tool, consider releasing it to the library community at large. This serves the dual goal of assisting others while paving the way for feedback from those who implement your solution, giving you the opportunity to improve your tool.

Operating Systems

While Windows is still the predominant OS used in libraries, many libraries have different stations using different systems. Some libraries have made a point to have public stations available for all types of computer users: Windows, Mac, and Linux. Other libraries are switching all of their public stations to OSS such as Linux, while leaving their staff machines running on Windows. With all of this variety in operating systems, it's important for systems librarians to be aware of the various applications on the market and at least have a general feel for how they all work.

Microsoft

Microsoft is still the most commonly used software publisher in libraries today, and many libraries' computing environments contain a mix of different Windows-based operating systems. If possible, try to standardize your institution's client machines on one version of an OS, which will simplify troubleshooting and provide a more stable and consistent environment for staff and users. Resist the urge to upgrade as soon as a new version of a Microsoft OS appears, since patches and service packs are sure to follow. Since stability is so important in a library environment, older technologies may suffice for quite some time.

Beyond their Windows-based client machines (see Figure 2.1), a number of libraries maintain a Windows server, or servers, at the

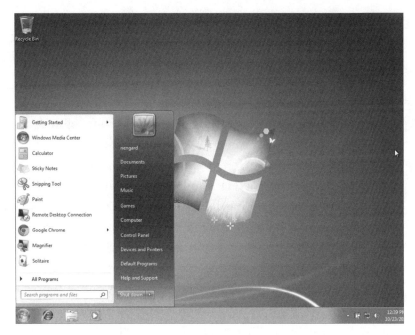

Figure 2.1 Windows 7 Start Menu

center of their local area networks. (Read more on networking later in this chapter.) Microsoft's tendency to heavily discount client access licenses and software used in educational, including academic and public library, environments is one factor in ensuring that the company's dominance in the library server market is likely to continue. Windows 2008 networks, furthermore, are comparatively easy to set up and maintain, making Windows-based servers a logical choice for libraries whose network administrators are also accidental systems librarians.

Microsoft's overall dominance, however, also makes it an attractive target for hackers, virus creators, and other malicious individuals. If you use a Windows-based server in your network, make it a priority to keep that server up-to-date with the latest security patches, service packs, and recommended updates. Many libraries have experienced heavy damage to their systems through hacker attacks (generally by disgruntled patrons or former staff members—it should go without saying that ex-staff members' access should be removed the day they depart from your institution). Others have fallen prey to opportunistic worms such as Conficker, which, for example, caused public computers to be inaccessible for a 10-day period at the Hartford (CT) Public Library in November 2009.[7]

At a minimum, you should faithfully update your antivirus software definitions, keep your servers behind a firewall, and patch your servers on a timely basis to reduce the likelihood of this occurring in your institution. You may wish to subscribe to a product such as kbAlertz (www.kbalertz.com), which will regularly email updates of knowledgebase additions on the products you choose. Also, familiarize yourself with Microsoft's online security center (www.microsoft.com/security) and be sure to visit often or sign up for its email notification service on security issues. While there, download the Microsoft Baseline Security Analyzer, which allows you to scan your systems for known vulnerabilities. Automated patch tools are worth investigating as well, although users have reported mixed experiences.

Since Microsoft products are so predominant, there are also plenty of resources available on their use. Beyond the official Microsoft support site and knowledgebase (www.support.micro soft.com), you may wish to investigate the following:

- Microsoft Support on Twitter (www.twitter.com/
  microsofthelps), through which professionals will answer
  your questions sent to their attention on Twitter
  (@MicrosoftHelps)

- Office Watch (news.office-watch.com), which provides
  email newsletters containing straightforward advice, tips,
  and tricks on Office, Windows, Access, and other
  products

- Annoyances.org (www.annoyances.org), which gives tips
  on customizing Windows, Windows usage, and getting rid
  of annoyances, as well as features downloads and
  discussions

Mac

While some public libraries are starting to add Macintosh computers to their public areas, you will find that Macs are predominately
used in school and university library environments. These libraries
usually have a mix of Macs and PCs on their networks, making
knowledge of the intricacies of Mac and PC networking a necessity.

When it comes to managing the software on your Mac computers, you'll find that many popular applications such as Microsoft
Office and Adobe products come in Mac varieties. While the software is the same, the interfaces are often different and may require
additional staff training time to help your librarians and patrons
get used to the Mac-style menus (see Figure 2.2).

The main source of support for Mac products is Apple's support
site (www.apple.com/support), which links you to the company's
knowledgebase, online forums, and so on. Other useful support
sites include:

- MacFixIt (reviews.cnet.com/macfixit), which contains
  online forums, a blog, troubleshooting reports, and
  downloads

- Macworld (www.macworld.com), which is the
  companion site to the magazine of the same name and
  includes product reviews, news, and discussion forums

- TidBITS (www.tidbits.com), which includes an
  enewsletter and forums devoted to Mac issues

Figure 2.2 Mac OSX Applications Menu

An Interview With Stef Johnson, Reference/Systems Librarian

Stef Johnson, reference/systems librarian at Butte-Silver Bow (MT) Public Library for the past 3 years, had experience as a library assistant and billing and phone support specialist before coming to her library. She talked to us about working in a library that uses mostly open source software.

Can you tell us a little bit about what your responsibilities are on a daily basis?

I'm in charge of planning and configuring the implementation of hardware and software, but of course on a daily basis, it's maintenance, maintenance, maintenance, and, oh yeah, training! We offer on-site "tech tip" group classes, one-on-one and phone support for public users, and review with staff regularly.

What first made your library start exploring OSS?

We had a painfully outdated, proprietary integrated library system (ILS) four years ago, and our director was reluctant to re-invest in the same cycle: ridiculous licensing fees, long waiting periods for updates and fixes, poor customer service, mandatory "upgrades" and mergers, etc. She researched open source ILSs and did a test migration with Koha (www.koha-community.org). She really liked that there was community support to assist with creating records that could migrate from our legacy ILS into Koha (2.2.9 at that time). Overall she liked the process of collaborating with other librarians. Koha fit our needs and was a huge improvement in the features offered, so we took the leap and it has been a great decision for us!

As my director points out regularly, open source and librarianship go hand in hand, providing greater access to information for all. Access to information in the digital age needs the input of librarians to insure no one is locked out. Who will protect access better than the champions of First Amendment rights? The librarian.

What open source software are you using?

We've been a Koha ILS library since 2008, and we installed a whole suite of FOSS on our public PCs including LibreOffice (www.libreoffice.org), Songbird (www.getsongbird.com), GIMP (www.gimp.org), and Firefox (www.firefox.com).

We have started replacing our Microsoft public computers with Ubuntu (currently 10.04), and, in the future, we plan to move to a thin client configuration to make updates more efficient. There is a sense of control and security in running a Linux-based OS and FOSS ILS. We are less vulnerable to viruses and malware (we use AVG antivirus). We also use WordPress (www.wordpress.org) for our library web page, which has served us well these past 4 years. The new Library Technology Reports from the American Library Association in April 2011, titled "Using WordPress as a Library Content Management System" (vol. 47/no. 3 by Kyle M. Jones and Polly-Alida Farrington), illustrates that FOSS is finally getting the nods from the library world it deserves.

What have you found to be the most challenging with using OSS in your library?

Staff and public are sometimes intimidated by the Ubuntu machines. I think the visual differences are a shock to users lacking a ton of computer experience. Folks have just gotten comfortable looking for the "blue 'e' with the swoosh around it" when they need to access the internet, and its absence confuses them. We've found that the majority of patrons jump in with very little assistance, but there's definitely a regular need to do some orientation using the Ubuntu interface.

While we are all dedicated to helping the public, not all staff are regular computer users outside the job; they're not getting much experience searching the web and using peripherals, etc. Skills disappear quickly when the only practice is the occasional question from a patron. It is a challenge to bring staff skills up and keep them honed to assist the public.

Staff training/experience has to be addressed when looking seriously at any implementation, due to the learning curve and variety of interfaces. But providing great service means taking a risk and learning new ways to be effective.

What have you found to be the most rewarding with using OSS in your library?

The first time I installed Ubuntu on a public machine, I plugged it back into the public network and it immediately self-installed the printer. I said "Yeah!" loud enough to startle everyone around me.

Seriously though, I'd call it a tie between: 1) the pleasure of putting Ubuntu on one of our antiques and having it run beautifully, and 2) the process of working with the Koha community. We are so lucky to work with software developers who are passionate about access and the need for information to be free to insure a free and informed society (and who actually want librarian input!).

Typically, I just didn't know where to look for my solution, but the point is that someone else had taken the time to help a stranger in need—that's the spirit of open source!

What tools/resources would you recommend to other systems librarians who are looking into OSS?

Koha for sure. I can't say enough about the supportive environment surrounding a really usable base product. Evergreen developers are also a great bunch to work with and depending on your needs, both have great features.

Ubuntu has been a terrific replacement for us: unbeatable price and it just wants to work! Especially over the past 5–6 years with everything becoming much more secure and usable in the cloud, even inexperienced users become comfortable in the Ubuntu interface pretty quickly.

Anything else you'd like to share (or wish I had asked)?

I can't say enough about the excellent communities surrounding open source. The astonishing part is that they are groups dedicated to making the product function better next time.

Every iteration is the result of the group doing its monumental best to encapsulate the most useful suggestions for improvement, while simultaneously keeping down the bloat of trying to be all things to all librarians.

Makes you wish everything worked this way!

Linux/Ubuntu

A common theme emerged in the survey of systems librarians: They wished they had been taught more about Linux, and many recommended that the next generation of systems librarians learn Linux before starting their careers. While in years past, Linux was an OS only considered by computer developers, Ubuntu (www.ubuntu.com) has made it possible for the average computer user to use an open source OS. This alternative to Windows has become very appealing in libraries, which have adopted it worldwide.

As already discussed, OSS gives users the freedom to use, modify, and distribute for any purpose, and as such, it can be a cost-effective and appealing alternative for libraries. Choosing Ubuntu (see Figure 2.3) to power your desktop systems means that you won't have licensing fees to worry about. While there are commercial support options, most people who use Ubuntu don't have to

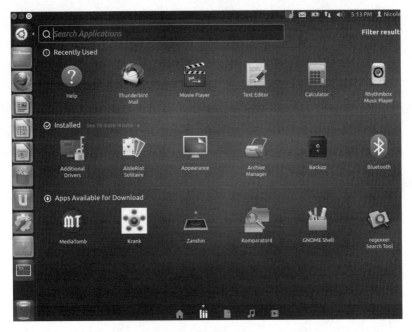

Figure 2.3 12.04 LTS Dash

make that investment. Ubuntu and open source applications like it have a huge worldwide network of people you can consult with if you have a problem installing or managing the system, making the need for a support vendor almost unnecessary.

While Ubuntu can be used on any type of computer in any type of organization, it also lets small libraries or libraries without the funds to upgrade computer hardware squeeze more life out of their older machines; the system requirements for Ubuntu can easily be met by older, less powerful machines. Ubuntu has actually become the popular choice among netbook users because, when the system has limited resources, you don't want your OS to soak up all of them.

To find additional Ubuntu support, you can visit the official support site (www.ubuntu.com/support) or try one of these outside sources:

- Ubuntu Geek (www.ubuntugeek.com), which offers tips, tricks, and help for using Ubuntu

- Planet Ubuntu (planet.ubuntu.com), which is a compilation of articles about Ubuntu written on several sites

Linux varieties can also be used to manage your library network and web servers. While Red Hat Linux is probably the most-talked-about option, the beauty of open source is that there are many different varieties, or distributions, of Linux to choose from to manage your network, desktops, and web servers. Take a look at the full distribution listing at Linux.com (www.linux.com/directory/Distributions).

Productivity Software

Most productivity software will work on several different operating systems. Microsoft Office, for example, works on both Windows and Mac OS. Keep that in mind while reviewing the productivity software options listed in this section.

While most librarians know all about Microsoft products, it's essential that a systems librarian be aware of alternatives that are often more cost-effective and less troublesome in terms of security concerns and usability. Your staff and administration will turn to you for suggestions on which applications best meet the library's needs, and it's important to review as many options as possible before making your decision.

Microsoft

Your institution likely makes use of the Microsoft Office software suite. Microsoft Office software is one area in which you may receive some assistance from other library staff members in answering questions and teaching other users. Its longevity as the predominant office suite has resulted in a large base of "power users" familiar with the ins and outs and tips and tricks of dealing with the software. Note, however, that documents created with newer versions of Office software are not always compatible with older software (Access 2007, for example, will not read all databases saved in Access 2010). This is another argument for standardizing on a particular version or setting newer versions of software to save automatically in older file formats, since it is important that users be able to share files in a library environment.

If you use Outlook as your email and productivity software, be on the alert for viruses and worms transmitted by email. (See more on protecting your users from such threats in the section on security in Chapter 4.) Outlook and Outlook Express are particularly susceptible to these threats due to two factors: They contain security holes that may not be necessarily present in other email programs, and Microsoft features an irresistibly large target for the creators of these exploits. This problem requires you to educate your library's staff on safe email usage and to keep your software patched and updated.

Mac

While you can use Microsoft Office products on Macs, you may instead choose to use Apple's office suite, iWork. As with other office suites, iWork comes with applications for word processing, spreadsheets, presentations, and database management. If iWork is on your public stations, it's likely that you'll have to offer some patron training to get them used to the menu systems. You might also want to set up the system to use Pages (iWork's word-processing application) as the default when opening Microsoft Word *.doc files.

For email, Mac users will generally be familiar with Mail. As with any email application, you'll want to keep up with the latest viruses. Many Mac fans will tell you that Mac OS is better than Windows simply because it gets fewer viruses, but there are two views on this theory. The first is that Macs are more secure in general; the other is that Mac OS isn't as popular as Windows, and it just doesn't get targeted as much. Whichever school of thought you believe and whichever OS you use, viruses are real and can destroy your systems. Always keep your protection software up-to-date.

Open Source

There is one way to make switching between operating systems easy for your patrons: Choose an open source productivity suite. LibreOffice, for example, works on Mac, Windows, and Ubuntu, and the interface doesn't change significantly when switching among the three. LibreOffice, which has been around for more than 20 years,[8] is a well-rounded, stable application. Like its competitors, it has a complete suite of applications to help manage your productivity needs. LibreOffice also lets you save files in formats that can be opened on other office suites, making it easy to create a file in the library and then open it up at home on another application. One way to ease your patrons' fears about using an alternative program such as LibreOffice is to change the default file format so it saves word-processing documents to *.doc, which they'll recognize from their experience with Microsoft Office.

When it comes to open source email clients, there are many to choose from, and the most well-known among librarians is Mozilla's Thunderbird. Thunderbird is often overlooked by larger organizations because of its lack of a built-in shared calendar. As with Firefox, however, Thunderbird supports add-ons for additional functionality and has calendars that can be integrated.

That being said, larger institutions might be more impressed with Zimbra, an open source email for the enterprise. As with any email client, though, you want to make sure that all of your security settings are up-to-date and your virus protection software has the latest definitions.

Online

Since many people now have more than one internet-connected device, online productivity applications have grown more popular.

Google Docs and Zoho Office are two alternatives to the desktop productivity suites. While Google Docs (docs.google.com) is more popular, Zoho (www.zoho.com) offers more application options. Both of these office suites offer freely accessible web-based word processing, spreadsheet, and presentation applications, allowing you to log in to create and edit your documents from nearly any internet-enabled device. Teaching patrons about online office suites such as these will save them money and let them access files they have created at home while they are in the library.

In addition to its free Docs service, Google offers Google Apps for Business (apps.google.com) as a pay service to businesses. Google Apps provides access to all of Google's web-based productivity applications on your own domain. This means members of your institution can share calendars and documents hosted by Google, but they can keep these private, restricted to only those logged in on the domain.

Many people have email addresses on a free web-based service such as Gmail or Yahoo! Mail. Even email addresses provided through home internet service providers (ISPs) these days are web-based. These web-based email addresses can usually be imported into a desktop client such as Outlook, Mail, Thunderbird, or Zimbra, but they can also be read in the browser. When it comes to security and web-based email boxes, you're depending on your web browser's security settings and desktop virus protection to keep you safe.

If you choose to use online productivity software, use backup utilities to download the content from the web to your desktop or external hard drive so that problems with the service provider won't cause you to lose important documents and/or emails.

Web Browsers

Whenever you visit small-town public libraries, you'll always have to wait for one resource: internet terminals. In their survey on the use of internet in public libraries, Samantha Becker, et al., found that "internet access is now one of the most sought after public library services, and it is used by nearly half of all visitors."[9] This makes the web browser one of the key pieces of software in libraries.

Microsoft

Many libraries still depend on Internet Explorer (IE) as their primary browser on both staff and public machines. Using IE on public workstations in the library creates a particular set of challenges. Since the software is primarily intended for home use, it can be difficult to lock down in a library environment and to prevent multiple users from changing settings, adding plug-ins, and altering the software for their own purposes. See the section on security in Chapter 4, and look at Microsoft's Internet Explorer Administration Kit (technet.microsoft. com/en-us/ie/bb219517), which provides additional tools for customizing and locking down the browser. You might also turn to Public Web Browser (www.teamsoftwaresolutions.com/projects. html), which, although based on IE, is specifically intended for use in a public environment.

Open Source

A better option, and one that many libraries have chosen, is to switch to Mozilla Firefox (www.firefox.com) on all computers that can access the internet, regardless of operating system. Firefox is an open source browser that has more security built into it right out of the box than many alternatives. It also offers hundreds of plug-ins to extend your security and privacy settings, making it the perfect option for public machines. In 2008, Brian Herzog, a reference librarian at the Chelmsford Public Library in Chelmsford, MA, switched his library's computers to Firefox, stating that "[t]he reason we're switching is a simple one: Firefox is just cooler. It lets us have more control over how the browser functions, and lets us offer more tools integrated right into the browser. Better for us, better for patrons."[10]

In addition to being "cooler," Firefox has been proven to be more secure than IE time after time, making it the logical choice for keeping your library network free of viruses and malware. Add-ons such as NoScript (addons.mozilla.org/en-US/firefox/addon/noscript) and Flashblock (addons.mozilla.org/en-US/firefox/add on/flashblock) stop scripts from running on pages without you saying that it's OK first. Firefox's private browsing functionality (www.support.mozilla.com/en-US/kb/Private%20Browsing) keeps information safe from being stored by the browser—in essence, by the library.

Another browser option is Google Chrome (www.google.com/chrome), another open source browser built with security in mind. Some proponents say that Chrome runs more smoothly than Firefox, but at the time of this writing, it doesn't yet have all of the plug-ins that Firefox has.

Endnotes

1. Steve Krug, *Don't Make Me Think!: A Common Sense Approach to Web Usability*, 2nd ed. (Berkeley, CA: New Riders Publishing, 2006).
2. Eric Lease Morgan, "Open Source Software in Libraries," Infomotions, LLC, June 8, 2001, accessed May 22, 2012, www.info motions.com/musings/ossnlibraries.
3. Eric Steven Raymond, "The Cathedral and the Bazaar," September 2000, accessed May 22, 2012, www.catb.org/~esr/writings/cathedral-bazaar/cathedral-bazaar.
4. While the GPL is the most commonly seen in the library arena, there are nearly 50 open source licenses to choose from. See www.open source.org/licenses.
5. View the current version of the GPL at www.opensource.org/licenses/gpl-license.
6. Blake Carver is the creator of LISNews (www.lisnews.org). Rules reproduced with permission.
7. "Hartford Public Library Chief Executive Officer's Report," March 2010, accessed May 22, 2012, www.hplct.org/assets/uploads/files/about/CEOReportMarch2010.pdf.
8. Previously, it was known as OpenOffice.

9. Samantha Becker, Michael Crandall, Karen Fisher, Bo Kinney, Carol Landry, and Anita Rocha, *Opportunity for All: How the American Public Benefits from Internet Access at U.S. Libraries*, U.S. Impact Study (Seattle, WA: Technology & Social Change Group, March 2010), accessed May 22, 2012, www.tascha.washington.edu/usimpact/us-public-library-study.html.

10. Brian Herzog, "Using Firefox On Our Public Computers" Swiss Army Librarian (blog), May 8, 2008, accessed May 22, 2012, www.swissarmylibrarian.net/2008/05/08/using-firefox-on-our-public-computers.

Chapter 3

Systems Librarianship 103: Web Applications You May Need to Master

> *Engaging with library users on the web is no*
> *longer restricted to simply putting a static HTML*
> *file on a server and calling it a successful website.*
> —Kyle Jones and Polly-Alida Farrington[1]

With more than half of Americans accessing the internet wirelessly,[2] a library's web presence has become more important than ever. This responsibility may ultimately fall into the hands of the systems librarian.

Web Design

Libraries have been creating institutional websites since the launch of the graphical internet, extending their traditional roles as disseminators and organizers of information. While such sites generally started as static collections of information about the library's hours and services, many libraries now take advantage of newer web technologies and techniques to create dynamically generated sites that house digital collections, provide off-site access to electronic subscription resources, and so on.

Due to the changing nature of library sites, web librarians have experienced a corresponding change in duties and expectations. Whereas many librarians began creating and maintaining their library's web presence on an ad hoc basis, with just a minimal knowledge of HTML or of entry-level editors such as Adobe Dreamweaver, the rising expectations of internet users and the ability to facilitate a library's mission through interactive technologies have raised the bar in many institutions.

Many library web designers now face multiple challenges, such as the need to provide sites that meet users' growing expectations while still remaining accessible to users with disabilities, the onus for creating a selection policy for links, the need to make tough decisions as to which parts of the enterprise will be emphasized on the library's front page, the responsibility to make the site usable on mobile devices, and the necessity of supporting more advanced technologies including database-driven sites, personalization, distance learning portals, and streaming webcasts.

Much of this can now be done with powerful (and open source) content management systems (CMSs), reducing the need for additional programming skills. Webmasters in some institutions, however, will still need to acquire skills ranging from programming and database design to graphics creation and video creation. Depending on the tools your library uses to manage the website, you may also need to familiarize yourself with languages beyond basic HTML, such as PHP, JavaScript, AJAX, Perl, XHTML, Ruby, and CSS. Tangential, although not specifically technical, issues for library webmasters include online copyright and privacy issues, linking development, and public internet usage policies.

Any aspiring web librarian should subscribe to the Web4Lib mailing list (www.web4lib.org), the Code4Lib community (www.code 4lib.org) and journal (journal.code4lib.org), and the *Journal of Web Librarianship* (www.lib.jmu.edu/org/jwl). Also examine A List Apart (www.alistapart.com) for design tips and W3Schools (www.w3 schools.com) or Lynda.com (www.lynda. com) for tutorials on almost any language you might need.

You may also be involved in creating an intranet for library staff in order to facilitate access to internal and external staff resources.

This intranet, which can be hosted on your internal network server and made accessible only to staff machines, is a useful way to post and share staff documents such as personnel codes and library policies, training materials, answers to commonly asked reference questions, and schedules and calendars. This is a great time to take advantage of a CMS to give your staff the freedom to create and add their own content to the intranet without having to consult with you before making additions or changes.

Content Management Systems

A CMS is a tool that can be used to manage an entire website or collection of websites. Jones and Farrington sum up CMSs in their guide to using WordPress in libraries:

> Structurally, a CMS is a type of software that allows for the online publishing and management of content, where content is defined by the author. The content is flexible and extensible, and it may exist or be created in a variety of sources but can be somehow interacted with by the CMS.[3]

CMSs can be huge time savers for systems librarians who are swamped with other responsibilities and tend to let the library's website fall by the wayside. Since "always on" wireless internet access (via smartphones, tablet computers, and laptops) has become so prevalent, our websites need to provide all of the information our patrons are looking for in a modern, easy-to-navigate package. CMSs can do just that with little effort on your part.

While you have your choice of many proprietary CMSs, libraries have flocked to open source offerings instead. The three major open source CMSs in libraries are Drupal (www.drupal.org), Joomla (www.joomla.org), and WordPress (www.wordpress.org; see Figure 3.1). Of these tools, WordPress and Drupal have their own library-specific communities[4] that you can turn to for advice

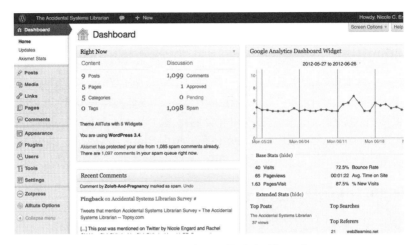

Figure 3.1 WordPress CMS dashboard

and support. All three are widely used and well-documented online. Any one of these tools can be installed on a web server at the library or hosted off site, and each can be used to set up your library website so that staff members have the power to create and edit content without having to consult with a web professional.

Blogs

Libraries are also embracing the power of blogs to deliver updates to patrons. In *Blogging and RSS: A Librarian's Guide*, Michael Sauers points out that "Today, librarians use blogs to share their experiences with their peers, while libraries as institutions use blogs to get information out to patrons. In some cases blogs are the core of a library's website."[5]

Most CMSs (including those just mentioned) provide the option of including a blog on the library website, either right out of the box or by using a plug-in. If your library already has a website and is just looking to link to or import content from a blog, you can take advantage of free hosted options such as WordPress.com (www.wordpress.com) or Blogger (www.blogger.com). Another option is to install a tool such as WordPress on your own web servers and use it to host a blog on your own domain.

While a full discussion of blogs is beyond the scope of this book, it's important to be aware that blogs are used in libraries for more than just sharing opinions and original thoughts. A blog, for instance, can be an easy way to share information about events, book club news, and new acquisitions at the library. Always remember to see what other libraries are doing with these tools and learn from their successes. David Lee King offers some great insights to successful blogging language styles in Chapter 2 of his book *Face2Face: Using Facebook, Twitter, and Other Social Media Tools to Create Great Customer Connections.*[6]

Wikis

Wikis are among the other popular tools that systems librarians need to learn about. A wiki is another web-based application that you can install on your library's web servers (or host outside of the library) to allow your colleagues to work together to create content. Many libraries use a wiki as the base for their entire intranet (as I did in the first library I worked in), giving staff members complete power to add pages and edit content on their own. This also promotes sharing and collaboration without too much effort from the systems librarian. Two popular and freely available wiki products are licensed under the GPL: MediaWiki (www.mediawiki.org) and DokuWiki (www.dokuwiki.org). You can also look into hosted options such as PBworks (www.pbworks.com) or Wetpaint Central (www.wetpaintcentral.com). The Library Success wiki (www.lib success.org), for example, uses MediaWiki to allow librarians to share their success stories (see Figure 3.2).

Mashups

Finally, when creating content for your library websites and intranets, remember that there are many free sources of data that you can use to enhance your content—and your website as a

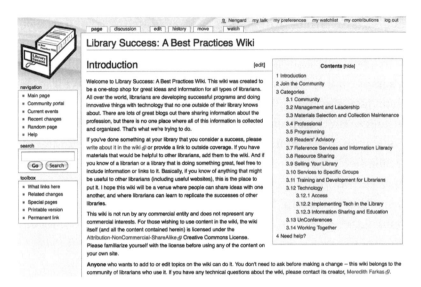

Figure 3.2 The Library Success wiki

whole. Mashups are simply web applications that pull data from more than one source and bring them together as one tool.[7] Libraries can use mashups to enhance their own data or to bring completely new information in to their websites. For more on mashups, see *Library Mashups: Exploring New Ways to Deliver Library Data* by Nicole C. Engard (Information Today, Inc., 2009) and mashups.web2learning.net.

Web 2.0

While the label "Web 2.0" has been beaten to death, there is no easier way to lump together the multitude of social web applications that you may need to understand in your role as systems librarian. If you're managing your library's web presence, then you'll need to be aware of the many ways you can push library data out to the web. Social tools such as Facebook (www.facebook.com), Pinterest (www.pinterest.com), Google+ (plus.google.com), and Twitter (www.twitter.com) let libraries promote their services wherever their patrons are.

As a systems librarian, you may need to make sure that your library is present on popular social networking or Web 2.0 sites, write policies for participating in such sites, and manage the content posted by patrons or the general public on library-branded pages.

Programming

While programming skills are a luxury in many smaller institutions, some programming knowledge will be useful in larger environments (or in those requiring homegrown solutions). Whether you are writing original scripts to extend the functionality of your ILS or adding personalization features to your webpage, programming skills can be useful to many institutions. More systems librarian job ads are now specifying some sort of programming or scripting expertise, particularly knowledge of web technologies and related languages such as PHP and Ruby-on-Rails. Look to the programming titles provided by O'Reilly publishers for assistance in learning new languages quickly. Evaluate the market and the type of library you wish to work in before making a significant investment in shoring up your programming skills, but you should realize that there are situations in which such skills will come in handy.

Cloud Computing

Another technology that systems librarians need to be aware of is cloud computing. John Horrigan defines cloud computing as "an emerging architecture by which data and applications reside in cyberspace, allowing users to access them through any web-connected device."[8]

The proliferation of wireless devices creates the need to store our information in one place and access it from everywhere. This is where cloud computing comes into play. For libraries, this means that more of our patrons will be coming to our libraries to access their files on web-based servers. It also means that more of our patrons will expect to store the data they find at the library in the cloud.

Finally, libraries are seeing more and more services offered as software-as-a-service, which is just a fancy way of saying "we're hosting your software and data in the cloud." It is for these reasons that today's systems librarian needs to at least be aware of the term *cloud computing* and know what this means for any products the library has under consideration.

Virtual Reference

Virtual reference services can range from supporting emailed reference questions to implementing a live environment involving chat or instant messaging and the ability to "push" websites and other resources to remote users. The latter requires your attention to details ranging from selecting and setting up software and webpages, to training reference staff to interact in the online environment, to managing logs gathered from such live interactions.

Endnotes

1. Kyle Jones and Polly-Alida Farrington, *Using WordPress as a Library Content Management System*, Vol. 47, Library Technology Reports 3 (Chicago: ALA TechSource, 2011.), 5.
2. Aaron Smith, *Mobile Access 2010* (Washington, DC: Pew Internet & American Life Project, 2010), July 7, 2010, accessed May 22, 2012, www.pewinternet.org/Reports/2010/Mobile-Access-2010.aspx.
3. Jones and Farrington, *Using WordPress as a Library Content Management System*, 5.
4. For Drupal, there is Drupalib (drupalib.interoperating.info) and the Drupal4Lib mailing list (drupalib.interoperating.info/node/88). For WordPress, visit WP4Lib (www.wp4lib.bluwiki.com) and be sure to join the WordPress and Librarians Facebook group (www.face book.com/groups/214139591937761).

5.   Michael Sauers, *Blogging and RSS: A Librarian's Guide,* 2nd ed. (Medford, NJ: Information Today, Inc., 2010), xi.

6.   David Lee King, *Face2Face: Using Facebook, Twitter, and Other Social Media Tools to Create Great Customer Connections* (Medford, NJ: Information Today, Inc., 2012), davidleeking.com/face2face.

7.   Nicole C. Engard, *Library Mashups: Exploring New Ways to Deliver Library Data* (Medford, NJ: Information Today, Inc., 2009).

8.   John Horrigan, *Use of Cloud Computing Applications and Services* (Washington, DC: Pew Internet & American Life Project, 2008), September 12, 2008, accessed May 22, 2012, www.pewinternet. org/Reports/2008/Use-of-Cloud-Computing-Applications-and-Services.aspx.

Chapter 4

Systems Librarianship 104: Other Technical Areas You May Need to Master

*All you need is the ability to read books, the desire
to learn, and the time to do it.*
                    —Eric Lease Morgan[1]

While there is no way to know all the specific tasks you will be assigned (or need to take on) in your role as systems librarian, the previous three chapters have given you a good overview of tools and technologies. In this chapter, we'll touch on a few additional issues that you should be aware of, starting with the most important application in your library: the integrated library system.

Integrated Library System Management

Integrated library system (ILS) management is one area in which your library background will be essential. Without an understanding of cataloging fundamentals, for example, it is nearly impossible to understand the ILS needs of a cataloging department. As one library systems coordinator stated, "I couldn't do this job effectively without prior knowledge of MARC or cataloguing standards—everything else I can see learning on the job."

Managing an ILS requires attention to issues as varied as:

- Regularly backing up patron and bibliographic data
- Maintaining the ILS server and database

- Creating and running reports

- Technical support for ILS users

- Customizing the display of your public access catalog

- Managing access to and setting up security for staff modules

- Installing client software on staff workstations

- Serving as the liaison between your library and an ILS vendor

- Keeping current with new versions and features, and coordinating any needed upgrades

- Testing connections between the ILS and any linked external databases

- Setting up policies in conjunction with other library staff

- Implementing new or additional modules

In many cases, ILS management will usually be carried out by staff at your library system or consortium, and you will serve as their local liaison. In a stand-alone library, however, someone needs to take responsibility for each of the areas in the preceding list, as well as for any other ILS issues that may arise.

For a discussion of managing an ILS migration, see Chapter 11.

Mobile Computing

Mobile devices are not given enough attention in most libraries. In his report on mobile computing in libraries, Cody Hansen asks librarians what it will take for us to consider mobile computing as more than a passing fad:

> What evidence would provide a good indication that the day had come for your library to focus concerted efforts

on mobile services? If nearly all Americans owned cell phones? Maybe if a large percentage of those phone owners demonstrably used their device to access the internet? Perhaps if smartphone sales began to approach sales of PCs? If major information service providers were shifting their focus from the desktop to mobile devices? If the trend turned away from mobile devices mimicking the functions of desktop computers, and instead desktops began to emulate mobiles? Maybe if there was evidence that traditional desktop connectivity wasn't reaching people who could be reached on their mobile devices?

   If so, then that day is today.[2]

In May 2011, 84 percent of smartphone users and 15 percent of other cell phone users in the U.S. reported that they use the internet on a cell phone.[3] Libraries should be providing services to our patrons on these devices, and it falls to the systems librarian to explore what devices are out there, what makes them different, and which ones the library needs to focus on going forward.

   Just as in the PC market, the smartphone market has several different operating systems, each of which comes with its own strengths, limitations, and—let's not forget—application store. Some libraries, such as the Hennepin County (MN) Library System, offer mobile library apps to cater to as many operating systems as possible (www.hclib.org/pub/info/mobileapp.cfm). Others, such as the (Washington) DC Public Library, start with an iPhone app (dclibrary.org/appstore) and then see what their patrons demand. Your job will be to evaluate your options (considering both tablet computers and mobile phones), compare them to the usage patterns of your patron base, and decide what's best for your library.

Preparing the library for mobile users starts with making our website and catalogs mobile device–friendly. One study found that mobile device users visiting a mobile-friendly version of a site were successful (i.e., were able to complete the task at hand) 64 percent of the time. However, mobile users who had to navigate the full (desktop version) of the site were only 58 percent successful.[4] This means that we need to revisit our websites and online catalogs, and create mobile-friendly versions to help our patrons find what they're looking for more efficiently on their mobile devices. Once that initial step is done, it's time to consider designing apps for mobile devices; the same study found that users' success rate jumped to 76 percent when they used an app to complete the task.

With so many different mobile devices to design for, it can be overwhelming to try and figure out where to start. Many web design blogs have helpful posts and guides to help you get started:

- Smashing Magazine (www.smashingmagazine.com) is a great place to look for design tips, and it even has a "Best of" category where you can find a list of links to articles on mobile web development (www.smashingmagazine. com/guidelines-for-mobile-web-development) or browse its series of articles on current trends in design (www.smashingmagazine.com/tag/trends) to see what other organizations are doing.

- Six Revisions (www.sixrevisions.com) provides articles and tutorials on web design trends, including those related to creating mobile websites and apps. Its article on building web apps the right way (www.sixrevisions.com/web-applications/building-mobile-web-apps-the-right-way-tips-and-techniques) and its best practices guide (www.sixrevisions.com/web-development/mobile-web-design-best-practices) are just two of the many handy guides you'll find.

- Mashable (www.mashable.com) is one of my favorite
  sites for learning about new tools to make my job easier.
  Its list of tools for creating a mobile version of your
  website (www.mashable.com/2010/12/16/create-mobile-
  site-tools) in particular can help you in your efforts to
  provide a mobile-friendly site.

For library-specific resources related to mobile web and application development, check out Lori Barile's article in *College &
Research Libraries*.[5] You can also review what other libraries have
done in the mobile arena by checking out the Library Success
Wiki's M-Libraries page (www.libsuccess.org/index.php?title=M-
Libraries), which lists libraries that have mobile applications, websites, or other mobile services.

In addition to thinking about how best to serve our patrons who
use mobile devices, we need to consider how we can use these new
systems to improve library services. For example, when the staff
members at the University of Northern British Columbia's Geoffrey
R. Weller Library noticed that in-person reference questions were
decreasing, they decided to experiment with a roving reference
model with the help of handheld tablets.[6]

Networking

Networking in libraries can encompass a variety of issues; as
always, the specific networking knowledge you'll need depends on
the needs and technological environment of your institution. In all
but the smallest library, you will probably at least be involved with
administering an internet-connected local area network (LAN). At
a minimum, this network requires ensuring that the server(s)
operate consistently, that users can access the internet, and that
the client machines (whether there are five or 500 of these) can
connect to the server and access shared resources such as files and
printers. Depending on your institutional environment, you also

may be involved in ensuring your network security through the deployment of a hardware or software firewall, while ensuring that the firewall is flexible enough to allow authorized access to online subscription databases and other desired resources. (In larger or consortial environments, the firewall may be maintained at the system's end.)

Software packages such as Microsoft Office may also be installed on your server and accessed by the client machines, rather than being installed and used from the hard drive of each client. Decisions on what to make available through your network will usually depend on the size and needs of your library and the reliability of your network server and connections.

Most libraries currently employ some form of Ethernet network, but some institutions are moving toward replacing or supplementing standard Ethernet cabling with fiber connections, and many are adding wireless connectivity. This network may be small enough to run off of one server, or it may employ multiple servers and server software packages (including Linux and Microsoft). If your website and/or email server is locally hosted, you will need to support internet services, as well as local functions on your network. You may also wish to set up some related locally hosted services, such as email lists or newsletters for your staff and/or patrons.

Client machines may be full-fledged workstations running a client operating system such as Windows, OSX, or Ubuntu, or they may be thin client machines that only gain functionality when they are connected to your network. If you need to add cabling and additional workstations, you may also be involved in planning for new wiring centers, or you'll need to at least add switches to expand the number of clients you can support. Here, you will also need to be cognizant of licensing issues. On a Microsoft-based network, for example, you will need to purchase a client access license for each additional workstation you connect to your server. If you are interviewing for a systems librarian position, be sure to ask questions about the type and size of network you'll be responsible for supporting.

Wireless networks are becoming the norm in many organizations. This is a useful way to avoid the annoyance of running cable everywhere you want to drop a network node—and, of course, as a way to let patrons use their own devices to connect to the internet. In a wireless environment, infrared or radio signals are used to transmit network data between network nodes and a wireless access point (which works much the same way as a traditional network hub), allowing you to place workstations and other devices with wireless network adapters throughout your building—and move them around without having to drop new cable. Wireless networks can also be combined with existing wired versions, providing an alternative method of network expansion.

Useful resources for those interested in establishing wireless LANs in libraries include Bill Drew's Wireless Librarian blog (archived at www.billthelibrarian.com/category/wireless-libraries-blog), which contains vendor information, article citations, and useful links. Also check out The Wireless Networking for Libraries pathfinder at WebJunction (www.webjunction.org/content/web junction/documents/wj/WebJunction_Pathfinder_Wireless_Net working_for_Libraries.html), which provides access to many resources on the topic. Other sources include:

- "Wireless Success Stories" through WebJunction, resourcesharing.webjunction.org/wireless-success

- *Wireless Networks in Libraries* (Library Technology Reports v. 41, no. 5) by Marshall Breeding (Chicago: ALA TechSource, 2005)

- "Look Ma, No Wires! Or the Ten Steps of Wireless Networking" by James L. Glover (*Computers in Libraries,*

March 2001, www.infotoday.com/cilmag/mar01/
glover.htm)

- The Joy of Computing: Recipes for a 5-Star Library by
  Chris Peters (San Francisco: MaintainIT Project of
  TechSoup, www.techsoupforlibraries.org/cookbooks/
  recipes-for-a-5-star-library)

- "Create a Smart Wireless Network for Your Library" by
  Louise Alcorn (WebJunction, January 10, 2012, www.web
  junction.org/content/webjunction/documents/web
  junction/Create_a_Smart_Wireless_Network_for_Your_
  Library.html)

If you are thinking about creating a wireless LAN in your institution, you should also be aware of the potential security implications. First and foremost, change default names, set passwords, and create a separate network for library staff from the one that is accessible by the public. This way, patrons are less likely to access something you don't want them to access.

Related networking issues involve providing consistent access for your library community, whether users are on- or off-site. Your library or consortium may choose, for example, to run remote requests for access to IP-restricted licensed databases through a proxy server so that you can authenticate such requests against your patron database (or by username and password). Proxy servers permit remote access by handling remote requests and passing them through to vendor databases as if the requests were originating from an IP address within your network. Software proxies such as EZproxy (www.oclc.org/ezproxy) that run on an institution's server (bypassing any requirement for users to make modifications to the proxy settings in their individual browser software) are popular in all types of libraries. These also let you gather statistics on remote usage of your electronic resources. Some ILS vendors also provide their own remote authentication products.

Lastly, you might be involved in creating a virtual private network (VPN) environment for library staff if you have a number of telecommuters or others who need access to local resources from remote locations. A VPN allows users coming in over the internet to be recognized as if they were coming from within the local network, while adding encryption to protect your institution's data while it is being transmitted over the public internet. In this way, a cataloger working from home who logs in to your VPN, for example, will have access to modify item records in your ILS database just as if she were working on location at your institution.

An Interview with Ruth Kneale, Systems Librarian

Ruth Kneale, systems librarian, joined the Advanced Technology Solar Telescope (ATST) at the National Solar Observatory (NSO) 9 years ago, after serving as the librarian/webmaster at the Gemini Observatory for 11 years. She talked to us about being a "jack of all trades" systems librarian.

Tell us a bit about your library.

I don't have a library in any traditional sense of the word. I have a bookcase with one shelf of books, mainly conference proceedings and computer manuals, but that's it. I do have a well-populated online library and archive for my staff (spread out over three states), so distributed information delivery is very important. I serve neither the public nor any academic researchers, only the observatory staff, but those services can run the gamut from obtaining a list of citation references to installing a new printer.

Are you the only person working in systems? Do you have to deal with a separate IT staff?

I am, and I do. I provide systems support for my project team, but we are part of a larger organization that I must interface with regularly for services like email accounts, network security, etc. For example, I may spec up and order a new server or workstation, but I then interact with the Computing Infrastructure Services (CIS) department to get an IP address assigned within our subnet, verify the wires at my end are connected to the right router at their end, and add them to the domain. I make sure that all my staff's computers are running the latest enterprise antivirus software, but the licenses we use are provided by CIS.

And anytime I need to move the servers around in the computer lab—or move a server into the lab—I have to coordinate the space I use in our rack with the CIS manager. I have developed good relationships with the CIS staff I work with regularly, and I've learned a lot from them over the years.

Do you deal with the vendors who provide your systems or do you have an administrator who does that?

While I suspect my vendors are not the same as in most libraries, I do deal with them directly and provide the administrative support. For example, we use a proprietary product data management system for our electronic documentation processes, we store all of our files in the "vault," and we use a workflow process to manage our reviews, approvals, and esignatures. I deal directly with the vendor to get our yearly maintenance renewal pricing and then provide that to our procurement department. I administer the system on our servers, including setting up accounts and permissions, and setting up, maintaining, and changing the workflow as we need. When we have a problem I can't solve, I deal directly with technical support and apply any fixes or patches to the server myself.

Can you tell us a little bit about your typical day as a systems librarian?

The one thing I can count on in my job is that I rarely have a typical day! Some of the tasks I'm regularly given include:

- Administer and/or troubleshoot our electronic document management system or other client software packages (including things like getting webcams set up, helping configure backup programs, installing software, configuring printers, etc.)

- Find published papers or help complete a bibliographic reference list for a paper going in for publication

- Administer and manage ATST's web content management system, Drupal (www.drupal.com), and maintain the website (which can range from a quick 30-second update of a page to a dedicated chunk of time setting up a restricted website for an upcoming review and everything in between)

- Administer, manage, and maintain the NSO websites and migrate them into Drupal

- Provide configuration management process support to the staff by shepherding critical documents through our workflow and tracking their progress

- Administer and update our systems database, which is a one-stop-shop for information about all our project documentation, such as reports, technical notes, specifications, drawings, staff publications, and all the other documents generated by a construction project

Most of my days involve at least half of these tasks.

What have you learned on the job that you wish someone had told you in library school?

That working as a nontraditional librarian can be just as satisfying and purposeful as working as a traditional one—and it does *not* mean I'm not a librarian.

What is your advice to other "jack of all trades" systems librarians?

Keep your calm, pace yourself, and take breaks. Expect crises to come in bunches, and practice your juggling. Keep your mind open—many times a solution to a problem won't come from where you expected it. Never underestimate the importance of playing with technology. Don't be afraid to ask for help!

What is your favorite part of your job?

The fact I almost never get a chance to be bored. I definitely do not do the same thing every day, and even when the tasks I work on fall within a certain category, I can guarantee that today's issue is completely different from yesterday's issue. I also love that I get to play with technology and then demonstrate it to our team. Many things the staff thought were not useful in the workplace I have been able to show otherwise, and now they're in common use.

Least favorite?

Software upgrades and system rebuilds, by far!

Where is your favorite place to turn for assistance and information related to systems (specific websites, groups, etc.)?

I get a lot of general systems-related news from the SYSLIB-L list. Being a Drupal administrator, I also belong to several Drupal-related listservs and get a lot of help and information from those. I also have been known to use Lifehacker (www.lifehacker.com) as a starting point for problem research. I have plenty of O'Reilly tech books on my reference shelf, and there isn't a knowledgebase I've met yet that I can't get some useful information from.

Anything else you want to share with us? Anything else you think future systems (or accidental systems) librarians should know about?

This is a great profession where you can let your geek flag fly in tandem with your librarian one! You are not alone—there may not be a lot of us out there, but we are there, and we're happy to help you.

Troubleshooting

As is true of all electronic equipment, computer components and hardware inevitably fail, experience glitches, and require upgrading in order to take advantage of more current technology. Especially if you are in a larger institution with hundreds of workstations, sending machines out for repair or upgrade whenever needed can become prohibitively expensive and time-consuming. Luckily, many common tasks, from adding RAM to swapping cables to installing network cards, are easy to master. A willingness to tinker is often all that is needed to give you a solid background in maintaining computer hardware and resolving hardware issues.

As academic systems librarian Terry Ballard noted even back in 1994, "When a piece of equipment is broken, the only procedure is to send it out for repair. However, I have found that only one percent of my cases need to be sent out. As someone with no technical background and little formal education in computer science, I feel pretty good about that score. The point is not that I am an extraordinary troubleshooter—it's that if I can learn to do this anybody can."[7]

You can begin hardware troubleshooting with a fairly basic set of tools; for many jobs, all you will need is a Phillips screwdriver. If you find that you often need to delve into your machines' innards, you may wish to invest in a small computer technician's toolkit, flashlight, and other basics. Familiarize yourself with the basic layout of PCs; take the time to open and explore a case before you need to do so in an emergency. You can use older, discarded machines to practice on or to strip for parts—and newer PCs are often lighter, easier to open, and better-laid-out, which means that working on them will be a breeze if you have learned on older machines.

You will also need to become comfortable troubleshooting common problems with computer software and configurations. (Find more on researching such issues in Chapter 6.) Some preventative maintenance will go a long way toward preventing many system problems, as will regular backups or drive imaging. On internet-connected terminals, make it a habit to remove spyware, malware, and adware with a program such as Ad-Aware (www.lavasoft. com/products/ad_aware.php) because these unwanted programs can make machines run sluggishly after a while. Defragment disks, back up Windows registries, and otherwise make a habit of maintaining your PCs. Much of this can be automated to run at night in a network environment when it will be least disruptive to staff and patrons.

If you are in a large, spread-out institution, or if you have WAN (wide area network) responsibilities, look into remote-access software such as pcAnywhere (www.symantec.com/business/pcany where) or its free competitor, VNC (www.realvnc.com/products/ free/4.1).[8] These programs will allow you to access both your server and clients from your own desktop, saving you the time and trouble of having to visit a malfunctioning workstation on your own or to sit at the server to make configuration changes or add users.

Antivirus and Workstation Security

In an open environment such as a library, ensuring the security of the computing environment is integral to the smooth functioning of library systems. Whether by accident or by design, patrons are prone to wreaking havoc with unprotected machines, changing settings, releasing viruses, deleting files, or saving pornographic images to the desktop. Since PCs by default assume that their users have certain access to their machines, you need to prevent such problems by locking down public workstations and protecting them from patron interference.

In a Windows environment, for example, start by setting a BIOS password on all machines and set all of your public PCs to boot off of the hard drive before accessing any other drive. Your attempts at locking down a Windows desktop, for example, will be futile if users can simply insert a system disk and boot to a command prompt.

There are a number of ways to control a desktop, which may be used alone or in combination, according to your situation. You may also wish to use these methods in conjunction with software such as Norton Ghost (us.norton.com/ghost) or Clonezilla (www.clonezilla.org), which allow for easy imaging and restoration of workstations. Another option is to invest in a program such as Fortres Grand: Clean Slate (www.fortresgrand.com/products/ cls/cls.htm) or Faronics Deep Freeze (www.faronics.com/enter prise/deep-freeze), each of which restores your original system configuration, settings, and files with each reboot. Such software might be most useful in a computer lab environment, when you wish to allow access to Windows functions for training purposes but still want to keep users from permanently damaging settings or configurations.

The first approach to securing public machines is installing a public PC management application, which locks unauthorized users out of such danger zones as My Computer and the Windows Start menu. Realize that you will have to do some configuring so that patrons can still access the programs and services you want them to be free to access. You should be able to install security software on your server and configure group settings, so you don't have to create new settings for each machine you want to protect. Such security software has been discussed at length on Web4Lib; search the archives (www.web4lib.org) of the list for testimonials and warnings. (Find information on mailing lists for systems librarians in Chapter 7.)

You might also decide to control access to the desktop through setting network rights and permissions for certain users and groups. For example, use group policies to lock patron logins out of changing settings, and/or limit their logins to accessing only one program (such as Firefox on catalog terminals or internet stations). It should go without saying that you need to discourage library staff from leaving staff passwords on display or making their passwords simple to guess. Create written policies for your institution that delineate what users will be allowed to do on public machines; you will probably want to prohibit anyone from loading personal software onto library workstations, for example.

Security software or network policies, however, are insufficient protection for your workstations. Protect each computer in your building, as well as your network server, with reputable antivirus software and be sure to keep your virus definitions updated daily. (You can probably download definitions onto your server and then update workstations from the local network.) Major antivirus vendors include Symantec (Norton Antivirus), Kaspersky, and BitDefender. Invest in a site license or in sufficient client licenses to protect all of your machines. With the proliferation of email-borne viruses, you can also protect staff machines from infection by stripping off any executable file attachments (such those with .exe, .pif, and .bat extensions) at the mail server end. Staff should have no reason to be receiving these types of files and removing such attachments before they are received will go a long way toward protecting your network. Be sure to set your virus scanner to check all drives on access, since this is another major method of infection.

While software security is important, you'll need to recognize the necessity of protecting the physical security of your equipment. Consider the possibility of equipment theft, especially if your library is open late and/or understaffed. If this is an issue for your institution, consider investing in lock-down cables to prevent users from removing expensive printers, monitors, and CPUs. Users in some libraries have even to taken the balls from unprotected mice, and staff members have resorted to gluing them shut (although this can make cleaning them difficult) or have switched to optical versions. Protect against power surges with UPS/surge protectors at each workstation, if possible. Create emergency startup disks for your workstations and back up important data. This is less of an issue on public machines where users should not be storing personal data in the first place, but staff should be encouraged to save all documents to network drives, which should be backed up each night. Check the integrity of your network backup on a regular basis by attempting to restore files off tape to ensure that your data has not been corrupted and that files are actually backing up.

Miscellaneous Issues

You may also need to support a number of newer and more library-specific technologies and services in your institution. These include:

- *Ebook distribution:* Issues here include selecting platforms and formats the library will support, assisting the cataloging department in deciding when and how to catalog ebooks, delivering content to handheld devices, and deciding when and how to circulate ebooks and ebook readers.

- *Digitization projects:* Digitization encompasses a variety of issues, discussions of which could easily fill up an entire volume. Libraries involved in digitization projects are usually concerned with preserving and making historical materials available. A sampling of what you may need to deal with includes the process of converting documents, photographs, and/or videos to digital format; creating cataloging records and metadata; ensuring accessibility, storage, and usability; and attending to the copyright protection and adherence of your digitized collections.

- *Distance learning:* If the university in which your library is located provides distance learning opportunities to its students, your library will need to provide distance learning support for these classes. This can include creating webpages and providing and promoting online resources, creating electronic reserves, snail-mailing course materials to students enrolled in distance learning courses, and supporting interactive courseware.

- *Electronic resource licensing and management:* Your duties here can range from selecting subscription databases to negotiating license agreements with vendors to training staff and patrons on the use of various resources to arranging on- and off-site access to a variety of databases. In larger institutions, you might want to create reports and identify which full-text database contains a desired journal by using tools such as Serials Solutions (www.serialssolutions.com). When selecting and maintaining electronic resources for your library, always remember that formats may change, but your goal is to provide library users with the information and resources that will be most useful to them.

- *Public internet access:* See the Web Browsers section in Chapter 2 for a brief discussion on deploying web browsers in a public environment. Beyond the browser, however, systems librarians supporting public internet access must make decisions such as which plug-ins to install and support; what headphones to buy that will be both sanitary and unlikely to break easily; whether to allow access to chat, gaming, and similar activities; and how often and how extensively to offer patron training. Internet filtering is a separate issue that is beyond the scope of this book, but it's important to realize that you might be involved both in discussions with your administration and/or the public on filtering advisability and effectiveness and in implementing a filtering solution, if your library chooses to use one. Many libraries will also decide to implement time metering and/or print management software, which you will also need to research and support.

- *Adaptive technologies:* Public and university libraries have a responsibility to provide open access to all users and part of providing such access is making library computer technology accessible to all. Your institution might, for example, invest in screen reader or zooming software for the visually impaired. You will wish to ensure that at least some of your workstations are wheelchair-accessible—do not locate all of your catalog and electronic resource stations at stand-up carrels.

- *Mobile access:* Some libraries extend the traditional concept of a bookmobile to include "cybermobiles," which can provide roving internet access, computer training classes, and online database access on the road. You will need to research connectivity options such as satellite internet access or cellular modem solutions.

The preceding descriptions, while insufficient to describe all the duties that a systems librarian's job truly entails, should give you an idea of the common tasks and background shared by many. If you are thinking of becoming a systems librarian, consider whether you have an existing aptitude for, knowledge of, or willingness to learn more about one or more of these areas. Try not to be intimidated by the sheer variety of tasks described in this chapter; you will not need to be an expert in every area and much depends on the needs of your particular institution.

Endnotes

1. Eric Lease Morgan, "Technical Skills of Librarianship," LITA Blog, August 7, 2005, accessed May 22, 2012, www.litablog.org/2005/08/technical-skills-of-librarianship.

2. Cody Hansen, *Libraries and the Mobile Web*, Library Technology Reports 47:2 (Chicago: ALA TechSource, 2011), accessed May 22, 2012, www.alatechsource.org/taxonomy/term/106/libraries-and-the-mobile-web.

3. Aaron Smith, *Americans and Their Cell Phones* (Washington, DC: Pew Research Center's Internet & American Life Project, 2011), August 15, 2011, accessed May 22, 2012, www.pewinternet.org/Reports/2011/Cell-Phones.aspx.

4. Jakob Nielsen, "Mobile Usability Update," Jakob Nielsen's Alertbox (blog), September 26, 2011, accessed May 22, 2012, www.useit.com/alertbox/mobile-usability.html.

5. Lori Barile, "Mobile Technologies for Libraries," *College & Research Libraries* 72, no. 4 (April 2011): 222–228, accessed May 22, 2012, crln.acrl.org/content/72/4/222.

6. James MacDonald and Kealin McCabe, "iRoam: Leveraging Mobile Technology to Provide Innovative Point of Need Reference Services," *The Code4Lib Journal* no. 13 (April 11, 2011), accessed May 22, 2012, journal.code4lib.org/articles/5038.

7. Terry Ballard, "Zen in the Art of Troubleshooting," *American Libraries* 25, no. 1 (January 1994): 108–110, ccbs.ntu.edu.tw/FULL TEXT/JR-EPT/ballard.htm.

8. Learn more about these tools and others like them from MaintainIT at www.techsoupforlibraries.org/cookbook-3/maintaining-and-sustaining-technology/remote-desktop-software.

Chapter 5

Organization of Knowledge

*Proper planning and prioritization is critical to
meeting the technological demands of library
users successfully.*
> —Karen Knox[1]

Many noncatalogers look back on their required cataloging
courses with a mingled sense of relief and disbelief. The organization of human knowledge, however, remains one of the foundations of librarianship, and, whether we retain a personal fondness
for the intricacies of the MARC record, most librarians still love
order. Cultivate the ability to organize the IT knowledge of your
own department or organization, which will always stand you in
good stead. The very process of working in the computer field will
make you realize the importance of being able to find the correct
piece of information quickly, whether you are looking for vendor
contact information, system configurations, license numbers and
registration keys, documentation, or any of the multitude of other
details involved in managing technology in libraries.

Each institution will have its own mix of hardware, software,
and other computer technology, as well as varying levels of complexity in keeping accurate track of technological resources. It is
not necessary to catalog your technology holdings in full MARC
format, but some type of organizational system is necessary
whether you keep your records entered in a variety of databases or
written down and filed in manila folders. This chapter contains
suggestions on recordkeeping and statistics collection that you'll
need to do in all libraries; you can modify these requirements or

methods of organization to fit your own institution's needs. Find discussions on inventorying computer systems, tracking software licenses, maintaining support information, keeping good statistics on electronic usage, and creating useful documentation for others.

Inventorying

Maintaining an accurate tally of your computing assets is critical for a number of reasons. First, when you are creating a technology or strategic plan for your institution, you will need to be able to paint a complete picture of your library's current computing environment. (For more on technology plans, see Chapter 10.) If you have not made a habit of keeping accurate records that describe how computer equipment and software are being deployed throughout your institution as these products and services are added, then you will need to conduct an inventory from scratch when it's time to compose your planning documents. Maintaining an ongoing inventory (that can be modified whenever you purchase or modify computer hardware or software) will simplify the planning process and allow you to see an outline of your technology holdings at a glance.

You also may be required to keep an inventory of computer equipment as part of your library's annual audit. An auditor will need to be told, and perhaps be shown, the locations of all major computer equipment you purchase during a given year to ensure that these purchases are actually being made for and used by your library. In a larger institution where it is not as easy to spot a newer item after the fact, it's important to keep accurate records of where you have installed or replaced hardware in your library during any given year and to match up your inventory with purchase orders and invoices.

Each piece of equipment and each computer system in your institution can be labeled with an inventory number or a bar code, which can also be kept with invoices, documentation, and mainte-nance histories for easier match up. Any method that allows you to locate equipment quickly and to match it up with its information and invoices will suffice. There are other advantages for those who are willing to maintain inventory records. For example, an ongoing inventory will also help you keep track of the library's computing environment and to know where and when you need to update, upgrade, or replace hardware and software. If you keep mainte-nance records as part of your inventory, you will be able to recog-nize at a glance which machines have been behaving poorly. You can identify how many printers you have and their particular make and model, which will help determine how many specific toner car-tridges you may need to keep in stock. You can easily see when each machine was purchased, which helps you keep to a set replacement cycle and to tell at a glance if a machine is under warranty or a sup-port contract. Although these points may seem minor, each piece of documentation is helpful to keep your library technology running smoothly and will save you time in the long run.

Licensing

You or your department's staff will likely be responsible for track-ing the software licenses your institution purchases. It is a good practice to ensure that your library complies with licensing requirements for any software deployed in your library, which requires accurate recordkeeping as to the number of installations, licenses, versions, and locations of particular products. If you are using newer Microsoft products in your institution through open license agreements, you will also need to create a Microsoft Passport account (also referred to as a Windows Live ID) and keep track of that user name and password, as well as the license and grant numbers for each piece of software your library uses.

Whatever you may think of Passport's privacy and security implications, it remains a necessary evil for open license customers and many other institutions using current Microsoft software. To minimize your exposure and to ensure others have access to Passport records after you leave your institution, you may want to create a general library email account on your own mail server and use it solely for such registrations. It's better to not use a free email service for this purpose, since you aren't likely to receive any important messages regarding your registration if you fail to check and clean out your mailbox daily.

Grant and/or license numbers may also be necessary when you need to contact technical support about certain software. For example, if your antivirus software fails, machines are infected, or your server is somehow failing to download and install regular updates, then you can contact tech support immediately, but this often requires you to be able to locate and provide this information.

Ensuring licensing compliance will also prevent your institution from running into legal problems in the future. Software associations and companies are not generally swayed by either claims of poverty or of ignorance, and it is your responsibility as a systems librarian to be sure that your library is in compliance. This is one reason (other than the obvious support and ethical issues) to be wary of letting users install and use their own software; they may not think to put the good of the institution above their own convenience. You may wish to conduct a regular audit of installed software; you should create a policy stating that only systems staff may install software. At the very least, make sure to require staff to clear software installations with the systems department, or with you, if there is no formal IT department, before adding any programs to their machines. It is important to get the backing of your administration on this issue; describing the consequences in terms of possible fines for licensing violations and potential damage to users' systems from illegal and unapproved software will help you make your point. (For more on ethical issues and systems librarianship, see Chapter 12.)

You may also be required to register software in order to activate it. While this process might seem to be an annoyance, especially if you need to register multiple installations, registering all software in your name with the general email address you're using for such registrations will ensure you are on a vendor's mailing list for upgrades and related offers (as well as for unrelated offers and junk mail, but that is another issue). Registration also allows vendors to inform you of patches and security issues with your software and of trials of new versions; some vendors will even offer free online seminars or other perks for registered users. For instance, Citrix Online (www.citrixonline.com), which produces GoToMeeting and GoToWebinar (among other products), emails registered users about opportunities such as online seminars and classes on how to hold effective meetings. If you fail to register your products, you may miss out on useful training opportunities. (See more on independent study in Chapter 9.)

Lastly, keep careful track of all registration keys for your purchased software. This is especially important if you have downloaded and registered software online. If the computer on which you have installed the registered version crashes or if you migrate to newer hardware, you will need the key to reinstall and unlock the software. Often, especially if you have purchased shareware from smaller independent vendors, you cannot count on their records to be accurate if you need to contact them and request that they reissue such a key. Smaller vendors might even go out of business before you need them again, so keep your keys and registration numbers in a safe place.

Support Information

Accurate recordkeeping is also crucial for you to support your library's technology adequately. Beyond keeping track of where computer hardware and software are installed throughout your institution, it is useful to have system information handy for each machine, especially when you need to do an emergency reinstallation of hardware drivers or operating system. You will also need to know your systems' hardware specifications when upgrading to a newer OS, such as when you move from Windows 7 to Windows 8. This will allow you to research whether a system will be capable of running a new OS smoothly before you begin the actual installation process and to locate and install device drivers that will work in your new operating environment.

At a minimum, keep track of items for each machine such as:

- Installed RAM

- Operating system version

- Network card model and manufacturer

- Wireless card model and manufacturer

- Video card model and manufacturer

- Clock speed

- Purchase date and system manufacturer

- Sound card model and manufacturer

This information is most easily recorded when you first buy the machine, but much of it can be retrieved from the system information found in the device manager. Also record IP addresses for each workstation; if these are set as static, as well as those for your network printers, it will allow easier setup when installing that printer on a newly purchased system.

You can keep your system information in an inventory database such as the one from Spiceworks (www.spiceworks.com/free-pc-network-inventory-software), or, if you are in a smaller institution, simply write it down (or keep it in a simple spreadsheet) and file it in a binder. If you are creating your own database or spreadsheet, use your inventory number or bar code as your primary key (or unique identifier) or file system information in order by number for easy retrieval. It will also be useful to keep a current detailed list of any maintenance and troubleshooting that has been done on these machines; this will help you identify "problem children," see what has already been done, and keep track of how your time (and, if applicable, that of your staff) has been spent. (See the sidebar Sample System Information Sheet for a Microsoft Environment.)

Sample System Information Sheet for a Microsoft Environment

Number: Date Purchased: Manufacturer:

RAM: Processor Speed: Location:

Windows Version: Windows OEM Number:

Hard Drive Model/Size:

Network Card:

Sound Card:

Wireless Card:

Video Driver:

Printer(s):

Maintenance Record (include date, problem, and resolution):

If you have the storage space, keep each computer system's driver software and manuals together in its original box and label each with its inventory number. This way, if you need to work on the system, you will have everything you need close at hand. In your box, you may also wish to keep boot disks, warranty information, and any other useful material for that system.

Beyond keeping support information handy for each machine, you will also want to collocate your vendor contact information so that it is easily retrievable when you need to contact tech support. Make sure you have current phone numbers, website addresses, and email support addresses for all of your major software and hardware vendors. Keep track of when and why you have called each vendor and print out or file any webpages or emailed fixes and documentation they send you for future reference.

Statistics

Circulation statistics have long been a traditional measure of libraries' usage. In an internet era, however, statistics on the usage of electronic resources and library public access computer equipment are equally as important as, if not more important than, traditional counts. A patron accessing an online database, visiting your website, emailing a reference question, or spending an hour typing a document on an in-house computer is using library resources, just as the patron who comes in to check out a book or ask a question at the reference desk is. In many libraries, electronic resources have replaced traditional print-based references; online full-text journal databases predominate rather than shelves of periodical indexes, for example. Yet, libraries often lack an accurate picture of how these nontraditional resources are being used.

Given the costs of online database subscriptions and other computer-based resources, having statistics on their use (and on any increase in their use) will help justify their recurring expense. These statistics will also help you plan for the future, since you can see which resources are being used most and how usage patterns change over time. If an expensive resource sees little use, you can either choose to publicize its availability and to offer training on its usage or to cancel your subscription and replace it with a database that will be more useful to your patrons. If you are continually maxing out your allowed simultaneous connections to a resource, you may want to invest in additional licenses. Statistics on electronic usage will also help you make decisions on which print resources to maintain; if users prefer electronic editions, for example, do you wish to maintain both versions?

Keeping track of statistics generated by your integrated library system (ILS) will be another useful way of seeing how people are using the library in nontraditional ways. What if in-person interlibrary loan (ILL) requests at the reference desk are down? Are they being replaced by patron-generated requests through the OPAC? Take advantage of any statistics you can generate or retrieve and use them to plan your future path. Run regular reports against your ILS database to get a picture of how these patterns change over time.

Most database vendors will supply monthly usage reports for their products. Unfortunately, note that these reports are not standardized across vendors and resources, so it can be difficult to use these vendor-supplied numbers to make strict comparisons between databases. Typical measurements include:

- Number of queries or searches

- Number of logins: This may be broken down into in-house and remote logins. If your database vendor is unable to distinguish remote logins made through your proxy server from in-house connections, you may need to compile your own statistics.

- Number of times users were denied access: If your license allows a limited number of simultaneous connections, this will give you an idea of whether you need to increase your allowed level.

- Number of items retrieved: For example, these might be individual full-text articles or abstracts viewed.

- Number of citations displayed

- Number of items retrieved, separated by title

- Number of items emailed

- Number of items printed

- Number of logins by time of day, day of week: This can be useful for seeing if your library is fulfilling the promise of 24/7 access and the use patrons are making of remote resources during nonlibrary hours.

- Amount of time used monthly

If your vendor does not seem to provide statistics in a timely fashion, you may be able to create your own rough measures by logging the traffic that passes through your proxy server. While this method will not provide an accurate picture of finer measurements, such as total numbers of searches and what types of articles are being accessed, it at least can let you know the number of times a database has been accessed from inside and outside your institution. Before resorting to this as your only measurement, however, check with the vendor; some supply statistics only upon request.

When deciding how to compile statistics on electronic resource usage, you may find the Useful Links compiled by the Statistics and Evaluation section of International Federation of Library Associations (www.ifla.org/en/statistics-and-evaluation/useful-links) helpful. It consists of a bibliography on maintaining statistics in libraries and links to helpful sites in several countries.

You also may wish to monitor statistics on the number of full-text journals the library provides access to through such electronic databases. Again, these numbers should be available upon request or regularly provided by the database vendor; they will help you demonstrate how the addition of electronic resources extends the library's physical collection. You should also be able to access (or maintain) lists of journal titles that are included in the databases so that patrons can see whether and where a particular source they are trying to access is available. If you have purchased separate subscriptions to individual online journals, keep track of how these are being used as well.

Keeping similar statistics on the usage patterns of your website will help you make the argument for additional funding when it comes time to devote more resources to your online presence. These statistics will also let you target your efforts to enhance the areas that site visitors find most useful, or publicizing and reorganizing areas that receive little traffic. Patterns will be easier to track if you have first structured your website in a logical manner, as most major statistical packages such as Analytics from Webtrends (www.webtrends.com) track usage by directory (among other methods). These analytics products form the information from your web server's logs into useful reports. These packages also generally provide useful information on the browser and operating system versions your visitors are using, which will help you make decisions about what browser versions to support when designing your library's site. These reports are sometimes customizable, so you may need to work with your own reports or with your outside host to ensure that you are seeing the results that will be most useful for your purposes.

If you have your site hosted at an external web hosting company, note that most providers run a site analysis package on their servers and will be able to provide you with a URL where you can access regular (generally monthly) reports. If you are hosting your site on your own server, you will need to invest in such a package. Install a free log analyzer such as AWStats (www.awstats.source forge.net) or choose a hosted solution such as Google Analytics (www.google.com/analytics; see Figure 5.1).

See if the majority of your website traffic originates in-house or if you tend to serve large numbers of remote users. As patterns change and more visitors come from the outside, you might need to increase the number of resources you provide to off-site users. If you do not seem to be serving remote users, you may have a publicity problem and will need to work on getting your site in search engines and directories, as well as increasing awareness among your patron base of the resources accessible from outside your physical institution. Provide these numbers to your administration and your publicity and reference departments to help them make decisions on how best to publicize electronic resources.

If you have an internal site search function, keep track of what visitors are searching for. Tracking can give you ideas of commonly used areas you may wish to beef up or items you might wish to add to your site. It can also give you an indication of whether your users are confusing your site search with general internet search engines and whether you might need to more clearly describe your search box or link. Note that some free search services (such as Atomz.com, for sites less than 10,000 pages) will keep search records and generate limited reports for you, but they usually require you to visit their site to generate a new index every time you make a change to your own webpages. Most content management

Figure 5.1 Sample Google Analytics for this book's companion website

systems have a built-in search engine already, and you simply need to choose the right plug-in to extract the data from it. Find a number of options for site search tools for your website and/or intranet at Search Tools for Web Sites and Enterprise (www.searchtools. com).When tracking your website usage, you may also wish to compile statistics on what type of connection (dialup, broadband, or mobile) your patrons are using to access your site remotely. For these types of "soft" statistics, you will likely need to survey your user population; consider posting such a survey on your website using a tool such as LimeSurvey (www.limesurvey.org). Other uses for surveys include finding out whether users are actually retrieving what they need from your electronic databases, whether they are able to identify which database will be useful by referring to your online descriptions before starting their search, and whether they find the online help screens to be user-friendly.

Keeping track of patron use of remote resources also extends to tracking how they are using your ILS. Are patrons using the personalization features of your web-based OPAC to check their accounts, place holds, renew items, and pay fines? (If not, what can you do to publicize the availability of these services?) What percentage of your OPAC access stems from outside your institution? You may also be responsible for using built-in ILS capabilities to create and run reports for other departments on more traditional library usage measures, such as number of items circulated, number of patrons registered, and so on.

Public and academic libraries will wish to track how public access computers are being used within the library. If you use signup sheets for internet access, for example, or if your time-management software compiles usage statistics, keep track of how many patrons use your internet terminals on a monthly and yearly basis. (You might also wish to keep track of how many people are turned away or how often users must wait for a machine when all terminals are in use, which can help you see if additional stations might be needed.) If you teach public classes on basic productivity applications, internet use, and/or OPAC functionality, keep track of how many people attend each. These numbers provide a rough measure to help you see whether you need to add more terminals or classes. Note how often patrons need computer help and the common questions that arise. This can let you see whether you need to create documentation answering frequently asked questions (FAQs) or whether you need to increase staffing levels on certain days in computer labs or public service areas.

You may want (or be required) to keep other statistics, depending on the population your library serves. If you have a number of distance education students making use of library resources, for example, you will probably want to track their use of automated ILL services and of any online email or chat-based reference services that your institution offers, as well as tracking how many technical support questions IT staff handles from distance education students. (Here, see whether there are common questions that may be better answered by composing an FAQ and making it available on the library's website or by providing a technical orientation at the beginning of distance learners' course of study.)

Documentation

Although you may not initially view the process of creating documentation for your library's computer systems and services in terms of the organization of knowledge, your efforts at documenting will actually go a long way toward the effective organization and management of technology in your institution. Documentation in this sense includes organizing, collocating, and disseminating the knowledge that will help you and others succeed in your library's technological environment.

Creating useful documentation for general users requires an awareness of the mindset of those who might be using a particular piece of hardware or software for the first time. Construct your documentation in a clear, logical manner and be sure to provide step-by-step instructions for common tasks. Be liberal with screenshots so that users can follow along in pictures and words to see if they are in the right place in your sequence of instructions. Most modern operating systems have some sort of built-in screen-capture capability, allowing you to select just a section of your screen for capture. There are also a number of low-cost screen-capture programs that allow "capture with cursor" and the capture of sections of the screen; see for example Snagit (www.tech smith.com). Basic word-processing software is sufficient to create printed documentation in most library environments. If you're looking to create more professional-looking handouts or guides, you can look into an open source desktop publishing application such as Scribus (www.scribus.net).

Documentation will be useful for both library staff and library users, although it may take different formats and levels of complexity for your different audiences. For library users, consider creating "cheat sheets" on accomplishing specific, common tasks, such as attaching a resume to email or looking up a title in your online catalog. You can supplement printed cheat sheets with more extensive online directions or direct users to resources (such as your catalog vendor's online help screens) and titles your library owns on using specific pieces of software.

For library staff, you can consider posting relevant documentation on your institution's intranet (this is where a wiki comes in handy) so that it is accessible to any staff member from any point inside the library. In a system or consortium where members use much of the same software, try collaborating with your peers in other institutions and sharing the documentation you create. There is no sense in reinventing the wheel if someone else has already produced a usable or easily modifiable document. In his survey response, Ata ur Rehman, head of the library at the National

Centre for Physics Islamabad, noted: "Do not re-invent the wheel for any library need. ... First try to find already available tools or techniques." So before starting fresh, be sure to ask your colleagues on your online networks and mailing lists to share documentation they have written.

You may also wish to create a pool of documentation that you (and your systems staff) can draw upon. Document any support issues and their resolution so that if the situation arises again, it can be dealt with quickly. If you find you have a lot of these issues to document, you can try using a help desk ticketing system such as Request Tracker (www.bestpractical.com/rt) to track problems and keep a knowledgebase. Documenting server and network configurations will benefit you at a later date when you might not remember how you set up particular system. This will also benefit any systems person who steps into your position if and when you decide to move on. Think of the information that would have made your job easier and provide it for yourself, your staff, and your successor.

Overall, any organizational efforts you undertake are designed to make life simpler for you and your fellow staff members. As in the rest of systems work, your goal is to keep technology running smoothly and serving the good of the institution. Taking the time to keep track of how this is done will make everyone's job easier. Taken together, all of your documentation, statistics, maintenance, and inventory information provide a concrete pool of evidence for you to point to in describing the importance of your department's function to your institution. This information paints a picture of what you have done and of the technological environment that needs supporting.

Endnote

1. Karen C. Knox, *Implementing Technology Solutions in Libraries: Techniques, Tools, and Tips From the Trenches* (Medford, NJ: Information Today, Inc., 2011). Visit the book's website at www.karen cknox.com/ITSiL.php.

Chapter 6

Research Techniques

I believe "passing it on" isn't something to be done once you've "made it." Rather it is something everyone should do from the beginning.
—Jill Hurst-Wahl[1]

Systems librarians have an inherent advantage over IT personnel in nearly any other type of institution for one simple reason: We know how to find answers. The increasing complexity of computer systems and software ensures that no one person automatically possesses the right response for every situation. We rely on a diversity of resources, such as vendor knowledgebases, our past experiences with technology, and our colleagues in other institutions, to help us resolve technological issues and to create usable and useful computing environments for library staff and patrons. In systems librarianship, as in librarianship in general, take heart in remembering Mary Ellen Bates's maxim: "Whatever the question, you can either find the information or find someone who can find it."[2]

Systems work and troubleshooting will give you a new appreciation for the way in which your library background builds a foundation for successfully finding and implementing technical information. The usefulness of the experience you have built up in areas such as online searching and reference work extends to systems work as well. As David Ratledge, associate professor and head of systems at the University of Tennessee, noted in his survey response: "Technology requires a lot of research. I put the search skills I have acquired as a librarian to constant use." Margaret Hazel, virtual branch and innovative tech manager at Eugene

Public Library, concurred: "I use reference interview skills all the time to get more information out of the folks who are truly geeky, and to help people troubleshoot the problems they are reporting. I also use my web-searching skills often to find answers to thorny problems."

Another advantage stemming from a background in librarianship is the ability to critically evaluate the technical resources we find. We understand not only how to find information, but also how to interpret and evaluate that information. When researching technical issues, you may uncover a great deal of misinformation and half-truths. Use your research techniques and skills to evaluate the reliability of any information you find, particularly online— where anyone can easily masquerade as a technical expert. Ask questions: Is the answer from a trusted source? Is it current? Does it match up with my existing store of knowledge about this product? Does it match up with my past experience? Can this information be verified with another source?

Our inherent skepticism and willingness to dig deeper can save us from acting on misinformation that may be not only unhelpful but damaging to library equipment and software. Some recent internet virus hoaxes, for example, have taken the form of email insisting that your account will be deleted if you don't provide updated information. However, providing that information gives hackers access to your account, rendering it unusable—or worse. Most librarians, even if they are newer to systems work, have developed critical thinking skills that prevent them from taking such rumors at face value. They should be able to consult authoritative sources to verify any such information before acting on it.

The sections in this chapter provide strategies and resources to help streamline your technical research and include information on where and how to locate answers, as well as on when and why research becomes necessary. The emphasis is on internet resources because these tend to be more up-to-date and because of the huge support community available online. Recognize, however, that opening up your support toolbox to include online resources requires that you give special attention to nurturing the critical thinking skills previously mentioned. Also in this chapter, you will find tips on dealing with vendor technical support as a last-ditch reference resource, conducting support interviews with your own users and staff to help determine the root of a given technical problem, and researching technology purchases.

Resources

The right mix of resources for locating solutions to your systems issues will be unique to your institution. You will want to maintain your own technical knowledge management environment, organizing and maintaining the resources that are likely to be most useful to you. Familiarize yourself with your selected resources and arrange them in a way that makes sense to you in order to minimize the time you need to spend later searching for answers to common problems. Know which source is likely to contain the answer to specific types of problems.

A number of important and commonly used resources will be relevant to systems work in nearly every type and size of library. Supplement more general resources such as those listed in the sidebar Favorite Tech Support Resources with those specific to your institution's needs, such as your integrated library system (ILS) vendor's email list and support website, any customized support pages for your system hardware, and those for your proxy, firewall, and/or filtering software vendors.

Online resources can also be supplemented with more traditional print versions. Here again, you may have an existing advantage because your institution probably owns a number of computer books already that you can consult. Technical titles from O'Reilly Media, Apress, and Que come highly recommended as solid resources for systems librarians, as do a number of the guides from Information Today, Inc. and Neal-Schuman on issues more specific to libraries. When you are researching or learning more about a technical issue, look for topical guides from your library associations, which have the advantage of being short, focused, and library-specific. Library Information Technology Association, for example, publishes monographs on topics from open source software for libraries to the usability of library websites (www.ala.org/lita/publications). Develop your own tech support bookshelf that you can turn to when your internet access is down or when it is easier to sit a book next to your terminal than to switch between screens when looking up answers online. At the very least, keep vendor documentation handy for each system and program, although this is now more often available only online. Check vendor documentation first in the event that yours is a common issue.

Favorite Tech Support Resources: Systems Librarianship Survey

Respondents to the systems librarianship survey were each asked to list a favorite tech support resource. The overwhelming winning answers to this question emphasized the importance of building networks with others using social networks and mailing lists; the top five answers were some variation on Google, email lists, IT departments, library systems journals, and colleagues/staff. (For more on networking with others, see Chapter 7.) Many respondents did, however, mention specific resources (including specific lists). Online resources were clear favorites, and some of the top picks are listed here:

- TechRepublic (www.techrepublic.com) includes handy technology news, tutorials, articles, and software suggestions.

- O'Reilly Media's (www.oreilly.com) solid print titles and thorough technical information mean that it has useful offerings for all library technical personnel.

- Web4Lib (www.web4lib.org) and Code4Lib (www.code4lib.org) email discussion lists for library web managers were mentioned along with the Code4Lib IRC channel (www.code4lib.org/irc), where you can chat in real time with fellow systems librarians.

- Popular technology blogs such as Lifehacker (www.lifehacker.com) and Engadget (www.engadget.com) were presented as good resources for finding tips and new software applications.

- Microsoft Support (www.support.microsoft.com) and TechNet (technet.microsoft.com) were mentioned by several librarians. Although various operating systems are in use in different library environments, Microsoft's overall predominance makes its site a favored destination. Realize also that you may find different answers at the support and TechNet sites; it is worth searching both on a particularly recalcitrant issue.

- While not free, Experts Exchange (www.experts-exchange.com) was mentioned by several respondents as a place to find answers.

- For those working with original programming, Stack Overflow (www.stackoverflow.com) was referenced as a good resource.

Techniques

When one of your systems has a tech support issue, you may find that dredging the right piece of information out of an online knowledgebase or elsewhere will be more difficult than you might expect. This is an increasing problem as software becomes more complex and as the number of (both known and unknown) issues grows. Many issues stem from the interaction of one vendor's piece of software with another vendor's product, so you will need to examine your operating environment as a whole when problems arise. If you have a failure in one program, it will often be due to a conflict with other software or hardware you have recently installed, so your first step might be to think about what changes you have recently made to a misbehaving system. Consult both the new vendor's and the older product's support information to see if there are known issues between the new product and your existing software. Also realize that the complexity of software and the sheer number of products out there can make navigating vendor websites treacherous at best.

Viewing support issues from a reference standpoint, however, can help you dissect these problems. First, you will need to get a handle on a good starting point for your search. As one survey respondent noted: "I think librarians are so well-versed in teasing out any applicable knowledge from a problem. Systems can often be like patrons, with their vague messages and insufficiently communicated demands, that teasing out the information failure of a system vs. a patron often involves the same skill set. A good reference interview, between myself and the system, or sometimes just myself, will often lead to a solution."

Is the system generating an error message? Write it down or drag it out of the affected user and search on the specific phrase or event ID number. Start with the vendor's online knowledgebase. If you have had difficulty locating information in a poorly organized or badly indexed knowledgebase in the past, or if your search uncovers no documents, try your phrase search in a major search engine such as Google (see Figure 6.1), which serves as an index to online knowledgebases such as Microsoft's. A useful trick here is to restrict your Google search to a particular vendor's site by using the syntax *site:* within your query (e.g., site:ubuntu.com). Note that no search engine indexes the entire web and be willing to extend your search with either other general engines or specific tech support sites.

If the knowledgebase doesn't seem to have the answer to your query, check to see if the vendor maintains online discussion forums or an email support group and repeat your search or ask your question there. You can also try asking your question on a relevant library discussion list (see Chapter 7) or in a chat room, because your peers in other institutions may have resolved similar issues or have other ideas on where to search. Other options include opening your search up on a major search engine to see if a nonvendor website has addressed the issue. Here, always be careful to evaluate the reliability of your source before acting on any advice. Also check your print resources and any documentation to see if your issue is described there.

Remember to avoid relying entirely on one source, whether it's a knowledgebase or a favorite manual. Often a source will contain just part of an answer and putting its clues together with other sources' suggestions and/or your own experience will help you find a solution. Some situations will lend themselves to online searching, others to contacting technical support, still others to printed documentation and/or your own maintenance records. As

Figure 6.1 Limiting a Google search to a specific support site

you become a more experienced troubleshooter, you will be able to ascertain more easily the appropriate starting point for your searches and use the knowledge you have gained from resolving previously related problems for solutions to try.

If the affected system is not generating a specific error message you can search for, you will then need to research its behavior. This may take a number of tries before you can sort out the correct terminology for your situation. While systems issues fail to come with a set of controlled vocabulary, there are terms and concepts that will be unique to particular products, situations, and vendors. Locating the right terms for your search is a process similar to realizing the necessity of looking in your OPAC under *Costume— China* instead of the straightforward *customary dress in China*. Each profession has its quirks, and the tendency of vendors to try to minimize problems by disguising knowledgebase articles under innocuous-sounding headings merely exacerbates this issue.

Our willingness to dig through these various sources until we find an answer, by brute force if necessary, also makes us effective systems librarians. One survey respondent noted: "I use my inquisitive nature to come at a problem from different angles and ask a lot of questions to come up with solutions or learn how to do different things." As with reference librarians, systems librarians cannot afford to give up before an issue is entirely resolved or to settle for the first apparent answer without verifying the information and being willing to dig deeper.

When testing your hypotheses, remember the importance of testing one element at a time. If one method fails, reverse your steps before trying another fix. If you keep adding potential fix on top of fix, or if you try several solutions simultaneously, you may end up inadvertently creating a larger problem than the one you were originally trying to resolve. You also create an undocumented situation, in which you might be trying to resolve an unrelated issue months later and not remember that (or how) you previously changed a specific setting. Always know how to put a system back to its original state, and either do so or keep a record of the changes you have made.

Every time we find a working solution for a technical problem, we add to our existing stores of knowledge and provide ourselves with additional background for later, related problems. As in librarianship in general, everything you ever learn about computers will at some point come in handy during your career as a systems librarian. Each support interaction is a potential learning opportunity, and after each, you will be better prepared for the troubleshooting activities that follow. While some computer issues may seem truly unique, most occur with some regularity—and if you have kept track of how you previously resolved the same or a similar problem, you will be able to dispatch an issue much more quickly. Terry Ballard's description of the proper state of mind when contemplating troubleshooting issues may be helpful here:

"1. The problem can be solved. 2. It is my job to solve it, so the buck stops here. 3. Once it is solved, that will be one more thing that I know how to do."[3] Developing a similar attitude will help you approach your library's technical issues with greater equanimity.

Finally, remember that your librarian-honed research skills are integral to successful troubleshooting. As one librarian noted in the survey response: "Librarianship first, technical expertise second."

Dealing With Technical Support

There will inevitably come a time (or hundreds) during your career as a systems librarian when you will need to pry answers from a company's technical support personnel. Getting to the right information by talking to technical support requires an entire additional level of understanding beyond simply looking up answers online or in print. It's certainly similar to locating and dealing with the appropriate expert when you're asked a particularly complicated reference question. You may go through a number of unhelpful individuals before finding your expert, and your expert, once located, might be easily distracted or seem to be speaking some private, indecipherable language. But when you locate the person who is willing to resolve your query, the search suddenly becomes worthwhile.

Try not to be reluctant to call tech support because you are less than familiar with their product; tech teams have dealt with plenty of users who have less product knowledge than you. As technology librarian at the Federal Courts Libraries for the Eleventh Circuit, Carol Bean pointed out in her survey response: "IT (seems to) trust me because I speak 'systems.'" As in many other aspects of systems librarianship, a familiarity with the basic concepts and facility for clear communication (in explaining what you have already tried and the specific behavior the system is exhibiting) will help when dealing with support personnel.

Calling or emailing tech support will often be your last resort when information cannot be located through other sources. It is also an option when you suspect that a quick and simple solution exists and that contacting support directly will let you resolve a situation quickly. Before dialing or writing, however, realize that most frontline technical support personnel are used to dealing primarily with computer novices. Be patient if you are asked whether your computer is plugged in, your monitor is turned on, and any of the other basic and seemingly insulting questions that come with the territory. (And remember to think about asking such basic questions when trying to resolve issues on your own; do not assume that a problem always has a complicated answer!) If you get an automated or irrelevant response to your first email, answer with additional details or pick up the phone. Persevere with patience, and your (likely more complicated) issue will eventually be forwarded to someone along the line who can help. More knowledgeable personnel will not be answering phones on the frontlines because their time would be wasted by having to focus on the preponderance of calls dealing with easily resolvable issues.

When dealing with technical support, also document your issue as extensively as possible. If your system is giving an error, for example, technical support will need to know exactly what that error message is, so write it down. Have you dealt with technical support before on the same (or a similar) issue? Have it documented and get the names of representatives you deal with and incident numbers, if applicable. (See Chapter 5 for more on the importance of keeping thorough documentation.)

Your institution may also wish to invest in a cell phone or portable phone for your use while dealing with tech support, so that you can call while near PCs that lack accessible phone lines.

Often another support option is to look for answers (or post your question) on a vendor's technical support online forum or email discussion list. (See more on networking online in Chapter

7.) Many companies host online forums on their support sites, which are optimally staffed by technical support personnel. You can browse through previously asked questions to see if other users have encountered a similar issue or ask your own question of the support rep monitoring that forum. An added bonus is that you may often find your question answered by another user who has encountered the same problem and is willing to take the time to explain how it was resolved.

Many companies today have Twitter accounts where you can get quick answers to your questions. Sometimes these Twitter accounts are monitored more often than the forums and get you quicker answers than waiting on hold on the phone. Check to see if the vendor in question has a Twitter account and send your question to it using the @ (at sign) notation. If not, it might help to send a tweet out to your followers asking if they've seen the error you're experiencing. For my quick technical questions this has often been the most efficient way to get answers.

Lastly, find out what technical support options are available from your larger institution, system, or consortium. If your system headquarters or campus computing center, for example, employs a networking expert whose responsibilities include resolving network issues among member libraries, contact that individual first if a LAN problem looks too difficult or time-consuming for you to resolve locally. Be sure to contact them first if your issue seems to affect the system rather than just your institution or if it affects equipment they have provided or software they have installed. Develop a relationship with the systems staff members there so that you are able to draw upon their expertise when needed, and so that you are less likely to be left out of the loop when it is time to make systemwide decisions that will affect your local network and/or computing environment. Find out which types of issues are appropriate to escalate and refrain from referring every minor problem, but be sure to know when it is necessary to call on your larger institution for help. Also find out who to contact at your larger institution when you need changes made that affect your local network; for example, you may need additions to your proxy server or to your filtering software in cases where these are hosted at the system end.

If possible, always push an issue to your larger institution before paying for technical support from a vendor. If you are faced with making the decision as to when to contact pay-for-support, a good rough guideline is to estimate the number of hours you have spent—or seem likely to spend—resolving the problem in-house. What is your (or your staff's) time worth to your library? Multiply the number of hours you spend on a problem by your hourly salary, and, if you are spending more by keeping the work in-house than you would on the support call, you are not really saving your institution any money. While you are tied up resolving one issue, other tasks may go undone. Do realize that many pay-for-support options will require a credit card number, which libraries tend to dole out sparingly. Be prepared to explain your need to the appropriate manager or business office employee.

The Support Interview

Systems librarians are generally in the position of having to deal with outside technical support, as well as serving as help desk or technical support in their own institution. Again, you will tend to find yourself in the role of liaison, translating vendor-speak, contacting tech support for an affected user, and identifying the real problem behind a given user's request.

Any librarian who has been through introductory reference coursework—or who has worked at a public services desk—is familiar with the concept of the reference interview. Your background in ferreting out the real question behind an initial encounter will come in handy when a staff member or library patron begins a technical support interaction with the statement: "This computer isn't working!" Now it is your turn to be on the other side of that tech support call. Viewing your technical support encounter as a reference interview will also help you view this process as a collaborative effort between yourself and the affected patron or staff member. Your main goal in a support encounter will be to resolve the problem to the user's satisfaction, but your secondary goals can include identifying the real issue, identifying whether there are related or underlying issues that might also need resolving, and identifying opportunities to use the encounter as a learning opportunity. (Of course, these aspects are ideal, and in a busy library environment, you may often be satisfied with just getting a user's computer up and running again.)

The first step in your technical support interview will be to get a detailed description of the problem. Start from the statement "This computer isn't working!" and ask targeted questions to ascertain the real issue. Useful questions to help narrow down the exact problem include "What exactly is it doing?", "Is it displaying an error message?", "What were you doing when the problem occurred?", and so on. If this is a recurring glitch, try to have your staff members or patrons recreate the issue. Have them show you exactly what they are doing when the situation occurs. Try to ascertain specific error messages, identify the specific software and version they are using, find out when the problem started, see if they have installed software or otherwise modified their machine without your knowledge, and ask if the machine has been experiencing minor problems for a long time, which now have escalated to the point where the user cannot function.

It will often be easier to observe an individual's actual workflow than to have her try to explain her exact sequence of actions when a problem occurs. As Gem Stone-Logan, IT application engineer at High Plains Library District noted in the survey: "I think the reference interview is one of the most powerful tools any librarian is given. Before you can fix a problem, you have to understand what the problem is. Reference librarians are taught not to assume the initial question is really what the patron wants to know. Similarly, when a staff member reports a problem or I see an error message, it's important not to jump to assumptions about the problem."

If you are in a larger institution and feel confident in your ability to train your coworkers to report problems accurately, or if there are often times when no systems staff is available to resolve technical issues, you may want to develop a standardized method of reporting computer problems. Create a printed fill-in-the-blank form that can be kept at central locations such as the reference and circulation desks, and use this form to coax usable information out of the reporting staff member. Include space for the date, the location of the affected machine (here your inventory numbering system will be useful in easily identifying which system needs work), the name of the staff member, any error messages generated, a description of the issue, and anything the staff member may have done (e.g., reboot, change settings) to try to resolve the problem on her own. Many computer repair shops use a similar form to describe problems when items are dropped off for repair; you may be able to borrow ideas from your local vendor and adapt the format for use in your library.

Some libraries find it useful to use the back of their standard "Out of Service" signs for these reports, so that the person tagging a piece of equipment as being out of order is also responsible for filling out the form. Others prefer submitting forms electronically through a web-based help desk application so that it goes directly to the systems librarian or support department; this way the situation can be dealt with as quickly as possible and an archive of the solution can be kept. Make sure that all staff know to whom they should report computer outages. If you have several systems personnel, make it clear whether staff should report problems to different individuals or whether you prefer centralized reporting.

Remember also that it is often more difficult for users to describe a problem in writing than in person and take the time to speak directly with the reporting staff member before attempting to resolve the situation if the written report seems unclear or incomplete.

If working in an environment where it's hard for you (the systems librarian) to see what the librarian is doing or experiencing on his computer, ask for screenshots or screencasts of the error. Some of the easiest support requests to answer come with a visual of what the person on the other end is experiencing on his machine. This might also be a good time to use an application that gives you remote control of the problem computer, especially if you're in a large, spread-out institution where it's not easy to visit each affected machine.

Sample Computer Problem Report

Date: Reported By:

Inventory Number: Item Location:

Please describe the problem, in as much detail as
    possible:

List any specific error messages the system is
    generating:

List any steps you have already taken to try to resolve
    this issue:

You can keep these reports on file to help you identify machines that constantly act up and may need more drastic fixing or replacing. You might also want to create a maintenance reporting form for yourself and/or your systems staff that gives the date and resolution of each of these issues. This completed form can then be kept on file with your inventory or in each system's motherboard box so that you have both a record of what has been done and a reference to consult if the issue occurs again in the future. Some help desk applications have knowledgebases or ways to track this type of information electronically as well.

Try to create an environment in which library staff feel comfortable approaching you and/or your staff with their computer problems. While many staff members might seem to approach you with every minor issue, others will not want to waste your time or may feel they are exposing their technological ignorance by asking for help. If not dealt with, however, minor issues tend to evolve into major ones. Users who have become frustrated by constant minor annoyances will tend to be less comfortable with technology and more resistant to change. This is another reason why people skills are so important. Always ensure that staff members understand that these problems lie with the computer, not with them, and that you want them to come to your department with even seemingly minor issues.

Back up this request with a willingness to deal with such issues as swiftly as possible. This response requires developing the ability to prioritize your time and to differentiate actual issues from minor glitches that may just require a reboot. (See more on teaching staff to do minor troubleshooting and identify real problems in Chapter 8.) Make sure that if you have several systems people on site, all staff members know who they can go to with their computer problems. For example, if one systems person is in charge of networking and one is a printer whiz, make this information accessible to all staff so that the right person can resolve a given issue quickly. (If you are a one-person shop, then all queries will come directly to you, of course.)

You may need to be more proactive at first; set a regular time to go around the building and talk to staff about their computing environment, their needs, and their issues. Those who will not come to you directly might be willing to share their frustrations if you show your openness by first coming to them. While making your rounds, take the opportunity to engage in some preventative maintenance; bring some canned air and clean out case fans, defragment hard drives, and open up mice and dislodge any dust and lint. While it might be difficult to fit proactive maintenance into your schedule, setting aside a couple of hours each week will help prevent larger and more time-consuming problems in the future, as well as help you become acquainted with other library staff members and their specific needs.

Researching Technology Purchases

Any savvy consumer knows the importance of doing research before making any major purchases. This is doubly important when you are dealing with your institution's somewhat larger budget, and recommending and approving the purchase of software, products, and services on which your staff and users must rely and which you are responsible for maintaining. Researching and providing specs on technology purchases and getting competitive quotes from vendors will also be necessary in many libraries, especially when a purchase will be funded with grant or other specially acquired funding. It will be easier to recommend technology purchases if you develop the habit of keeping yourself continually informed about recent technological developments and possibilities. (See more on this in Chapter 9.) If you know your institution will be in the market for a particular technology solution in the foreseeable future, watch for articles on and mentions of that technology in your daily reading.

Also develop a collection of resources you can consult when researching such purchases. These resources can include websites, discussion lists and list archives, colleagues in other institutions, journal articles, product reviews, and so on. Outside sources and those who have used a particular product or service can help you evaluate its merits before committing to its purchase. Recommendations from your peers on software purchases can be especially useful; the library environment presents special challenges so programs can be deployed and run smoothly. Your colleagues may be able to notify you about problems with particular packages in a public access environment or to any adverse interactions between popular security software and the products you are evaluating.

As in systems librarianship in general, your previous experiences and your network of resources provide the foundation for evaluating potential purchases in terms of your library's needs. Your past experiences that include the time and aggravation involved in maintaining and troubleshooting generic, lower-priced PCs, for example, may lead you to investigate name-brand replacements in the future even if the initial cost may seem higher. Your experience with machines that were not easily upgradeable may lead you to ask questions about expansion slots and case design. Your experience with poorly designed navigation and search schemes may lead you to request trial access to an online database and allow public services staff to experiment with its usability before committing to its purchase. When evaluating any technology purchase, consider the total cost of ownership, which includes the time taken by staff in maintaining, learning, and effectively using the product. This is doubly important if you are a solo systems librarian because your time could be better spent than in repeatedly troubleshooting the same off-brand or poorly designed systems.

When evaluating these purchases, investigate both the reliability of a given vendor and its reputation for providing technical support. The annual Perceptions report conducted by Marshall Breeding,[4] for instance, is worth reviewing if you're in the market for a new ILS; it provides customer opinions about the major ILS products and vendors. Breeding also offers the Guide to Integrated

Library System Marketshare and Migrations (www.librarytechnology. org/web/breeding/ILS-marketshare-migrations). This lists the products and vendors that libraries have switched to and from.

If you have limited support from your larger institution and/or no other systems staff in your library, you will need to rely on support from your outside vendors. Again, consult systems librarian lists for comments on specific vendors, read comparative articles in computer journals, and ask others about their support experiences. If you read nightmare stories about others' support interactions with a given vendor, you might reconsider purchasing that vendor's product. Even if that product initially seems the most cost-effective solution for your institution, it may end up costing you more in terms of your time and your users' lost productivity in the long run. Try to look at the big picture and not only a single issue, such as price or initial convenience. Also pay attention to warranty periods on hardware (which should be at least one year) and ascertain whether support is included in the initial pricing or whether on-site or telephone support is only provided at additional cost.

When evaluating software and database purchases, be alert to offers of free demo software, onsite or online vendor demos, and other opportunities to try before you buy so that you can better see if a particular piece of software will meet your institution's needs. Demos may also let you see how the software will work in your environment, under your security software, and with the other programs on your network before you commit to a purchase. Always ask for trial access to online databases and other electronic resources; never commit to purchasing an expensive electronic database without having an opportunity to evaluate the product in your own institution. Peruse vendor websites for trial offers or contact the sales department at a specific vendor to see what options you have. Look for reviews of electronic resources and online databases to help you evaluate products before purchasing, since many library review journals now include coverage of these products in their review sections.

Researching purchases also involves researching different departments' technological needs. If you have kept the lines of communication open between yourself and nonsystems staff, you will have a better idea of the library's true needs. Involving other departments, especially in the purchase of electronic resources that they may be using on a daily basis, also helps avoid the impression that decisions are coming from on high without an opportunity for staff input. While you will provide the technical expertise behind a purchase decision, involving others is essential in making sure that these purchases serve the needs of your institution.

It may help to approach researching technology purchases as you would approach researching any large collection development purchase. You can apply similar criteria as to cost, suitability for your library's population, timeliness, and so on, and use review sources to help you make a decision just as you would in researching the purchase of, say, a major art encyclopedia. Also evaluate products and services in terms of your current computing environment and what you have previously purchased, just as you would when adding to the rest of your collection.

If you work in an academic, public, or school library, your institution is also eligible for academic or government discounts on most software and some hardware purchases. Sometimes these discounts can be substantial and will allow your library to purchase packages and equipment it could never otherwise afford. Websites such as TechSoup (www.techsoup.org) offer many popular software titles to nonprofits at a steep discount, and it's well worth consulting when it comes time to upgrade to a new version or purchase a new application. Always investigate academic/ governmental pricing options, whether from the vendor or from approved resellers such as Dell's governmental divisions. Some software is even free for nonprofit and/or academic use; check the license agreements of your shareware programs for such clauses.

Another factor to consider when researching purchases is deciding when and whether technology purchases, especially replacements of existing hardware and software, are actually necessary. While old equipment may still function perfectly well for its original purpose, you need to ask questions to find out whether it is time to upgrade: Do users need new software for compatibility purposes, or is it because you are upgrading the ILS or otherwise changing the computing atmosphere? Can your older hardware handle the newer software you are installing? Can older hardware be upgraded or repurposed? Is it cost-effective to do so? Does newer software offer features that will be useful to staff or patrons, or do they spend time working around issues created by older programs so that it is affecting productivity? Have vendors ceased supporting the older hardware or software? What funding is available for upgrades and can alternative sources be found? Is older hardware requiring constant maintenance?

The answers to these questions will help you determine the appropriate replacement cycle. Be sure to look at overall costs of using older equipment and programs, including reduced productivity of staff and users, as well as your and your department's time. Your inventory and maintenance records will be useful in determining the existing state of computing equipment and provide answers to some of these questions. Knowing your department's level of funding will help you determine whether you can realistically keep to an ideal replacement cycle or whether you will need to seek out alternative sources of revenue.

Overall, knowing where and how to look for an answer will be one of the most important building blocks in your successful systems librarian career. Take time to develop the research and critical thinking skills necessary for resolving the issues that will inevitably arise.

Endnotes

1. Ulla De Stricker and Jill Hurst-Wahl, *Information and Knowledge Professional's Career Handbook: Define and Create Your Success* (Oxford: Chandos Publishing, 2011), 185.
2. Mary Ellen Bates, "The Newly Minted MLS: What Do We Need To Know Today?" *Searcher* 6, no. 5 (1998): 30–33.
3. Terry Ballard, "Zen in the Art of Troubleshooting," *American Libraries* 25, no. 1 (January 1994): 108–110; ccbs.ntu.edu.tw/FULL TEXT/JR-EPT/ballard.htm.
4. The 2011 report (which links to previous years) can be found at www.librarytechnology.org/perceptions2011.pl.

Chapter 7

Networking

> *No matter how great you think you are, you can't*
> *do it all alone. When you can get a large group to*
> *collaborate, you can achieve monumental tasks*
> *that may have been previously impossible.*
> —Chris Brogan and Julien Smith[1]

Successful systems librarians know that networking extends far beyond deciding where to drop the Ethernet cable. One of the most important factors in our ongoing achievement is the array of professional and social networks we foster among our peers, vendors, and colleagues. While we can use the skills honed in our research techniques lessons to independently find answers to many problems, the best source of support will often be a colleague or other professional who has already been there. Interacting with other systems experts can also give us ideas for ways to improve the technological environment in our own institutions, to reduce our own workloads, and to provide answers to questions that we may not even have thought to ask. Lastly, networking with other systems professionals helps us understand that we are not alone and that others are experiencing similar frustrations and stresses—and successes. Both formal and informal networking groups provide opportunities for brainstorming, resource sharing, and showcasing examples of what other libraries are doing and can do with technology.

Systems librarians can find plenty of opportunities to interact with others in similar situations, both online and offline. The following pages offer recommendations on locating online discussion groups and in-person technology interest groups and associations, effectively interacting through such groups, and cultivating informal support networks with peers, staff, and colleagues. Each of these networking methods is essential to your success (and sanity); there is no single way to connect with other systems librarians. Survey respondent Andy Ekins, senior library systems officer at Canterbury Christ Church University, recommended that new and aspiring systems librarians "get connected to as many people as you can through Twitter, blogs, networks, conferences," and another librarian backed him up by stating quite simply, "You must connect with other systems librarians!"

Online Discussion Groups

As you might expect, there are a number of online forums where library systems workers can interact and share their knowledge. Online email lists and other discussion forums have the advantage of leveling the field: Systems staff members in the smallest, most underfunded library are equally able to participate in these conversations with those in larger institutions who have the funding to attend costly in-person conferences and workshops. Lists provide venues for discussions with colleagues even when no other systems personnel are handy to consult within our own institution.

Lists can provide a place for quick feedback on your systems questions; you can fit these interactions into your schedule since you can post a technical question or comment and then return at your leisure for a response. They are also a source for keeping track of virus and security alerts on common library applications, which can allow you to forestall technical problems in your own institution.

Beyond troubleshooting assistance, systems lists also let systems librarians discuss broader issues facing systems librarians and create a source of community for those, especially solo systems librarians, who may otherwise have a tendency to get bogged down in day-to-day technical tasks.

Selected Online Discussion Groups for Systems Librarians

Code4Lib (dewey.library.nd.edu/mailing-lists/ code4lib): Librarian developers and system administrators can discuss new technologies and provide support for one another.

Digital Libraries Research or DIGLIB (infoserv.inist.fr/ wwsympa.fcgi/subrequest/diglib): This list promotes discussion of digitization in libraries.

Drupal4Lib (listserv.uic.edu/archives/drupal4lib.html): This list helps librarians communicate with other librarians about the Drupal content management system.

Electronic Resources in Libraries or ERIL-L (listserv.binghamton.edu/scripts/wa.exe?A0=eril-l): This list deals with the selection and management of electronic resources in libraries; it covers issues such as collection development, statistics, and licensing.

LIBNT-L (listserv.utk.edu/archives/libnt-l.html): Discussions here center around the use and management of Windows server and client releases in libraries.

LITA-L (lists.ala.org/sympa/arc/lita-l). Librarians can find announcements and discussions relating to the interests of LITA (Library Information and Technology Association).

NETTRAIN (www.lsoft.com/scripts/wl.exe?SL1=NET
  TRAIN-L&H=UNM.EDU): This email discussion list
  is designed for internet and computer trainers not
  specifically focused on libraries.

PACS-L (www.lsoft.com/scripts/wl.exe?SL1=PACS-
  L&H=LISTSERV.UH.EDU): Here's one place to
  discuss end user computer systems in libraries,
  including OPACs and electronic databases.

Perl4Lib (perl4lib.perl.org): This site is designed to
  exchange programs and ideas from Perl
  programmers in libraries.

SYSLIB-L (iulist.indiana.edu/sympa/arc/syslib-1): This
  list for systems librarians channels discussions to
  topics related to their field.

Web4Lib (lists.webjunction.org/web4lib): Library web
  managers can talk about web design issues,
  managing public internet access, and training staff
  and users to use the web and/or web resources; its
  online archives are a great resource for designers and
  for those managing servers and sites at their libraries.

wp4lib (www.wp4lib.bluwiki.com): This discussion
  forum for librarians uses the WordPress content
  management system.

XML4Lib (lists.webjunction.org/xml4lib): Discussions
  here focus on the use of XML in the library
  environment.

See the above sidebar Selected Online Discussion Groups for
Systems Librarians for suggestions on systems lists to join. Find
additional groups by asking colleagues to recommend groups they

find helpful. But don't limit yourself entirely to lists for systems librarians; lists for IT professionals, technology trainers, and web designers may be just as useful to you. For more general lists, try searching by subject on CataList (www.lsoft.com/catalist.html). If your ILS vendor offers a list (or lists), consider joining or at least ensure that someone on your system staff or at the consortial level follows the discussions and forwards pertinent information. Your larger system or consortium may also have a list to support a technical task force or user group, along with national library associations and their subgroups.

Successful online interaction requires a few simple ground rules: When you first join an online discussion group, read any introductory messages carefully (and the FAQ, if available). These messages will provide the scope of appropriate discussion on the particular list or forum, and adhering to these guidelines will prevent you from asking off-topic questions or making comments that might be more appropriate in another venue. The guidelines will also provide instructions for leaving the group at a later date. (Never post repeatedly to an online group—especially a systems group—asking how to unsubscribe; you will succeed merely in annoying its members.) Before making your first post, read some previous discussions, and, if asking for help, check the group's online archives to see if your question has already been answered. The rest is common sense: Treat other group members with professional courtesy and respect, and lend your own expertise if you are able to answer a question posed by another member. Finally, Reply All when asking further questions or providing answers so that the entire group is kept in the loop. At least some systems people on these lists have been online longer, possess more expertise, and have likely exhausted their tolerance for breaches of netiquette, so participate appropriately.

Managing your time online requires the mastery of the grand art of skimming; read and file what is appropriate for your situation and ignore (or delete) the rest. Do not feel compelled to read every message that comes through every list. No one will know! If the traffic on a particular list gets to be too much for you, unsubscribe. You can always schedule periodic trips to its online archives to pull out any relevant material you may have missed. (If you do make a habit of skimming, be sure to read recent archives before posting to ensure that you are not repeating a point someone else has just made.) Finally, I file messages from lists directly into folders instead of cluttering up my inbox, but they are there to refer to when I have the time or inclination. In web-based clients such as Gmail, I have my messages go right to the labels I've set up and skip my inbox entirely.

Lists provide the perfect opportunity for learning from other technology librarians' experiences. The number of discussion group participants is large enough that others have probably resolved similar problems or worked with similar situations. Having group members willing to share these experiences and their expertise creates a true online community of experts, and no systems librarian can afford to remain outside this community. Once you have made online contact with group members, you may strike up an "off-list" conversation and develop a more personal relationship with group members in similar situations. Beyond providing a forum for group discussions, email is also exceedingly useful for one-on-one communication. Building a personal list of experts will give you a community to call upon for technical and personal support, and you may also locate potential mentors in other institutions.

This pool of colleagues and experts is especially useful to an accidental systems librarian who lacks a ready source of technical support in her own institution. It is easy to feel professionally isolated when you are the only systems person in your institution, and online participation can help reduce those feelings. As you can see from the sidebar earlier in this chapter, there are lists focusing on nearly every topic of interest to library systems personnel; systems librarians in all types of libraries appreciate the support and collegiality that these groups provide. Many systems questions may lend themselves to being answered via email, as group members can easily point to online resources and examples. Further, groups allow you to ask questions on newer or more library-specific issues that may not be retrievable from an easily accessible print or online resource.

Beyond email lists, system-specific web-based support forums and systems discussion groups provide another opportunity for learning and for building community. While most of these are not specifically focused on the library environment, they will still prove useful to technology librarians in all sorts of situations. Take the opportunity online resources provide to broaden your scope and to interact with systems peers in other environments.

Social Networks

One of the top ways systems librarians keep up with technology news and each other is by using social networking sites such as Facebook (www.facebook.com), Twitter (www.twitter.com), LinkedIn (www.linkedin.com), and Google+ (plus.google.com). Which is the top favorite tool of librarians answering our survey? Twitter.

Twitter is one of those tools that people love to hate. I like the way Seth Godin describes it in his book *Tribes*:

> Most people who see Twitter.com don't get it. It seems invasive or time consuming or even dumb.
>
> The converts, though, understand the true power of Twitter. Twitter is deceptively simple: It's a web protocol that makes it easy to instant message people with short

notes like "going to the gym." In fact, the limit is 140 characters, about half the length of this paragraph.

The difference between an instant message and [tweets], though, is that your instant message goes to one person and a [tweet] goes to anyone who has chosen to follow you.[2]

Using a tool such as Twitter to connect with your fellow systems librarians worldwide is a great way to see what new projects they're taking on, and it's a great way to get your question out to the masses. I have asked several systems (and nonsystems) questions on Twitter, and I always get at least one helpful answer but usually more. With Twitter, you can also expand your network to include nonlibrarian-specific sources for information—find those relevant to your own duties. In my role as director of open source education, for instance, I like to follow as many open source-related companies and authors as possible. If your focus is on security, for example, you can follow popular security companies such as Norton on Twitter (www.twitter.com/nortononline).

Facebook offers a convenient way to connect with the right people and gather information. I set up a list of contacts who work in libraries and have another for those who work with systems. This lets me easily see what new things people in specific fields are sharing. Sometimes I find the greatest new tools and tips simply by reading my news feed on Facebook.

Facebook also lets you create both public and private groups, which can be used to gather your most trusted systems librarian colleagues to share information and answer questions. This can be used either in conjunction with a mailing list or as a replacement, depending on the preferences of your colleagues.

LinkedIn focuses primarily on professional networking and job hunting, but did you know that it also has a section titled Answers (www.linkedin.com/answers) where you can ask and answer questions in your field of expertise? Why limit your network to librarians? Sometimes getting a fresh nonlibrarian perspective is just what you need to make your project run more efficiently. As on Facebook, you can also set up groups on LinkedIn, giving you yet another avenue for communicating with your colleagues.

Finally, the newest tool to join the social network arena is Google+, which approaches networks slightly differently than other similar sites. It asks that you put the people you connect with into Circles, which are supposed to imitate your social circles in real life. For example, I have a Library World Circle and a Family Circle. One complaint my family has about my Facebook page is that it's full of links to articles and topics that confuse them, but, by using Circles on Google+, I can share my library-related research with my Library World Circle and pictures of my dogs with my Family Circle.

The main drawback to Google+ is that it's still new, and librarians haven't quite figured out how to fit it in with the other networks they're using already. So, activity on Google+ has been sparse, but I'm seeing new colleagues sign up daily. Its use is likely to increase, so systems librarians should be aware of Google+ as another way to network with colleagues around the world.

Interest Groups

Online discussion groups and social networking sites present invaluable networking opportunities, especially for busy professionals whose duties allow little time for in-person communication. But there are also times when more old-fashioned networking is necessary—if only for the opportunity to get out from behind the computer screen. Technology interest groups (sometimes called committees, user groups, special interest groups, or forums) provide a built-in forum for networking, and members who meet in this way can then keep in touch between in-person meetings through email, social networking sites, and other online tools.

An Interview With Ellen Druda, TIF Member

Ellen Druda, internet services, at Half Hollow Hills Community Library in Dix Hills, New York, for the past 4 years (she was previously a media librarian and a reference librarian), talked to us about her experiences with the Technology Information Forum (TIF) in Suffolk County, New York.

Could you briefly describe your technology interest group and its purpose, number of members, and regular activities? When was the group established and what prompted its formation?

The group really goes back to the mid-1990s, when our library system pioneered the role of internet service provider (ISP) for county residents. We offered dial-up access and an email address for anyone with a library card. And with that came the responsibility of helping folks figure out how to get online, how to use email, and all that comes with it. Our library system began holding regular meetings for member libraries and their staff who were on the front lines. We're out of the ISP business now, but we never stopped having the need to brainstorm problems and cheer each other's successes.

We're now called TIF (Technology Information Forum), and we rotate monthly meetings at different libraries in Suffolk County. With about 50 public libraries in the county, we generally get about 20 or 30 people each month, and we also communicate on an active listserv in between meetings. The meetings can consist of a formal agenda with speakers or just a round table of conversation and group-think about new problems and projects.

What does a typical meeting look like? Who attends? What's discussed?

Typically, we gather in a meeting room (coffee and breakfast provided by the host library), and there will be a laptop connected to a projector. It's available for demonstrations or presentations. If you looked around the room, you'd see many people with netbooks, iPads, smartphones, and so on taking notes or trying things for themselves. It's a friendly group—many of us have been around for 10 or more years.

Do you have any sort of online meeting place—blog, social network, etc.—where members can communicate between meetings? If so, can you give some examples of topics that have been discussed/shared (and any public URLs)?

We have an old website that hasn't been updated in a while and a forum that doesn't get used too much; it seems the email list satisfies all our need to communicate between meetings. Although I like the idea of a blog or Facebook page—I should look into that! Email is used quite a lot; we ask for help, advice, post questions about new services, or comment about exciting news in technology. Since we all share a common OPAC and ILS, it's helpful to have a group to turn to that will respond quickly.

What types of programs does your group plan to offer in the future?

One of our members just finished creating an app for our county libraries, so that will be a future discussion. Computer security, best vendors for hardware, and ideas for managing time and print privileges are always popular topics.

What benefits do you see accruing to group members?
Networking is the big one. I know when I have a problem, I can send out an email and I'll get several responses. As a librarian, I find it extremely valuable to keep my foot in the techie-geeky world this way, because I hear ideas about different and creative solutions to issues I might be struggling with. Because we are mix of IT staff and librarians, the boundaries between us that we struggle with seem to disappear when we are all in a room sharing food and good will. The librarians get a chance to see things from the IT point of view, and vice versa.

Is there anything else you'd like to share about the group that has not been covered here?
We're lucky that this group grew under different leaders with distinctive styles, but always with the focus being the exchange of ideas in an open forum. If you're thinking about starting a group like this, it will build bridges and open doors. Go for it!

Interest groups may be subgroups of larger, more general associations, or they may be more informal networking groups formed by like-minded information professionals. Systems librarians in a large library system or city may be able to join a local technology group, but most systems librarians should begin searching for relevant technology interest groups at their state library association. (See more on association involvement in the next section.) Joining a technology interest group in your state provides in-person networking opportunities with nearby systems personnel. You may also be more likely to gain institutional funding and/or administrative backing if you attend local meetings with such groups rather than those of national organizations, which will generally require a bigger travel budget. If your system, area, or state association lacks a technology interest group, consider starting one. Rest assured that there will be systems librarians who are eager to attend and to share their expertise.

The Technology Information Forum (TIF) in Suffolk County, New York (see the sidebar in this chapter, An Interview With Ellen Druda), serves as an example of such a local networking group. Most members attend at least some of the group's regular meetings, which are held in different locations around the county to attract nearby systems personnel. This in-person contact adds another dimension to the group's online discussion list, as most members know each other from having met at conferences, meetings, and workshops. In-person meetings add a level of understanding of each other's circumstances that can be more difficult to achieve in a purely online environment.

Also consider joining a technology interest subgroup of a larger, national association. Examples of these smaller subgroups include two from LITA: Heads of Library Technology and Open Source Systems. (However, note that as with other divisions and roundtables, American Library Association [ALA] membership is currently required before you can join LITA. This imposes a double dues burden, and you end up paying for both groups. See if your library will pick up the tab for membership in one or both organizations.)

While you probably won't be able to meet in person with your colleagues as often as you might in a state or local group, you will be able to broaden the scope of your involvement and interact with other professionals nationwide. Especially if you are able to regularly attend the ALA annual meeting or other national conferences during the time these groups hold their meetings, smaller roundtables or interest groups provide a useful networking opportunity. Consider volunteering as a leader for such groups or participating in relevant subcommittees. Most of them are actively looking for volunteers, and your institution might also be more likely to provide financial support if you plan on attending meetings and as long as you can demonstrate your active involvement.

You may also consider joining local nonlibrary technology user groups, especially if you want to shore up or share your skills in a particular area. But these user groups may not be as useful as groups for librarians because members are not coming from the same background and will have different perspectives on how technology should be deployed.

Associations and Conferences

Several national associations are targeted to the needs of library systems staff. Chief among these are LITA and the American Society for Information Science and Technology (ASIST). Although it can be more difficult to attend in-person meetings of such groups, given the cost of conference fees, travel, and hotels, some associations are trying to bridge the gap by providing electronic archiving of conference presentations. (For example, see ASIST's 2011 annual conference proceedings at www.asis.org/asist2011/proceedings.) Associations such as LITA are also broadening their reach and educating others through Regional Institutes—one-day workshops that are held in different locations around the country and that focus on specific technology topics in libraries (past topics include Writing for the Web, User Centered Design, and Establishing Institutional Repositories). LITA also considers proposals for additional institutes or requests to develop an institute on a particular topic (www.ala.org/ala/mgrps/divs/lita/learning/ regional). Regional institutes and related programs can also let you pursue continuing education opportunities through your association beyond its annual conference.

As an association member, you will also be entitled to receive association publications, such as LITA's *Information Technology and Libraries* quarterly journal (a refereed publication focusing on all aspects of libraries and information technology) and ASIST's *Journal of the American Society for Information Science and Technology*. Such publications often contain articles of interest to working systems librarians and can serve as a content awareness tool. Other benefits for association members include the ability to join online discussion forums (which may be members-only) and to interact with fellow members between conferences. Members may also be able to get reduced conference fees and the opportunity to participate in decision making.

If you can attend out-of-state annual meetings, each of these association conferences provides useful in-person networking and learning opportunities. ASIST, for example, holds an annual conference mid-year and an annual summit on information architecture. Conference fees are heavily discounted for association members. LITA offers an annual national forum, and, since it is a division of ALA, also holds meetings at ALA Midwinter and Annual Conferences. This can be a useful way to combine your technical and general conference attendance and to network with systems colleagues while also attending less targeted programs and meetings. Also look for preconference sessions, which can provide opportunities to attend longer and more focused seminars on major topics including open source software.

Keep alert about opportunities for informal networking at such conferences during lunch breaks, talk tables, and encounters at exhibitors' booths. Make email or Facebook appointments to meet with your virtual colleagues at such events. Take time to approach a speaker you find particularly interesting after a presentation has concluded or email her after the convention with a question or comment on her talk. Conferences can also be a useful job-hunting tool (for more on this, see Chapter 12).

While evaluating whether to attend your association's conferences, consider attending one or more of the major technology-related conferences for librarians that are not linked to a particular association. Premiere among these is the annual Computers in Libraries conference, which generally includes sessions on topics that are relevant to systems librarianship. A sampling of topics from 2012 includes systems librarianship, user experience, web presence, ebooks, and mobile trends. Because such conferences are not tied to the agenda of any particular group and do not have to compete for space with general sessions as at conferences such as ALA Annual and Midwinter, all of the sessions and workshops can concentrate on practical, hands-on topics for systems librarians. Also keep an eye out for relevant library symposia on topics such as building digital collections and virtual reference service and for related conferences on technology, knowledge management, and digital information; these are often announced on topical email lists for systems librarians.

For a more intimate atmosphere, attend the annual Code4Lib conference (www.code4lib.org/conference) which brings together members of the Code4Lib community to discuss the newest systems topics, new developments, and plans for future systems. The great thing about the Code4Lib conference is that the talks are relatively short, so you can hear about many more topics in a day than at the larger conferences such as LITA or Computers in Libraries. To get a feel for the topics discussed at this conference, check out the slides and video recordings of past sessions on the respective conference pages.

Another networking opportunity presents itself in the form of your ILS user group meetings. What better common ground than running the same automation system, which means you will be encountering many of the same issues. The sessions at user group meetings also give a number of ideas for extending the functionality of your system, for training, and so on, and these ideas provide a number of conversational starting points.

You might even consider presenting at one of these association meetings or computer-related conferences. If your library has found an interesting use for technology or if you have resolved a common problem, why not share your knowledge with your colleagues? You can start small by volunteering to lead a talk table or serve on a panel at your state conference, which will help you build your confidence in front of a smaller group before presenting at a national meeting. Presenting provides additional networking opportunities, as well as the chance to add to your resume and demonstrate your speaking skills to future employers. Watch calls for papers and presenters on email discussion lists and in the print literature; these provide the opportunity for you to describe and test your theories and thoughts in interaction with a live audience. You can also keep an eye on LISEvents (www.lisevents.com), which offers a place for libraries to list events and links to calls for proposals.

Lastly, don't neglect to take the time to check out the vendor exhibits at every conference. This can be a great way to gain information on new and forthcoming products, talk to vendor representatives to get in-person insights, sign up for demos, and see in-person demonstrations of both hardware and software products. It may be easier to try a product out when a representative is present to answer any on-the-spot questions you have, and an exhibit hall also provides the perfect opportunity to compare several competing technologies side-by-side. You can generally find a list of exhibitors in preconference information provided online or in an association journal; use this to plan visits to specific vendors whose products interest you. Be mindful, however, that vendor demos at a conference may be somewhat misleading as to a product's actual performance in a real-world environment. Demos may work from a smaller database (with correspondingly fast retrieval times) or on customized or expensive equipment, under very controlled circumstances. Ask tough questions, and demo a product at your home institution if possible before purchasing.

Informal Networks

While formal associations and other technology-related groups have their places, the informal networks you create with other systems librarians, IT personnel, library staff, and colleagues in other libraries are also essential building blocks in your networking edifice. When asked what one piece of advice they would give to an aspiring library automation specialist, many survey respondents mentioned the importance of building these relationships. Typical comments included:

- "Find excellent mentors and friends who can help you. You can't keep up with all of the technology trends at once, but if you know the right people, you can all share your information and benefit together."

- "Network to leverage other people's expertise. Be flexible and be prepared to juggle multiple tasks at the same time."

- "Get to know the folks who use the same software you do."

- "You must connect with other systems librarians!"

- "Listservs related to your ILS/area of focus are invaluable. Learn from others."

- "Get involved in user groups and organizations. Colleagues are great resources for ideas and assistance."

- "Network! You can't do it all on your own, and a network can help you solve the problems."

Working with technology can have the unfortunate side effect of isolating you from fellow staff members and colleagues. It is easy to spend more time one-on-one with the computer screen than communicating with others, and it may seem that your nonsystems co-workers lack a common basis for understanding your positions and workload. Be on the alert for this and recognize the importance of promoting communication among all of these groups.

Consciously networking with other staff members in your institution, especially nonIT staff, helps keep you connected both to your co-workers and to larger institutional objectives. When working in IT, it is easy to become narrowly focused on the day-to-day tasks of keeping computer technology running; interacting with other librarians can help you re-ground yourself in the foundations of librarianship. You and your co-workers already share common goals, and if technology is not helping your co-workers meet these goals (or if it seems to frustrate their achievement of them), you need to be aware. Make sure that you are approachable and that you are also open to talking about noncomputer-related topics. Often staff members will not even know the questions to ask or what might be possible, so talking with them about their overall wishes and needs lets you show them how (or think of ways) technology might be able to meet those needs.

When you neglect the cultivation of your informal network with other librarians in your institution, you thwart the goal of serving as a liaison between IT personnel and others in your institution. Remember from Chapter 1: This integral role of systems librarians is to serve to bridge the gap between what is sometimes perceived as two completely different worlds. This gap can be exacerbated if your only contact with staff is in a tech support role. You may work in systems, but you are still first and foremost a librarian. Further, colleagues with an interest in technology can be valuable allies in smaller libraries where you do not have an official IT staff or systems department to assist you. Power users and tinkerers who have been there since a system was installed will often possess pockets of knowledge that you should not neglect to mine.

Beyond networking with library staff in your own institution, be sure to tap into your network of peers in neighboring libraries. Other systems librarians in your library system or consortium probably face similar issues; they may use the same automation system, do group buys of electronic resources and/or computer hardware, or belong to the same WAN. Because of these commonalities, these peers are often your best resource for both systems advice and commiseration.

Developing Networking Skills

It is easy to become isolated after graduating from library school, especially if you move out of state to take a position or find yourself in a smaller library with a limited pool of peers. Systems librarians can find themselves more isolated by the very nature of their work—it can be difficult for nonsystems people to understand your day-to-day struggles with technology, and much of your work will be done independently. These factors, however, make it all the more important to try to actively develop your networking skills and reach out to your colleagues on both the technical and nontechnical sides.

Here it can be helpful to learn from your connected peers. If you know another librarian who seems to know someone at any institution and who always has a wide network of colleagues to call upon, watch how she builds these relationships. As Mary Heiberger observes: "It may also be helpful to watch people who seem to have wide networks. What do they seem to do? How do they act at conferences? How do they act at departmental colloquia? What do you see them doing that you might want to emulate? Realize that behaviors that now look easy are habits that these people also had to work to develop."[3] Go to a conference with others from your institution or meet up with people you have talked to on mailing lists. Ask the colleagues you know to take some time to introduce you to their peers in other libraries. Ask intelligent questions about what they are doing at their institutions and share your work with them.

Note that networking implies a two-way process. Always be willing to serve as a resource for your colleagues just as you wish others to be a resource for you. Contribute your expertise and findings as appropriate on mailing lists and in both formal and informal discussions with your peers. Remember that you are part of the "invisible college" of systems librarians; both contributing to and drawing from a joint pool of expertise and experience.

Collaboration

Beyond networking for professional development purposes or to solve immediate issues, you might also find yourself collaborating with colleagues in other institutions or other departments within your own institution on certain large-scale projects. For example, you might need to work closely with your counterpart in another institution or library system to set up Z39.50 access to each other's online catalogs. You may work with a distance learning unit in your university to create websites that provide access to library-supported electronic resources. You may work with the systems department in your larger institution to track down a networking issue affecting your interconnected systems. You may cooperate with other institutions in selecting and sharing licensing costs for online databases—cooperation within a consortium can result in significant savings. You may collaborate with other libraries and historical societies in joint digitization projects. Even if you are a solo systems librarian in your own institution, in many cases, you will not always be working in isolation.

The necessity for cooperation and collaboration creates an additional incentive to create relationships, not only with other systems librarians, but with other departments and other institutions. When you embark on one of these collaborative efforts, ensure that your own institution will be able to reap some of the benefits—whether directly or in terms of publicity, good will, or increased use of electronic resources you wish to promote. Remember that you are representing your entire library in many of these projects so do not promise more than you can deliver. If you need to involve your library's administration in order to secure funding or institutional permission to proceed, do so, and make sure you are all on the same page.

Developing good networking skills will serve you well in every aspect of your career in systems librarianship. Foster your connections with others carefully and always remember that you are part of a number of larger communities.

Endnotes

1. Chris Brogan and Julien Smith, *Trust Agents: Using the Web to Build Influence, Improve Reputation, and Earn Trust* (Hoboken, NJ: John Wiley, 2010), 30.

2. Seth Godin, *Tribes: We Need You to Lead Us* (New York: Portfolio, 2008), 34.

3. Mary Morris Heiberger, and Julie Miller Vick, "Networking for Dummies," *Chronicle of Higher Education*, May 17, 2002, accessed May 31, 2012, www.chronicle.com/article/Networking-for-Dummies/46091.

Chapter 8

Instruction Techniques

The cybrarian's role of information advisor and
trainer necessitates proficiency in software
productivity tool skills and teaching abilities.
    —John H. Heinrichs and Nancy Czech[1]

Bibliographic instruction has always been one of librarians' basic tasks. We understand that it is less than desirable—and less than fair—to maintain buildings full of valuable resources without also providing the opportunity for our patrons to develop the skills needed to locate and make use of those resources. Given that we are more often than not accessing newer resources strictly online (e.g., via web-based OPACs and subscription databases), we now have a responsibility to our patrons to help them learn how to use today's library effectively. This means that we need to extend our traditional experience with bibliographic instruction to include technology instruction, from teaching basic operating-system skills and internet usage to providing training on specific databases and ebook subscription services, to teaching advanced search techniques, to educating them on the nature of social networking tools and their related privacy concerns.

While some librarians may worry that teaching technological literacy is tangential to the library's mission, it is our responsibility to give people the tools they need to participate in our institutions. Our interest in inculcating technological literacy extends our traditional interest in literacy and in information-seeking skills.

Staff members may also require training in these general areas, as well as on the use of the various modules of your automation system and on other library-specific technologies. In many libraries, you will find that technology has been added and upgraded bit by bit over the years but that staff members have received little formal training on its use and have had either little time to learn the ins and outs of library technology or little interest in developing skills on their own. In any library, staff members will be at various stages of technological savvy. Librarians, however, cannot realistically be expected to provide adequate service to patrons in a wired institution if they have never been given the tools to use technology effectively. One of your responsibilities as a systems librarian will be to raise the bar of skill levels for others in your organization. If sufficient training has not been provided in the past, you will also need to make up for your institution's previous shortcomings. Although dated, Karen Schneider's statement that "Some of these people [library staff] never recovered from the shock of having computers plunked down in their work areas without any accompanying rationale or training"[2] still holds true today. Although the technologies that are shocking our librarians are different, it's still important to remember that forcing a new technology on your staff without proper training or explanation is unacceptable.

In many cases, you and/or other systems staff members will be able to provide in-house training for your co-workers. In other cases, you may wish to find and send staff to affordable and reputable outside courses or bring in outside trainers for specific software packages. Many library and technology organizations also offer free and low-cost webinars that your staff members can attend right from their desks. (For more on finding online training, see the sidebar Free/Low-Cost Online Classes/Tutorials in Chapter 9.) In many areas, your library and librarians can join a library cooperative for both bulk buying discounts and free training.

You can also use an appropriate combination of these methods for your needs. For large systems such as your ILS, vendors may supply training for at least a limited number of people, and you should always ask about the potential for vendor training or demos for staff when you invest in a new subscription database or other expensive electronic library product.

As a systems librarian, you will likely be involved either directly as a trainer during patron and staff computer instructional sessions or with formulating the syllabus, methods, and format of such instruction. You will also often encounter opportunities to do more informal on-demand training, demonstrating on the spur of the moment how to accomplish a computer-related task. You'll be responsible for creating handouts and cheat sheets to help empower library staff and users to carry out such tasks independently. The effectiveness of all of these instructional activities goes back to your library background and your communication skills; as one survey respondent reminded us, "It's very helpful to have had years in public services and in technical services. I feel I can understand and communicate with librarians, technologists, and users in a way that programmers can't."

Adult Learners

Training adult learners requires a different approach than you may have been used to having in high school and other classes. First and foremost, you'll need to convince adult learners about the advantages that training will bring to them personally. If adult learners are not self-motivated and not convinced of the value of training, they will not learn. This is as true of your patrons as it is of your staff. Along with self-motivation, realize that adult learners also place a high value on their time, which they don't want to feel is being wasted. When training adults, refrain from spending a great deal of time on buildup or on covering material that is impractical or irrelevant to your trainees' immediate needs; they will merely tune you out. Particularly when it comes to technology training, you need to keep sessions practical and to the point. Avoid both theory and jargon as much as possible and try to relate training back to concrete examples of how they can use what you are showing them in their jobs or in their daily lives.

Adult learners also tend to learn best by analogy. They have had years to develop their knowledge and a mental map of their world, and the best way to reach them is by demonstrating the parallels between what you are trying to teach and what they already know. For instance, many smartphones and tablets allow you to move from screen to screen by "swiping"; this is analogous to physically turning a page in a book or magazine, and such a comparison can help a new user understand the interface more quickly. The more of these connections you can help your trainees, especially beginners, make to their pre-existing stores of knowledge, the more comfortable they will be with using new technology.

Lastly, it is important to develop training skills along with your technology skills. Merely knowing the ins and outs of a particular program is insufficient. Realize that many adult learners will be uncomfortable with or fearful of technology; some aspects of computers still hold a peculiar mystique in the minds of many adult learners, which you may need to work to overcome. Always keep in mind what it is like to confront a new application or technology for the first time and try to empathize with your trainees. Cultivate patience along with the communication skills discussed in Chapter 1.

Training Techniques

It is important to account for the different learning styles of individuals in your training sessions. Attendees tend to be at their best when learning in different ways; for example, some may be highly visual learners and will benefit from seeing you perform the actions for them before having to do it alone, while others may be auditory learners and will need to hear you explain a skill or process. Use a mixture of different methods in combination with hands-on practice in any training program and provide self-study materials for those who would prefer to learn on their own or to supplement training with individual study.

Always allow time for staff and patrons to review the material you have provided. For staff, this can mean working with department heads to set aside time for their staff members to practice on their own following training sessions. For patrons, this can mean reserving some time for hands-on practice at the end of a training session or providing an environment where they can go to review what they learned at a later date. To this end, you can consider posting training materials on your website or a course management system and providing handouts that trainees can take with them to review on their own. Always be sure to supply review materials and printed cheat sheets with step-by-step instructions on how to accomplish the common computer-related tasks that you have demonstrated in your training sessions. If possible, test these cheat sheets on someone without previous knowledge of how to complete the task to ensure that you do not leave out any steps. (Handouts will also be useful in the case of technical or equipment failure; at least attendees will not leave empty-handed, and you can use handouts to discuss at least some of the points you originally intended to cover.)

Keep handouts and training simple, as short as possible, and to the point. Remember that adult learners want to feel that they are using their time wisely and will not appreciate having to wade through superfluous and distracting information to find out what they need to know. Computers can be confusing enough without you adding to the situation! Try to create an environment where trainees feel comfortable asking questions. This can often mean being flexible with your outline in order to spend more time on areas that are causing greater confusion and/or fear. You do not want attendees leaving confused or feeling as if they did not learn what they expected to learn. Often trainees will come to a class with a specific goal or question in mind, which, although it may not be specifically what you intended to teach, will be useful to them in their daily lives or work. If such a question is appropriate and relevant to the subject at hand, answer it. If it is too tangential, offer to talk with the person after the training session. That way, you avoid holding up the class with too much extraneous information, while still showing your receptivity to trainees' needs. Pay attention to students; make eye contact and notice who is looking "lost" during class. If they are reluctant to ask questions, ask specifically if they would like a point clarified. Some students will feel embarrassed exposing what they see as their own ignorance in front of other trainees; be sensitive to this possibility and never make a questioner feel that a query is either inappropriate or uninformed.

Create realistic objectives for your training sessions, teach directly to these training objectives, and make sure that they are achievable in the time allotted. Computer training objectives need to be specific, practical, and measurable; you can see, for example, whether an attendee at a basic public internet training class can now type a web address into the browser's address bar to go to a website. You can observe whether a member of the reference staff after the class can place a hold for a patron using your ILS. Keep the number of objectives for any one class low; you cannot inculcate technological literacy in a single session. It will be more useful to present the same few objectives from several angles than to cram multiple objectives into a limited amount of time; repetition increases retention.

Training Staff

Training library staff members on computer usage presents a peculiar set of challenges. In any given library, the staff's level of technical competency and comfort with change will vary greatly. Some staff members who have graduated recently may have picked up a strong set of technical skills in a revamped library or information school program. Some may have graduated years ago before such skills were taught regularly or were taught then-current technologies such as punch cards and Apple BASIC that are less than relevant today. These librarians have had to learn technical skills on the job (or have avoided learning them on the job). Paraprofessional staff members may either have had an extensive technical background but lack the foundation in librarianship to go with it, or they may have worked in a library for years without receiving any formal training in or increasing their own comfort with technology. While library administrations increasingly desire technical skills in new employees, the wider range of options and salaries available to technically adept MLS holders means that those with these skills often go elsewhere—and the changing nature of library technology means that even those who arrive with such abilities will at some point need to upgrade or refresh their skills.

In a larger institution, you can find yourself needing to establish classes at various levels and to accommodate various learning styles. (This is integral: Pairing more advanced learners with beginners only serves to frustrate both groups because you are wasting the time for those who already know the material while also unintentionally convincing novices of their own ignorance compared to others.) This is a situation in which your competency checklists will come in handy, giving you a tool to assess the skill levels of various staff members and match them up with their peers.

Furthermore, with some staff members, you may face the challenge of convincing them of the need for training in the first place. If staff members enter training sessions with the mindset that they have already mastered all of the skills they need to serve patrons adequately, whether in library school or through their years on the job, they will be less likely to retain material from technology training or to revisit the skills they have learned after sessions have ended (which is an essential factor in retaining knowledge). If they begin by viewing computers as toys, interlopers, or machines that constantly break or otherwise frustrate their "real" work, they will not be receptive to learning. So, your first task with such staff members will be to convince them that training is indeed important and that a certain level of comfort and facility with technology is now essential to serving patrons effectively.

When training those who are less than convinced of the value of computer technology in serving patrons or serving the needs of the library, it is important to show them how their new skills can be put into practice with their daily tasks. This can be best accomplished through concrete examples. For example, show how specific patron questions can be resolved through the use of a new online database. Ask for suggestions of real-life problems or questions staff have encountered and show how computer technology can help resolve those problems. Provide scheduled times to practice these new skills after the session, so staff members don't feel that they are taking time away from their jobs to spend on technology. Provide follow-up sessions for staff members to reinforce the skills they have learned and give them an opportunity to share any instances in which their new knowledge has helped them on the job. Create online tutorials or practice sessions and post them on your intranet to help staff members develop their skills outside of formal training sessions. Create printed handouts to distribute at your sessions, as well as printed cheat sheets, assessments, and exercises that they can use at their own pace. Remember, those who are less familiar with technology might also be more comfortable with using print resources.

Training should be just one component in an entire campaign to convince staff members of the importance of technology in the day-to-day running of the modern library and to familiarize them with technology as an everyday concept. Remember from previous chapters the importance of communication in imparting the value of technology and in minimizing your co-workers' fear of change. Use venues such as a technology tips newsletter, your library's internal blog, and informal conversation to help show others how technology can be used effectively and how it is intertwined with daily library operations. If you have created technology competencies for staff, show how the knowledge of these particular areas can help make their jobs easier. One common complaint about technology training is that it takes time away from an already short workday, especially in those institutions facing declining staffing levels and increasing workloads. (Ironically, the expense of keeping up technologically can exacerbate these staffing issues.) Showing how familiarity with various aspects of the library's technological environment can make staff's jobs easier in the long run and allow them to complete tasks and/or help patrons more quickly will go a long way toward countering such objections.

As your training program progresses, staff who have benefited from earlier training sessions will be more receptive to future opportunities. Much of the stress inherent in dealing with technology in libraries comes from a feeling of not being able to keep up and from lack of knowledge of how to use and deal with these resources. By giving staff the tools to deal with computers and to integrate technology into their daily lives, you can reduce that level of anxiety tremendously and help them deal with the inevitable changes to come. You also help reduce the digital divide among staff members—which we worry greatly about among our patrons, but sometimes neglect to pay attention to among our own staff. Merely providing access to technology is insufficient if staff members are not prepared to use and benefit from such technology; the gap between those who are informed about, open to, and use computers and those who do not may seem to be as insurmountable as the gap between those who have access to the internet or computing technology and those who do not.

While some staff may resist learning about technology, others will welcome the opportunity—and well-thought-out training opportunities can also be a selling point for your library when it comes to hiring and retaining staff. Libraries that invest in their staff's professional development, including technical development, will serve both staff and patrons more effectively in the long run. Also make sure to provide training opportunities for new hires who may begin their positions some time after formal training is completed on a new product or service; it is unfair to expect them to pick up the usage of a system on an ad hoc basis when everyone else has received training. If you are in a larger institution, you may consider creating a training program specifically for new employees, or you can tailor their training on a more personalized basis after they have completed your set of competency tests. As Michele Boule reminds us, "Regardless of why you have chosen this particular tech training topic, always stress that your intention is to make the lives of your staff, patrons, and community easier, better, and sunnier. Remember that in the long run, this is the reason why most of us stick with certain technologies. We like them because they make our lives easier or richer in some way."[3]

While your role in creating and facilitating training is integral, note that in-house training may be only one component. A forward-thinking library should also make it possible for staff to pursue outside continuing education opportunities, and should especially encourage systems librarians and other technical staff to take advantage of appropriate opportunities to shore up their skills. (For more on finding classes for yourself and other systems staff, see Chapter 9.)

Try to make it as easy as possible for staff to participate in technology training sessions. To avoid overwhelming staffers and for the sake of scheduling convenience for others, consider varying your class offerings. As a supplement to longer classes, you might provide short, half-hour sessions once a week on specific topics such as blogging basics or new ILS features, for instance. Staff members can shore up their skills as needed. Provide online tutorials on your intranet to supplement in-person training so your coworkers can learn or practice on their own. (See more on creating online training later in this chapter.) This will be especially useful to part-timers who may not easily be able to adjust their schedules to attend in-person training sessions. Coordinate with department heads and supervisors so that they understand the value and necessity of both training itself and allowing staff time to review later on their own, and try to work your class offerings into their schedules. You want to remove as many obstacles to training as you can.

One training technique that has been successful in recent years is to offer self-directed learning programs. These types of programs give general guidelines and topics to the learner, but they still let people complete the tasks at their own pace. The most popular of these was started by Helene Blowers at the Public Library of Charlotte & Mecklenburg County in 2006.[4] Blowers set up a list of 23 things that she wanted her staff to learn and offered prizes to those who completed the tasks she set up. Over the past few years, many libraries have taken this idea and molded it to fit their own patron and staff needs, facilitating continued learning. Other training materials and ideas can be found on the Tech Training for Libraries page (www.coloradovirtuallibrary.org/techtraining) put together by the Colorado State Library.

Training Patrons

Patron training presents its own set of opportunities and challenges to the systems librarian/trainer. Patrons who attend computer classes at the library may be more self-motivated than staff members who often attend classes only because it is required, rather than out of any inherent interest in the subject. In some ways, this makes patrons easier to teach. Again, however, you will see a disparity in knowledge levels and expectations among patrons attending any computer classes you offer. Those who have not grown up with computers, access to the internet, or mobile devices or who have never learned basic skills may seek introductory Windows, word processing, and internet training (yes, these people do still exist), while those who are computer-savvy might benefit more from instruction on the use of your library's electronic databases and other online resources. Remember to never judge a book by its cover. Younger patrons who have had these tools their entire lives don't necessarily know how to use them. What makes a tech-savvy patron is not age, but experience and training.

Many libraries, therefore, might need to provide a variety of training sessions to patrons at different levels of computer expertise. The type and number of classes you offer will vary from library to library; some may choose to simply offer training sessions on the internet and/or the use of the library's OPAC and other electronic resources, while others may create full-fledged training programs on using gadgets such as ebook readers, tablet computers, or even digital cameras. It is up to you and/or your institution to determine how the goal of teaching technological literacy fits into the library's broader mission and what you can realistically support with the staff and resources you have.

Whatever types of training you choose, advertising is key. You'll want to make sure to announce the classes your library is offering on your website, social networks, and even in print. The Sachem Public Library (www.sachemlibrary.org), in Holbrook, New York, for example, publishes a monthly newsletter that announces new computer training sessions for patrons (see Figure 8.1).

COMPUTER SERVICES

Register online, in person or by phone at 588-5024, beginning Monday, April 25 at 9:30am. *Beginners can take either Domesticate Your Mouse or Computers for Beginners. Prerequisites apply to most programs; if you feel you have met the prerequisites, call the Technology Center to inquire about the possibility of having them waived. *The Domesticate Your Mouse session may be bypassed by successful completion of the online mouse test at:* **http://sachem.suffolk.lib.ny.us/mouse.htm.** *Take our online Microsoft Word test to bypass the Beginning Word 2007 session at:* **http://www.sachemlibrary.org/pages/tech_tips.aspx.**
All sessions are conducted in the Technology Center. Class duration is two hours, unless otherwise noted.
Classes are for district residents only. Seating is limited.

TECH 30
Technical Help in 30 Minutes
Call the Tech Center for an appointment. If you have a question about something that has you stumped while using a computer, call our Technology Center at 588-5024 to schedule a personalized 30-minute session with one of our tech-savvy staff members.

INTRODUCTORY

Domesticate Your Mouse
Thursday, May 5 • 12:00pm
Program code: SAEDYM
No experience with computers? Take this class first. If you already have mouse experience and wish to bypass this session, take our online mouse test at:
http://sachem.suffolk.lib.ny.us/mouse.htm
No prerequisite required.

Keyboard Confidence
Thursday, May 12 • 12:00pm
Program code: SAEKC
Not a typing class, this session is an introduction to unfamiliar computer keys.
Prerequisite: *Domesticate Your Mouse*

Internet for Beginners
Thursday, May 19 • 12:00pm
Program code: SAEIFB
Beginners learn the very basics of the Internet. Learn Internet history, terminology, and introductory searching techniques.
Prerequisite: *Domesticate Your Mouse*

Beginning Word 2010
Tuesdays, May 3 and 10 • 11:00am
Program code: SAEBMW
Word 2010 basics for beginners. (4 hours; two 2 hour sessions) **Prerequisite:** *Domesticate Your Mouse* or Computers for Beginners

INTERMEDIATE

Beginning Publisher 2010
Wednesday, May 11 • 6:00pm
Program code: SAEBMP
Create simple publications using Microsoft's 2010 version of Publisher. **Prerequisite:** *Beginning Word 2007 or 2010**

Word 2010: What's New?
Tuesday, May 17 • 11:00am
Program code: SAEWWN
What did Microsoft change in Word 2010? **Prerequisite:** *Any Word 2007 class taken at Sachem Public Library**

Word 2010: Format a Document
Wednesday, May 18 • 6:00pm
Program code: SAEMWFD
Learn how to change defaults to customize the look of your Word 2010 documents. **Prerequisite:** *Beginning Word 2010**

Intermediate Internet
Thursday, May 26 • 12:00pm
Program code: SAEII
This second-level Internet class introduces the Sachem Public Library's website as one entry point to topical information on the World Wide Web. **Prerequisite:** *Internet for Beginners or Computers for Beginners*

SPECIAL

Introduction to the Apple
Saturday, May 7 • 2:00pm
Program code: SAEIA
In this lecture and demo class, you will be introduced to the Apple computer. Learn all about the desktop, the elements of the computer, tools, and toolbars, and how to connect to the Internet. This program will be held in Community Room A on the lower level. *No prerequisite required.*

ADVANCED

Small Business Excel
Thursday, May 5, 12, 19 and 26 • 7:30pm
Program code: SAESBE
Learn to use Excel to plan, organize, manage, and report on all aspects of your small business dealings. This series will give you the hands-on experience to work confidently with dozens of the built-in functions, including IF, Lookups, and Financial Functions. You'll prepare basic financial statements with projections and presentation graphs. Explore the analytical tools that will help you spot trends and make informed decisions. (6 hours; four 90 minute sessions) **Prerequisites:** *NOT for the computer novice, these sessions require knowledge and current use of MS Excel.*

Searching the Web:
An Introduction to Search Engines
Saturday, May 21 • 11:00am
Program code: SAESTW
A third-level Internet class: Learn how to find and use Internet search engines to make your research easier. **Prerequisite:** *Internet for Beginners and Intermediate Internet.*

Intermediate Publisher 2010: Newsletters
Wednesday, May 25 • 6:00pm
Program code: SAEIPN
Learn to create newsletters in Publisher. **Prerequisite:** *Beginning Publisher 2007 or 2010 (If you have not taken this class with us, call the instructor for permission to waive this prerequisite)*

Figure 8.1 Sachem Public Library's monthly newsletter

Ad Hoc Opportunities

Watch for opportunities to do one-on-one, ad hoc training when the occasion presents itself. Many computer situations present a learning opportunity, and even the process of resolving a problem with someone's computer gives you an opening to explain why and how you are performing certain actions. Often, these informal occasions for learning can be more productive than a formal session, and those you are helping may learn without being aware that they are being taught. Computer users also may feel more comfortable asking questions one-on-one than during a more formal training session.

Ad hoc opportunities also provide the perfect environment for hands-on training, from which users are more likely to benefit. When you are showing people how to accomplish a task or resolve a minor issue, avoid taking over their machines if at all possible. Let them sit at the terminal, type, and click for themselves. Even if you are showing them how to proceed at every step, they will gain a feeling of accomplishment that they have "done it themselves" and will be more likely to remember the steps if they need to repeat the process later. Explaining the "why" behind your actions as you are showing them how to proceed will help them retain the steps as well. Patience is an essential attribute for a successful computer trainer; you have to be willing to watch users struggle, resist the urge to simply do tasks for them, and develop a sense of when and how it is appropriate to intervene.

Setting Up Sessions

The actual format of your training sessions depends largely on the equipment and facilities you have available, as well as on your attendees. If you have the opportunity to get involved in the design of an actual training or computer lab, seize the chance with delight. Consider factors such as room temperature and ambient noise, whether students can see a trainer from behind their monitors, standardizing consistent hardware and software, and whether you wish to purchase classroom control software that lets a trainer push materials to student desktops and keeps students from indulging in off-topic activities such as games and checking email while you are trying to conduct a session. Products here include LanSchool (www.lanschool.com), Net-Support School (www.netsupport-inc.com), and iTALC (italc.sourceforge.net), although there are a number of alternatives to consider.

If your library lacks a computer lab, you will need to be more creative in adapting to available resources. Do not use the lack of formal training facilities as an excuse not to provide any instruction. If you need to cluster smaller groups around one or two terminals, do so. If you have a meeting room, encourage attendees to bring their own laptops (supplementing with library-owned laptops) and provide power and internet access (wired or wireless). Training sessions taught this way will seem more informal and will reach fewer people at a time, but these sessions may also have the advantage of being less threatening for beginners and for those who fear the technology.

The space you have available will automatically influence the format and size of your classes. If you have a projector and lab available, you might wish to use a slideshow application such as PowerPoint, LibreOffice, or Prezi to demonstrate your points, and then provide an opportunity for hands-on practice. If you are clustering people around one terminal, you will probably want to avoid slides and lecturing, and simply demonstrate techniques. As always, be flexible and willing to adapt to the technology at hand.

Online Training

One advantage to working in a "wired institution" is that it provides an environment for you to post training and other tools online, allowing staff and patrons to pursue learning on their own. Many libraries simply post training materials to their intranets or library websites, and overlook course management tools under the assumption that these are too robust for their needs. But this isn't necessarily true. Even if you only offer small staff training sessions, a free, open source course management system such as Moodle (www.moodle.com) can often help you organize your materials more efficiently. Course management systems provide ways to share all sorts of training materials, allowing your staff and/or patrons to work at their own pace while still being able to communicate with you (the instructor) and each other.

Examples of training materials you can provide on the web or through your course management system include tutorials, quizzes, help documents, screencasts, and competency self-assessments. You can also easily link to outside online resources to give people the chance to read further on a technical topic of interest. While often not a complete substitute for in-person training, online training can help supplement your in-person efforts, provide an opportunity for people to practice their skills, and reach people who may be unwilling to attend a more formal session. These materials also give staff members or patrons a chance to engage in self-paced learning and to practice at their own convenience.

There are a number of useful tools to help you create online training materials. You can keep these online resources as simple as step-by-step instructions, with screenshots, on accomplishing common tasks, or you can create interactive quizzes and video tutorials for intranet or website users. (Most operating systems now offer a built-in screen capture tool, but if you're still using an older installation, a useful tool for screen captures is TechSmith's SnagIt at www.techsmith.com.) Here are a few cost-effective options to help you post training materials online, some of which are add-ins or extensions to software you might already own:

- TechSmith Camtasia Studio (www.techsmith.com/ camtasia): Create recordings of your computer interactions, including the ability to add an audio track so that you can simultaneously explain your actions.

- Moodle (www.moodle.com): An open source course management system that can run on your library's web servers to provide course materials, quizzes, forums, chat rooms, and much more.

- Jing (www.techsmith.com/jing): Free screen capture/screencasting tools that let you easily capture and save images and videos for web publishing.

- Prezi (www.prezi.com): A free and low cost web-based presentation maker that offers ways to create animated presentations and publish them to the web.

- Microsoft PowerPoint Producer Add-In from the Download Center (www.microsoft.com/downloads): This lets you create rich-media slides and publish them to the web. Note that PowerPoint's ability to output HTML versions of its slides provides the opportunity to publish tutorials online.

- LimeSurvey (www.limesurvey.org): This open source tool lives on your library's web servers and hosts surveys that can be used for self-assessment and simple quizzes.

Systems librarians who are comfortable with web scripting or programming might also choose to create their own tests and tools without relying on third-party options. If you want to keep things simple, you can create straight HTML tutorials sans interactivity—although these might be most useful as cheat sheets or as step-by-step instructions for straightforward tasks. If you have created slideshows, most desktop presentation applications easily convert these to HTML so that you can post them online.

When considering how best to create and format your online offerings, take a look at what other institutions have done. Examples include the University of Texas's TILT (The Information Literacy Tutorial; tilt.library.skagit.edu) and the Ann Arbor District Library's Computer Class Handouts (www.aadl.org/handouts).[5]

If you want to post tutorials or quizzes on a particular software package, ask your colleagues in other institutions or inquire on appropriate mailing lists whether others have created online training materials on a similar topic. Then you can see how those materials are structured before creating your own. You can also review presentations that have been licensed using the Creative Commons license on sites such as SlideShare (www.slideshare.net).

Interview With Chad Boeninger, Video Blogger and Librarian

Chad Boeninger has been the reference and instruction technology coordinator/business and economics subject specialist at Ohio University, Alden Library, for 9 years. He shares his experiences with managing a video blog at www.library.ohiou.edu/subjects/businessblog.

Can you tell us what prompted you to start your video blog?

As business librarian, I serve a college of approximately 1,800 students. In many cases, there will be 200–300 students working on the same project at the same time. I started making videos so that I could point students to them when I got those more frequently asked questions. Business resources can be very complex, and often the tutorials that are included from the vendor are not adequate for explaining how to use a database. Therefore, I started making videos that had more context to what the students were working on. Many of my videos cover the best ways to use a database based on the types of questions I have received over the years.

What is the process you follow when creating a new video? What tools do you use to produce your videos? How long does the process of creating one video usually take?

I have gotten a lot more efficient at making videos with more practice. My first video, produced prior to the existence of YouTube, took me about 6 hours to make. I can now make a 5-minute video in as little as 15–20 minutes. For one class, I once made four 5-minute videos in just under an hour, which included recording, editing, rendering, and uploading.

I use Screencast-O-Matic (www.screencast-o-matic. com) to record my on-screen actions and database demonstrations. I use the free version, as I don't really mind the watermark. (I should probably pay the $9.00 to support the product.) I like Screencast-O-Matic because it is web-based and very simple to use. Because it does not depend on a desktop application, I can produce videos on my office computer or on my personal laptop at home (or at the coffee shop). I usually record a screencast in one quick recording. If I mess up really bad, I'll re-record a section, but generally I am not aiming for perfection.

I record an introduction and a conclusion with a small handheld camera. I've used a small Canon point-and-shoot camera and a more-advanced Sanyo Xacti camcorder. I set the camera on my desk with a tripod, hit record, and start talking. I can generally record a 30-second introduction and a 15–20 second conclusion in one take. I have the recordings of me introducing the video because I like for the users to know my face and know who the expert is who is teaching them.

I splice the footage of me from the camera and the footage from Screencast-O-Matic with Windows Live Movie Maker. I generally just add fades and transitions and captions and then export the file. Nothing too fancy.

I use Blip (www.blip.tv) to host my videos. Blip has a huge number of features that I find a lot more useful than YouTube (www.youtube.com). Blip allows you to upload multiple video types, and you can even upload your own thumbnail or create your own [image] from the video footage on their site. Blip does automatic cross-posting to my WordPress blog and also can do automatic cross-posting to Facebook, YouTube, Vimeo (www.vimeo.com), iTunes, and more. The statistics features in Blip are very useful as well.

What were the hardest parts when you first started out with your video blog? Was there a big learning curve?

I think anyone who does video will tell you that the biggest challenge and learning curve is in understanding file formats and file compression. Fortunately, Blip, YouTube, and other hosts will accept almost any file type. The hard part now is making sure your computer will work with the file type from your camera. This is getting easier as time goes on. For example, Windows Movie Maker (the XP version) did not edit MP4 or MOV files. The newer Windows Live Movie Maker in Windows 7 now edits those files just fine. I spent a lot of my time trying to figure out which editors would work with which types of files, and being on a budget of zero meant that I had to have different workarounds for things. Once again, it's a lot easier now.

What kind of response have you seen from your students, faculty, and fellow staff members to the videos you post?

One faculty member recently responded to me via email: "You are a great TV star. I had no idea. BTW, great job. I had no idea about Mergent and how useful it is."

I also had a student email me out of the blue: "I'm a student in Professor Justin Davis' Business Strategy class (BA 470J). I'd like to thank you for providing the informational video describing where we can find the most helpful resources. I have begun writing my report and I'm able to find everything quickly and efficiently. Thanks again for your time, Chad."

What recommendations, suggestions, and tips of the trade would you like to share with others who might be interested in starting such a blog?

My main suggestion is that people should not attempt to try to be perfect with the videos they create. If you compare your videos with others who are more experienced, you are sure to be disappointed. I definitely recommend watching other videos to get ideas and learn, but don't try to copy someone else. As you get experience, you will develop your own style for doing things. I would also encourage others to watch other instructional videos from other areas besides librarianship. See how folks in other areas are doing things. If they are doing something really well, see how you can adopt it to your needs. When I remodeled the Business Blog last year to include more video content, I actually modeled a lot of the functionality of the blog after the Bicycle Tutor, a bicycle repair website at www.bicycle tutor.com. I saw what he had done with his site and how useful it was. I even adopted some of the same organization and learned how to use some of the WordPress plug-ins to do similar things to my site.

Anything else you'd like to share?

I'd say to make sure you explore as many options as you can before you get started. Learn which video hosts are going to give you the kind of flexibility you need. Understand that your workflow may need to change as technology changes. As an example, I used to use MediaWiki (www.mediawiki.org) for my site because it organized content better than WordPress. Last year I switched back to WordPress for my website content, as it had made several improvements as a content management system over the years. It took a good deal of work to make the switch, but it was well worth it. I also risked alienating my users and losing part of my brand, but I think the end result was well worth those risks.

Try to look for ways to improve. Once you get started, set a time in the future to go back and review your old videos. It may be painful to watch some of your first videos, but you'll get a good understanding of what you have learned. Have others watch your videos and give you feedback.

Screencasts and Video Blogs

Another great way to share learning materials with your staff and patrons is to create short screencasts that show how to perform a specific task. Chad Boeninger, the business librarian at Ohio University, set up a blog where he answers his patrons' (and students') questions by using short videos (www.library.ohiou.edu/subjects/businessblog). The Business Blog is a great way to help answer common research and technology questions that recur at the reference desk and promote the library's services to users searching the web. Sites that share resources such as these on a regular basis often get noticed by search engines, which helps move your library up in the rankings when people are searching for information on a topic you have in your video collection.

There are many tools to help you create screencasts to share with your patrons and staff. The first thing you're going to need is a good microphone, which can be found relatively inexpensively online. Next, you'll need to decide if you want to just record your voice over the actions on the screen or also your face. Each individual will be comfortable with different styles. My tutorial videos, for example, never show me, just the task at hand. Chad, on the other hand, likes to talk to the camera in addition to showing his screen. If you'd like to record yourself as well as your screen, you're going to need a camera in addition to the microphone. (Note that many laptops these days come with built-in web cams, so this may not be an issue.)

To record your screencasts, there are many tools to choose from. If you're on a tight budget, a free tool such as Jing or an open source option such as CamStudio (www.camstudio.org) might be worth consideration. If you have a bit more money to spend, you might want to investigate Camtasia Studio or ScreenFlow (www.telestream.net/screen-flow) for Mac.

Once you have your setup, you're also going to need a quiet place where you won't be interrupted. There is nothing more frustrating that getting partway through your video recording, only to be interrupted by a knock at the door or a ringing phone.

Your first few videos will probably be a bit clunky—but don't give up—practice makes perfect, after all! Try to come up with a schedule for posting your videos, especially if publishing to a blog, so that there are always new videos for your patrons. I post my tutorial videos every Wednesday afternoon at 2 PM. To make this happen, I record a bunch of videos in advance and use the scheduling tool on my blog to have the videos post on a regular basis. Remember that these don't have to be long productions; people don't have long attention spans to watch tutorials on the internet, and I have created tutorial videos that run less than two minutes.[6] The goal is to answer the question in the most efficient way possible.

Setting Boundaries

Systems librarians must learn to make tough decisions as to how much and what type of training they can realistically provide to both staff and patrons. This is especially important for those working in a smaller library and for solo systems librarians. You may choose, for example, to give public service staff members the skills to teach internet, OPAC, and basic word processing classes to patrons themselves, rather than trying to personally conduct all such training. You may provide staff members with training on library-specific applications such as ILS modules but require them to do some self-study or to take outside classes on applications such as office applications or your business office's accounting package. This approach also lessens your burden of learning all these applications sufficiently to teach them to others, when in-depth knowledge of these specific packages is not integral to your own job. Making these decisions will be part of your overall training plan for your institution, but you will likely be involved in creating or conducting some kind of training.

You'll also need to set boundaries regarding the type of training you and/or other systems personnel are able to provide to patrons. A large part of computer literacy, for example, involves learning the ability to critically evaluate the material that is available electronically. Information literacy is, of course, a useful skill, but perhaps one better taught by public services staff, leaving systems staff able to focus on training patrons and staff to use the technology itself. Set up a "train the trainer" program to provide other staff members with the foundation they need to develop their own classes. Provide them with any technical support they require, posting their training materials online or demonstrating the use of classroom control software, for example, but let them control the format and content of their training sessions. Remember that you and your colleagues are on the same side, and part of providing them the tools to deploy technology effectively involves providing the skills to pass those tools on to others.

Again, your communication, people, and library skills will come in handy here. IT people can have a hard time "letting go" and allowing others to take control of technology, but librarians understand that knowledge shared only grows.

Endnotes

1. John H. Heinrichs and Nancy Czech, "Training Cybrarians: The New Skill Requirements," in *Thinking Outside the Book: Essays for Innovative Librarians*, ed. Carol Smallwood (Jefferson, NC: McFarland, 2008), 259.
2. Karen Schneider, "The Old Guard and the New Technology," *Library Journal* (March 1, 1994): 64.
3. Michelle Boule, "Quick Tips for Technology Training," ALA TechSource, May 17, 2011, accessed May 25, 2012, www.alatech source.org/blog/2011/05/quick-tips-for-technology-training.html.
4. Michael Stephens, "Steal This Idea: Learning 2.0 at PLCMC," ALA TechSource, August 15, 2006, accessed May 25, 2012, www.alatech source.org/blog/2006/08/steal-this-idea-learning-20-at-plcmc. html.
5. Even more resources can be found in this article: Stephanie Gerding, "Fabulous Free Public Technology Training Materials," TechSoup for Libraries, January 28, 2011, accessed May 25, 2012, www.techsoup forlibraries.org/blog/fabulous-free-public-technology-training-materials.
6. My tutorial videos can be seen by visiting the ByWater Solutions channel at Blip (bywatersolutions.blip.tv).

Chapter 9

Independent Study

> *What we should take with us from library school*
> *is the ability to keep learning, to be comfortable*
> *trying new and difficult and sometimes*
> *threatening things, and to know that whatever we*
> *don't know, we can learn.*
> —Mary Ellen Bates[1]

Since library school cannot teach us everything associated with systems librarianship and since technology changes rapidly enough to make merely keeping up a constant challenge, one of your most important responsibilities as a systems librarian is to keep yourself current with the latest tools and techniques necessary to do your job effectively. The one certainty of systems librarianship is that there is always something more to learn, although the specific technologies you need to master will always vary depending on your institution and environment. Luckily, there are a number of options for extending your education beyond library school and giving yourself the tools you need to keep up-to-date.

Your foundation in the practices and principles of librarianship, built from library school coursework and from your professional activities, will inform the way you integrate the technological knowledge you acquire into your day-to-day tasks. Because of this, it is less important that you learn how to use specific technologies in library school (or before becoming a systems librarian) than that you embrace the capacity to learn and the principles of our profession. Try to learn something new every day and always be open to the possibility of expanding your personal knowledgebase. Your attitude and flexibility will let you gain the skills and information you need to adapt to new technological opportunities.

One truism of library work is that there is never enough money for everything your institution would like to purchase. Michael G. Sheehan, assistant director/database manager at Northern Waters Library Service, named the most frustrating part of systems work in his survey response: "Not having the physical staff support or money to provide the top level of service that large, well-funded institutions can. We cannot offer member libraries all the buttons, whistles, and gadgets we like or their patrons are sometimes requesting."

Unfortunately, this lack of funding also often extends to funding for education. So many systems librarians find themselves arguing for institutional support for formal computer training or using their own resources to further their education. This is the case for one frustrated survey respondent who states, "I am considering spending large amounts of my own money to get the training I need." Technology classes can also often be costly, which exacerbates the unwillingness of library administrations to spend a seemingly disproportionate amount of their training budget on technical coursework.

The following sections describe several ways of overcoming this funding gap and keeping current with new technological developments and changes in your institution's computing environment. These include locating free and low-cost online classes and tutorials, attending inexpensive local workshops or computer training center and community college courses, self-education, and current awareness. Note that several of these options are also appropriate as training alternatives for your staff; you can encourage the use of online tutorials and attendance at local training sessions, for example, as your co-workers begin to master your institution's set of computer competencies. Because free and low-cost options might not always be available, you need to be prepared to fight for funding for training opportunities. This includes writing memos to your administration, discussing the importance of learning opportunities with your board, and/or including funding for training in your technology grant proposals.

Other options for systems learning include attending local and national conferences and user group meetings, as well as joining and reading appropriate email discussion lists. (See more on groups, meetings, and online participation in Chapter 7.) Remember that every conference session and presentation you attend and each post you peruse is a potential learning opportunity; our best teachers are usually our colleagues who have faced similar challenges. Make a conscious effort to always keep learning, and make "keeping up" a priority—it is easy to allow the activities in this chapter to fall by the wayside when you get involved in pressing day-to-day dilemmas. But a commitment to lifelong learning will allow you to remain both effective in your day-to-day work and current in a changing technological environment.

Online Classes and Tutorials

Since internet technology has woven itself into every aspect of our lives, there is now an abundance of free and low-cost online classes and tutorials that serve the needs of those who want to learn more about using such technology. While a number of these online offerings are addressed to end users with limited previous technical knowledge, there are also affordable options for systems librarians who are set on improving their knowledge of a certain product or acquiring new skills such as programming or advanced web design techniques.

Free/Low-Cost Online Classes/Tutorials

The following websites each contain technology courses and/or tutorials on a variety of topics. For opportunities focused on a particular vendor's technology, be sure to check the vendor's website and watch its email discussion list and press releases; you can also search online for tutorials on specific topics. These sites are just a sampling of the online technical coursework and tutorials available; look also for sites devoted to learning specific topics or software packages.

- WebJunction (www.webjunction.org/catalog) is an online community that focuses in part on training librarians and offers free and for-pay courses, as well as many tutorials, articles, and resources to keep you up-to-date.

- MIT OpenCourseWare (www.ocw.mit.edu) offers freely accessible course materials from the Massachusetts Institute of Technology, covering topics such as management, computer science, literature, and technology.

- TechTraining for Libraries (www.coloradovirtual library.org/techtraining) offers ideas and materials for training on technology topics in libraries.

- TechTutorials (www.techtutorials.net) has free, searchable computer tutorials and white papers collected from around the web.

- TechSoup for Libraries (www.techsoupfor libraries.org) offers a growing collection of resources, articles, and webinars for librarians interested in new technologies.

- W3Schools Online (www.w3schools.com) is the place to go for free tutorials and quizzes on web development topics.

Beyond checking general online sources for learning more about technology, systems librarians should also look for internet-based classes at their local library systems, associations, and user groups. A number of these groups post tutorials online, webcast seminars, and are expanding into web-based instruction. Offerings from these groups sometimes have the advantage of teaching technological skills from a library perspective, and, in this sense, they might be preferred over more general options. They are also often subsidized by the sponsoring system or group, so they are more affordable than the online classes offered by library schools and computer training centers. (For more on taking advantage of local opportunities, see the Local Workshops section later in this chapter.)

Of course, online coursework can be supplemented with in-person classes, independent study of print resources, and on-the-job experience. However, any systems librarian should develop a certain level of comfort with online learning, both through formal online training sessions and through independent reading and self-paced tutorials. We just can't afford to neglect the learning opportunities that technology presents to us.

Community College and Computer Training Center Classes

Community colleges and local computer training centers offer in-person technical training classes if you prefer a more hands-on or instructor-led approach than those available online. While courses that are part of a certification track (such as Microsoft's MSCE or the A+ certification for computer technicians) may be somewhat pricier than others, the overall costs are generally reasonable. You can see which classes are more likely to meet your needs by doing some comparison shopping and examining course outlines. These outlines are sometimes available online; also watch for community colleges' printed class schedules in the mail or request syllabi/outlines directly from the school.

Note that computer training centers gear many of their course offerings toward those who are seeking technical certification. While there is nothing inherently wrong with such classes, you should realize that they may tend to "teach to the test," rather than focusing on the tasks that will be specifically useful in your daily activities. Chances are that they will also lack a library focus. If you intend to take a number of courses in one area of study, however, you might want to investigate the possibility of becoming certified in a subject that is relevant to your institution's needs. The O'Reilly School of Technology, for example, offers certification programs on various technology topics through the University of Illinois (www.oreillyschool.com/certificates). Your employer might also be more likely to fund classes toward certification than it will be to fund general computer training courses, since these classes are more easily compared to the Master of Library Science and Library Technical Assistant class work that the institution may already be accustomed to funding.

Certifications are also a way to prove to your employer that you take your systems responsibilities seriously, and any continuing education will provide you with a solid base from which to argue for increased compensation. (For more on compensation, see Chapter 12.)

Computer training centers are also now moving into the online market, offering their traditional in-person courses remotely in order to expand their customer base. Examine these courses carefully to ensure that you will be receiving the same instructor attention and interaction as you would at a class at the center's physical facility. Be wary of paying the same prices for online classes that are basically the equivalent of self-paced tutorials, because such tutorials are generally widely available elsewhere at little or no cost. While in-person courses may seem to require you to invest more time by sitting in a class, the hands-on experience and instructor attention can be worth it, especially when it comes to technical courses.

The most basic way to locate local computer training centers is by searching online. Once you find a center that looks promising, look for reviews online and ask your colleagues if they have had any experience with the group. It's also a good idea to look at the quality of the center's website design and organization as a possible indication of the coursework. (A technical school should have a useful and useable site.) Check for articles on the company, see if others have reported on their experiences, and use any other means possible to investigate a training center's reputation and reliability. Be sure to investigate before enrolling, especially if you intend to take several courses at one training center. If possible, see if a training center is in good financial shape, because some failing institutions have been known to close their doors without refunding student tuition. Ask if you can audit or sit in on part of a class to assess the quality of training before enrolling in a course. Some centers will give prospective customers certificates for free sample classes, although you will have to choose from their lower-cost (most likely end user) offerings.

Your local community college will also offer continuing education opportunities, which are generally listed separately from the college's courses for matriculated students. Continuing education courses are usually geared more toward working adults than classes for full-time students; these classes are usually more focused on how technology is used in the "real world." Community college classes are also usually affordable and are often scheduled on nights and weekends to accommodate the largest number of continuing education students.

Local Workshops

Look for statewide training opportunities from your state library, large library systems/consortia, and your state library association. Keep in mind, however, that many computer training classes and workshops offered by consortia will be fairly basic and aimed at inculcating technical literacy in general library staff rather than providing material that will be specifically useful to systems librarians. Examine the level of training advertised and see if you can preview a class outline before registering for such workshops. You want to avoid wasting your time covering topics you already know or those you could easily pick up from a book, or by spending time experimenting with individual software features.

The Metropolitan (METRO) New York Library Council, New York, for example, offers continuing education workshops on computer-related issues (see the catalog at metro.org/events/month). Classes range from those useful to systems librarians, such as "XML in Libraries," to options for other library staff, such as "Managing File Based Collections for Small Institutions." Check your own local consortia or systems for similar options. Workshops at local systems are particularly helpful because they are geared specifically toward the use of that technology in a library setting, although they still focus on technical topics. Other attendees are all working library staff. Further, coursework from METRO and similar systems/consortia is extremely affordable; costs range from free to generally less than $100 per workshop. Local workshops also provide an opportunity to network with other professionals who are usually at the same level of technological literacy as you are.

Local technology user groups sometimes also feature low-cost workshops and speakers on technical topics—another reason to stay involved and to keep informed. These groups will often advertise such opportunities in system or state library newsletters, and you may not need to be a member to attend. Note, however, that guest speakers will likely address broader trends rather than providing hands-on training. You may consider offering to present at one of these groups, if you have a topic you would like to share with your fellow professionals.

Library Schools

While library school coursework is often one of the more expensive continuing education options, it can also be the most targeted to working systems librarians and is most likely to be taught from the library perspective. Distance continuing education courses might be the most useful for far-flung students. For example, the offerings at the University of Wisconsin–Madison's School of Library and Information Studies (www.slis.wisc.edu/continueed.htm) often include courses in relevant systems-related topics such as metadata, virtual collection development, and digitization. The Simmons Graduate School of Library and Information Science offers similar, but on-site, continuing education courses (alanis.simmons.edu/ceweb) on topics ranging from technology grant writing to Zotero. These courses also qualify for continuing education credit.

Check with your local library school to see what it might offer in the way of continuing education coursework or certification classes. If you graduated from the institution, find out whether it offers alumni discounts on future courses. See whether you can take courses normally offered in the MLS track, if newer technical classes are being offered or if you were unable to attend these classes when you were pursuing your degree.

Self-Education

Any librarian should appreciate the power of reading and self-study. A number of resources are specifically geared toward self-education in the computer field, including test preparation guides for certifications such as the Microsoft Certified Solutions Expert and series such as the Sams "Teach Yourself ..." titles. If you purchase a new software package or upgrade to a new operating system, take time to work through the applicable self-study material in one of these resources. The hands-on exercises, quizzes, and review questions in these guides can help you gain valuable practice in a controlled setting before you have to deal with an emergency situation under pressure.

Self-education also includes on-the-job learning. As you progress in your career as a systems librarian, each experience you have, whether setting up a new server, troubleshooting an annoying systems issue, or negotiating a contract with a database vendor, presents an opportunity for learning. Once you have experienced something once, you are more prepared to handle similar situations in the future. Each time you educate yourself when researching a systems issue or purchase, you extend your own technical knowledgebase. If you are part of a larger systems department, you have the opportunity to learn from your colleagues and share knowledge and tips with others. This on-the-job learning is often superior to any classroom training, and formal class work still requires you to practice your skills in the real world before you can truly claim competence.

If you are interested in expanding your skills in a certain area, set aside a regular block of time for practice and research. Give yourself the tools to help you learn. If you wish to extend your knowledge of open source software, for example, why not take an older machine you would otherwise discard, download Linux, and experiment with setting up and configuring the operating system?

Find other ways to practice and extend your skills before you need to use them in a real-world environment.

Current Awareness

The best way to continue your education as a systems librarian is to adopt a constant attitude of attentive awareness. When you join email lists, read articles, subscribe to technology-related Twitter feeds, listen to announcements on the radio, or browse websites, be on the lookout for information that might benefit the technological environment in your library. File useful emails into folders for future reference. Bookmark useful websites, file them, tag them, and rename them with descriptive names. (I find Delicious, Instapaper, and Zotero very useful for these types of "clippings.") Clip magazine articles (or find their online equivalent and bookmark them) and file them by subject. Then, when a situation arises where your stored information is applicable, you may not remember the solution offhand, but you will likely remember having seen it and you'll be able to locate it easily in your personal knowledge management environment.

Online Opportunities

Due to their currency, frequently updated internet resources are the best way to keep up-to-date on technological topics. Subscribing to the RSS feeds on your favorite systems news websites and reading them regularly will help you find information on fast-moving topics such as virus alerts, new technologies, and security patches. If you take 15 minutes to read through your RSS feeds each morning, you will be less likely to miss important announcements that may affect your library and its users. Useful and frequently updated sites and blogs include:

- ALA TechSource Blog (www.alatechsource.org/blog), which has news and tips on technical issues for librarians. While much content is aimed at pushing their subscription products, you will also find useful news and links.

- David Lee King (www.davidleeking.com) writes about library website design and digital technologies, and he's a good source for information about emerging technologies and designing digital experiences in libraries.

- The Librarian in Black (www.librarianinblack.net) is Sarah Houghton's blog, containing news stories and commentary focusing on changes in the ways patrons and libraries receive information. This is a good source of new stories on ebooks and mobile devices.

- LISNews (www.lisnews.org) by Blake Carver focuses on issues for librarians and often discusses and links to information on technology topics.

- Mashable (www.mashable.com) is a multiauthor blog that covers all sorts of technology topics from social media to mobile technologies and open source.

- TechSoup for Libraries (www.techsoupforlibraries.org/ blog) is a multiauthor blog written specifically to give librarians technology information.

Supplement the sites on this list with your own favorites and ask your peers what they're reading.

If you feel ambitious, you can also set up your own blog or other online resource to help you (and/or your peers) keep current on new technology trends. Even if you do not choose to make your blog public and instead just host it privately or keep it on your personal machine, you can use blogging software's RSS features to create your own searchable and commented technology knowledge and news base. RSS lets you save time and collocate much of your daily reading in one place, and your RSS feed reader lets you read directly through the aggregator as if you were visiting each of these websites.

Beyond websites, one of the best ways to keep current is by signing up for free email newsletters on technology-related topics. These emailed newsletters "push" articles, summaries, and tips directly to your email box so you won't have to remember to go back to a site for the most current news. These daily or weekly newsletters can keep you aware of patches, virus alerts, tips, product releases, and ideas for using computer technology in your library. Be sure to sign up for general technical newsletters as well as library-related offerings. Some useful newsletters include:

- Information Today NewsBreaks (newsbreaks.info today.com) emails library-related breaking news, press releases, and conference reports.

- InfoWorld (www.infoworld.com/newsletters) lets you choose from newsletters on topics such as Microsoft, security issues, open source, web technology, networking, and other technology-related topics.

- LibraryJournal.com (www.libraryjournal.com/csp/ cms/sites/LJ/info/newsletterSubscription.csp) offers a series of newsletters to choose from on various library-specific topics.

- LockerGnome (www.lockergnome.com) lets you subscribe to its blog via email, which gives you access to all articles on mobile technology, computer software, online tools, and so on.

- NetworkWorld (www.networkworld.com/newsletters/ subscribe.html) offers subscriptions to any number of newsletters with news alerts on network and systems administration topics, product reviews, wireless, IT education, technology Q&A, Linux, Novell, Windows, and more.

- Windows Secrets (www.windowssecrets.com/newsletter) offers tips on hardware and software best practices, as well as insider tricks and information on known issues.

Note that some of these sites let you sign up for several newsletters at once. Be selective, and if past issues are available online, read a couple to find out if the content looks useful to you before subscribing. Supplement the newsletters in the list with your own findings and/or those specific to technology used in your library.

Offline Opportunities

In your quest to become and remain self-educated, you will also likely wish to subscribe to topical computer-related print magazines (or to read or skim those to which your library subscribes), as well as to faithfully read publications such as *Computers in Libraries, Searcher, Code4Lib Journal, Library Hi-Tech, D-Lib Magazine,* and *Information Today,* which are specifically intended for information professionals in systems positions. Urge your institution to invest in subscriptions to the major library-related technology publications. Join library technology organizations such as the Library Information Technology Association and read association journals such as *Information Technology and Libraries* and the *Journal of the American Society for Information Science and Technology.* If you cannot afford to join, read the relevant selected articles that are available free online or through your library's database subscriptions. The book reviews in such publications will give you more direction on avenues of self-study to help you improve your skills in supporting library technology.

Once your name is on a few mailing lists, you will also receive solicitations to subscribe to free weeklies and monthlies such as *Network World* and *InfoWorld.* Take advantage of these offers. While much of the content of such publications might be irrelevant to your particular situation, you are bound to encounter useful articles. Furthermore, skimming these magazines on a regular basis keeps you abreast of new technological developments and will offer tips and tricks to better manage your computing environment. You certainly don't have to read each issue word-for-word, but take even free publications seriously. If you see such an offer while surfing a relevant site, subscribe—you will probably have to fill out a long and annoying signup form, but the opportunities for learning make it worth your time. Read free publications critically, however, because their dependence on advertising dollars can influence the slant of their articles. Again, use these resources in conjunction with others and with your existing store of knowledge. Realize that these types of magazines are usually a better source for keeping current with broad technical trends and for product and software reviews than for developing specific skills. But they definitely have a place in your continuing quest to keep current. As always, ask your peers in other libraries what they read to keep current and watch for suggestions on email discussion lists.

Funding Training Opportunities

In an ideal world, all libraries would possess unlimited funding and all administrators would recognize the importance of lifelong learning. However, most librarians work under somewhat more realistic conditions, competing for a limited pool of funds. Unfortunately, a frequent byproduct of libraries' lack of sufficient funding is a tendency to skimp on professional development and training opportunities for library staff. While the methods described earlier in this chapter serve as lower-cost ways of bypassing this lack of funding, more formal and more costly classes and training opportunities also have their place.

If your institution already offers funding or full or partial tuition reimbursement for employees to attend library school, this will bolster your argument for receiving funding to attend computer training courses. These are equally as relevant to your job and your day-to-day duties as library school classes. Show how increasing your expertise will save your library the costs associated with system downtime, consulting fees, and repair in the long run.

If your library lacks a history of funding professional development opportunities, be prepared to point to pertinent studies and articles on increased employee retention and productivity among institutions that support continuing education. This will prove particularly effective if the library has grown dependent on your technological expertise and you can provide statistics on how a commitment to lifelong learning increases the retention of technical personnel.

Another way to fund technology training for yourself and for other staff members is to include training in any technology grant application you prepare. Most technology grants allow training as one of the areas they are willing to fund, so if you plan on using grant money to expand technology-related programs or services, always make staff training part of the package. Also investigate nontechnology-specific grants that can be used for activities such as staff development or guest speakers—either of these can focus on technology training. Take full advantage of the training provided in any grant you receive, such as the training supplied with Gates Grants, which focuses on training library staff to use and teach the grant-provided equipment. Look at Institute of Museum and Library Services grants distributed through the states, at American Library Association-funded grants, and at funding provided by large technology companies and charitable institutions.

Your library may want to subscribe to a resource like Technology Grant News (www.technologygrantnews.com) or other grant publications to keep current on what funding is being offered. Take advantage of any opportunity to extend your own learning and to encourage your institution to fund your technological professional development. Lifelong learning is essential to your success as a systems librarian.

Endnote

1. Mary Ellen Bates, "The Newly Minted MLS: What Do We Need to Know Today?" *Searcher* 6, no. 5 (1998): 30–33.

Chapter 10

Administration and Management

A library vendor is not quite as reliable as a good used car salesman. At least with the used car salesman, you can go somewhere else next time. With a vendor, your best quality is that latent streak of masochism that almost all systems librarians seem to develop on the job.

—Earl Lee[1]

Systems personnel in libraries often find themselves acting in an unofficial administrative capacity because administrators with little technical knowledge must involve their IT departments in planning and managing large technology projects. All computer services librarians need to understand the basics of project management and administration, and must be prepared to assume responsibility for the direction of technology in their library, whether or not they have technically been hired in an administrative role. This is especially important when your institution becomes involved in a major endeavor such as an automation system migration project (see more on this in Chapter 11), but administration and management skills will also be needed in such everyday tasks as negotiating a service contract for your library's printers. You will also probably be involved with the library's administration in either writing technology grants or implementing grant-funded projects. While the process of writing grants is beyond the scope of this chapter, there are a number of titles on grant-writing and library fundraising that can assist you if you do take on such a responsibility.

In larger institutions, systems librarians may also be lucky enough (depending on your perspective) to manage their own staff. The skills required to manage people are significantly different from those that are necessary in managing technology, and the process of managing nonlibrarian IT staff presents its own set of challenges. This is another situation in which your people skills and common sense will be as important as your technical knowledge—if not more so. As Mark Stover writes: "People skills are critical for information technology managers because their first allegiance is to human beings, not computers. True, they will be working with computers every day, but only in the context of working with the people who use those computers."[2]

The tasks of technology project management and people management, while requiring distinct skill sets, each involve a great deal of planning and care to achieve properly. In the following sections, you'll find discussions of the skill sets needed in systems administration and management, as well as descriptions of what you might expect to encounter and the steps you need to take in completing common IT projects. Begin with information on creating a technology plan, which is a necessary prerequisite to a number of large technology projects in libraries.

Creating a Technology Plan

Many libraries are required to create and submit a technology plan (usually covering a 1- to 3-year period) in order to satisfy state, board, or grant requirements. Technology plans are commonly required to receive E-Rate discounts and state per-capita equalization grants, for example. While only larger libraries tended to create such plans in the not-so-recent past, smaller and medium-size institutions are now recognizing the fact that managing the pace of technological change demands a more formal planning process. If you are required to create or contribute to a technology plan for a particular purpose, be sure to review the specific guidelines of the body requiring the plan. If your technology plan is for the use of your library staff or administration rather than for a granting body or your state library, keep your audience in mind; a major role for your document in this instance will be to provide the necessary information for others in your library so they can make informed technology decisions and use technology effectively in your institution.

In *Implementing Technology Solutions in Libraries*, Karen Knox explains why you need to create a technology plan regardless of your library type or size: "If you do not have a current technology plan for your library, take time to write one. … Technology needs to exist for both library customers and library staff. Take a look at the entire picture and prioritize what needs to be done. With a good plan, many things are possible."[3]

The basic purpose of a technology plan is to state the library's mission and goals/objectives, then to explain how the library will use technology to fulfill those goals and objectives in its mission. Your plan will need to include specifics on what you intend to do (with costs). Realize that your plan is not a "wish list" describing the technology you ideally would like to have but a statement of what your library intends to do with technology in the foreseeable future. The plan does not need to include the specific technology you plan on using, since we all know that technology will change during the time it takes you to write your plan, but it should be goal-oriented so that the tools can be chosen when you're ready to implement the new technology.

Depending on the size and nature of your institution, you may hold the entire responsibility for developing your plan, write it in conjunction with your director, be the liaison to a planning consultant, or be the technical liaison to or head of a technology planning committee composed of yourself and several other staff members. In any of these situations, however, the basic components and purpose of your plan remain the same.

Most technology plans contain several fairly standard sections. As you look through these, note how the earlier organizational and training tasks you have mastered in previous chapters will be useful in addressing these components. The standard areas of a technology plan are:

- Introduction: This brief section contains information on your library and on the plan's development, who was involved in its creation, and how it will be updated as needed.

- Vision statement: Keep this short and to the point, showing how technology will help the library meet its goals in terms of serving its community over the next few years.

- Background statement: You will need to build a foundation showing how technology has developed in your library, what technology you now own, and how it is currently used. This will be a much lengthier section and can include topics such as the way technology is integrated and used in general library functions, how much of the library's budget is allocated to technology, how staff and patrons use technology in the library, and the strengths and weaknesses of the library's existing technological environment.

- Goals and objectives: This section lists and prioritizes major institutional goals that will be accomplished through the use of technology. Objectives describe the specific way in which you will implement technology to accomplish these goals.

- Funding: Ask questions such as, How will the library fund these goals?, What percentage of funding will come from the library's own budget?, and What percentage is anticipated to come from grants or other outside sources?

- Training: How are staff and patrons currently trained to use technology, and how will they be trained to use the new technologies you plan to implement? This can also include an evaluation of the skills that your current systems staff have, and a list of areas in which they might need to take classes or otherwise increase their expertise.

- Evaluation: Many plans will require you to describe how you will evaluate whether your goals and objectives are implemented within a given timeframe. You may also need to include a section on how often you intend to update your technology plan.

- Conclusion: This is optional for most technology plans, and it just wraps up the library's intentions.

- Appendixes: These optional sections can include library-created, technology-related documents, such as handouts or class outlines.

If your library has created a technology plan in the past, you may only need to update it in terms of your current technological environment and needs. However, as many plans are updated only every 3 to 5 years, you may find that the older plan has outlived its usefulness or has failed to predict the current technological environment. In this case, you may be better off starting from scratch.

The New Jersey State Library compiled a useful list of resources related to technology planning (ldb.njstatelib.org/E-Rate/utech pln.php) for anyone to review. This guide includes links to specific planning guides from state libraries, sample plans, grants and funding opportunities that require technology plans, and other planning resources and guides. You can find additional useful resources related to technology planning at WebJunction (www.webjunction.org/techplan). Also consult Karen Knox's *Implementing Technology Solutions in Libraries* (www.karenc knox.com/ITSiL.php). This title includes a number of useful guides, as well as a sample technology plan.

Creating your technology plan will also be a test of how well you (and/or your department) can work with the library's administration. Since technology is now so tightly interwoven with all library functions, planning for the future of technology means planning for the future of the library itself. Dealing with the bureaucracy of creating a technology plan and applying for programs such as the E-Rate that require such a plan can be frustrating, partly because this removes you from the hands-on part of managing library technology and puts you right into the middle of a bureaucratic muddle.

But remember that a willingness to work at overcoming bureaucracy and politics is necessary to do your job effectively. Part of any systems librarian's administrative tasks will be to argue for increased shares of institutional funding and to allocate scarce resources in the most effective manner. Ensuring that technology serves the needs of the institution requires finding the appropriate funding to support technology. Working on a technology plan merely highlights this process.

Ensure that your technology plan is sensible and that it reflects the realities of time, goals, and funding at your institution. If you have historically had funding to replace computer equipment every 5 years, for example, it does little good to describe your library as being on a more ideal 3-year replacement cycle. (In this case, it would be better to describe the reality of the situation and to use your technology plan to show the necessity for increased funding so that you could move to a shorter replacement cycle.) The process of creating a technology plan presents an opportunity for you to learn how to market yourself and your department and to show the importance of allocating funding to technology in order to fulfill the library's mission and goals. Take advantage of that opportunity!

Buying Software

Earlier, we reviewed some of the various applications you might need to support in your library. You may also be included in administrative discussions on the different options available to your library, and, when making purchasing decisions, it is always important to shop around. While some products are only available from one provider, others can be purchased anywhere, putting you in the position of finding the best deal for the money.

Before making your purchase, you'll want to consider many factors. The first is the opinions of your peers. Talk with other systems librarians in libraries similar to yours, because the most helpful information is going to come from your colleagues. Talk to them about the staff's opinions of the software, how easy it was to make the change, how much training was required, how their patrons have reacted, and what they think of the company providing support. Next, you'll want to take advantage of demos. Having the opportunity to try the software out first will make your choice a bit easier. Finally, remember to look for providers who offer nonprofit discounts. For example, TechSoup (www.techsoup.org) offers discounts on software for libraries.

Resources

You are not the first librarian to feel the pain of planning an automation or new software project, and there are a number of guides, articles, and online resources to assist you throughout the process. Just a few selected resources are listed here, and you can find additional suggestions in Appendix B. Supplement these suggestions with your own research to find the most current guides before beginning your own IT project. You should also join and read your selected vendor's email discussion list and/or online forums to gather pointers from other institutions using the same software.

- Marshall Breeding, "Automation Marketplace 2012: Agents of Change," The Digital Shift, March 29, 2012 (www.thedigitalshift.com/2012/03/ila/automation-marketplace-2012-agents-of-change): This annual article surveys the automation marketplace over the past year and profiles a number of major vendors. It's a good starting point to locate vendor websites and get an overview of capabilities. It also includes helpful tables on sales to consortia, types of libraries using the system, and total numbers of installations.

- John M. Cohn and Ann L. Kelsey, *The Complete Library Technology Planner: A Guidebook With Sample Technology Plans and RFPs on CD-ROM* (New York: Neal-Schuman, 2010): In addition to walking public, academic, school, and special libraries through the technology planning process, the accompanying CD-ROM includes more than 35 RFP examples and technology plans to help you get started.

- Library Resource Guide (www.libraryresource.com): This resource offers a directory of library-specific vendors. Note that the vendors listed in this guide paid for their listings, which means that this list is not comprehensive, but it is still a good place to start.

- LisVendor.info (www.lisvendor.info): This new wiki lets librarians share information about the various vendors that their libraries have done business with. At the time of this writing, there isn't a lot of information, but watch for the site to grow.

- Marshall Breeding's Library Automation Companies listing (www.librarytechnology.org/companies.pl): This resource at Library Technology Guides provides press releases and statistics about many library automation vendors (simply click on the vendor's logo for more information).

Software Rollouts

The conversion to or addition of new software packages can be an extended process that encompasses aspects such as the selection of appropriate software for your institution's needs (see more on writing requests for proposals and other factors in choosing large-scale software packages in Chapter 11), upgrading or replacing outdated hardware that may not run the new packages effectively, software installation, and staff and/or patron training. You may choose to roll out new software gradually to give people a chance to use it before everyone needs to make the change.

In Chapter 1, we discussed the importance of communication in any systems librarian's work. One reason that library staff members are often resistant to a change in technology is that they were not involved in the decision-making process, and it therefore appears that their computing environment shifted arbitrarily without any advance notice. As Mark Stover writes: "People are mystified when they are expected to use a particular software application and are clueless about its functionality. People are mystified when changes appear in their computer systems (operating system, desktop, applications, hardware, etc.) without any advance notice. A good wired manager will prevent his or her employees from becoming mystified."[4] Demystify the process by giving people plenty of warning that the software environment will be changing. Explain why it is changing. Provide training on the upgraded or new program and the opportunity to practice with it. Ensure that staff members know who they can turn to for help with the new product.

Network Upgrades

Upgrading a computer network, another common major under-taking, requires attention to the same kinds of details as new software implementations. A network that is created and extended without proper planning can cause problems down the line, as connectivity and throughput become insufficient to support newer operating systems or the client modules of a new ILS, for example. While upgrading a network can be costly, grant money is often available for such a project. E-Rate funds, for example, can be used for cabling as well as connectivity, and many state libraries offer technology grant money specifically for upgrading networks.

Decisions to be made here include:

- The type of cabling to use: Should you invest in fiber? Cat 5E? Cat 6? Wireless? Pricing, ease of installation, and institutional needs will affect your choice.

- Where and how to configure wiring centers: This will depend largely on the size and layout of your institution and on the cabling you choose to use.

- How much future expansion to plan on: Realize that any networking solution quickly becomes insufficient or obsolete; plan to support many more network nodes than you currently intend to offer.

- The types of hardware and software upgrades that are needed: Are you upgrading your entire network to a new operating system? Do you need to invest in new servers, additional storage, additional RAM? Do you need to add wireless cards to your PCs?

The decisions you make here will determine the scope and expense of your networking project and can help you also decide the extent to which you will need to involve outside consultants or vendors.

Managing Systems Staff

In many larger libraries, systems responsibilities are split among several people. You may be the only librarian in charge of several computer technicians, or you may be a library systems administrator with the responsibility for managing other systems librarians in addition to library technology. This requires supervisory skills in addition to whatever technical knowledge you need to keep library systems running. Managing technical staff also requires different skills than managing librarians; IT can truly have its own culture, which means you need to work to bring your department into line with the larger library culture. Your IT staff may also lack the library background and values of other library staff members, which can create a communications gap between them and non-IT personnel. Your job is to bridge that gap and to give your employees the skills they need to interact more effectively with librarians and support library technology.

As an IT manager, you may be responsible for managing diverse groups, from other librarians to paraprofessional staff to nonlibrarian IT professionals to student workers—and even volunteers. Each of these groups brings a different outlook, skill set, and focus to systems work, and you may need to deal with them in different ways. Systems staff may be employed part-time or full-time, and there may be individuals you rarely see because they are responsible for covering the department on nights and weekends when you are not present.

Unfortunately, supervisory skills are not always taught in library schools, which focus more heavily on professional skills and theory rather than on the specific skills needed to manage people. Our background as members of a helper profession can also cause us to be a bit too helpful when it comes to managing our employees. The patron is always right, but your staff may not be.

Lastly, in most libraries, systems staff will be limited, and you will have a mix of hands-on and administrative duties that require you to add management expertise to your skills toolbox. As with the rest of systems work, responsibilities here tend to be additive; you will be a manager in addition to, rather than instead of, being a systems librarian.

Communicating

The same skills that serve you well as you are interacting with, training, and serving as a liaison to library staff and users will be your foundation as a successful manager. The key to a smoothly running department is communication and clarity; the relationship you build with your employees is equally as important as those you build with your superiors and peers. As Richard Warman points out: "At the top of most employees' gripe lists are problems in communication—not understanding what is expected of them, feeling excluded from important information, working under people who give vague and confusing instructions. When employees see their superiors as their main roadblock to getting their jobs done, the culprits are likely to be irrational or incompetent instruction-givers."[5]

The health of your department—and its relationship with other library departments—depends on your ability to maximize communication among your staff, yourself, other library employees, and patrons. Involve your staff in departmental decisions and recognize the value of their input, while clearly explaining your own motivations and positions. Communicate the importance of sharing knowledge with other library staff, which might be difficult for purely technical employees who may feel it is easier and quicker to resolve issues on their own and who underappreciate those without formal technical training. Explain these ideals in terms of the mission of the institution and try to pass on library values; your staff will appreciate being informed of the reasoning behind department policies and priorities. Technical staff can be especially sensitive to micromanagement and will appreciate the opportunity to extend themselves professionally. Your job will be to ensure that their actions serve library goals and to outline their responsibilities so that they have a framework to work within. Admire and hire people who can work independently but remember broader institutional needs.

Also draw on your own background with technology when communicating with your staff. Technical personnel have greater respect for those who can speak their language, and even if you have a better grasp of the larger picture than of the details, your technical knowledge will allow you to understand your staff's perspective and better communicate the library's needs.

Hiring and Staffing

In a larger institution, part of your responsibility as a systems librarian will be to deploy your staff effectively and to hire the right mix of people and skills to keep the technology in your library running smoothly. Unfortunately, finding money for technology and for sufficient staff is often a tradeoff in an era of fixed library budgets and insufficient funding. Here again, you will need to become politically savvy and learn how to market your department and its services, while arguing for sufficient funding to take care of yourself and your staff.

You will also need to master the skills involved in finding and hiring people who are the right fit for your institution. When looking for new systems staff, remember the skills, attitude, outlook, and capacity to learn and grow that have been important to your own success—these will be equally important to your staff's success. Specific technical skills are useful, but they can always be learned. As Roy Tennant emphasizes in a list of useful personality traits for digital library staff: "The capacity to learn constantly and quickly. I cannot make this point strongly enough. It does not matter what they know now. Can they assess a new technology and what it may do (or not do) for your library? Can they stay up-to-date? Can they

198 The Accidental Systems Librarian

learn a new technology without formal training? If they can't, they will find it difficult to do the job."[6] The ability to learn new technologies and to grow on the job is paramount. Joe Kirsch, senior control librarian of systems at Ekurhuleni Metropolitan Municipality, backs up Tennant's comments about being a systems librarian on his website by pointing out that "The more knowledge a systems librarian acquires, the stronger his background in both technology and librarianship, the more value he will be to the institution/council."[7] Remember your own need to extend your skills; your staff has a similar need. Learn again to fight for training dollars. While it is important that anyone you hire has the ability to learn independently, sometimes formal training will be necessary. Training and the opportunity for professional growth also always rank high on IT personnel's wish lists, so providing such opportunities will help you retain staff in an environment where you will likely be unable to pay the most competitive salaries.

If you are in an academic library, you may be responsible for supervising student workers, who are supposed to assist in troubleshooting, computer labs, and so on. Student workers may lack a commitment to the principles of librarianship and may require more supervision than other staff, although they may possess a great deal of technical knowledge that can be harnessed to help fulfill your institution's goals. Technical management here requires attention to the mix of employees and the optimal way to deploy them throughout the institution, which you will learn through time and experimentation. The right staffing mix depends largely on the type and scope of technology implemented in your library, as well as the technological comfort level of other library staff.

As a systems manager, you will be responsible for interviewing, hiring, and evaluating your employees. In any interview, remember that you and the candidate are actually interviewing one another to see if the institution and the position will be a good match for the candidate's skills and personality. In any hiring process, search not only for technical skills, but also for the ability to work well in a library environment, which includes communication skills and the ability to empathize with the library's mission. Search for people with whom you and other library staff can work well and who will help you fit technology into the library environment. When reviewing your staff, evaluate them in terms of goals such as: Do they support technology within the library well? Do they understand the library environment and arrange their priorities accordingly? Do they interact well with library staff and users? Can they work independently?

In all, you are seeking staff who share or can learn to adopt a similar outlook to yours, one that is based on the principles of librarianship and that melds library skills with technological savvy. You will need to work together to ensure that library technology serves the needs of your institution's users.

Endnotes

1. Earl Lee, *Libraries in the Age of Mediocrity* (Jefferson, NC: McFarland, 1998), 9.
2. Mark Stover, *Leading the Wired Organization: The Information Professional's Guide to Managing Technological Change* (New York: Neal-Schuman, 1999), 314.
3. Karen Knox, *Implementing Technology Solutions in Libraries: Techniques, Tools, and Tips From the Trenches* (Medford, NJ: Information Today, Inc., 2011), 3.
4. Stover, *Leading the Wired Organization*, 91.
5. Richard Wurman, Loring Leifer, David Sume, and Karen Whitehouse, *Information Anxiety 2* (Indianapolis, IN: Que, 2001), 225.
6. Roy Tennant, "The Most Important Management Decision: Hiring Staff for the New Millennium," *Library Journal* (February 15, 1998), accessed May 29, 2012, www.libraryjournal.com/article/CA156490.html. Tennant also notes the importance of flexibility and the ability to foster change among his list of useful traits.
7. Joe Kirsch, "Systems Librarian," 2010, www.systemslibrarian.co.za.

Chapter 11

Integrated Library System Migration

[A]s libraries, our relationship with ILS vendors is the most important technical relationship we have. We need to be approaching it from the point of view of software partners.
—John Blyberg[1]

Whether or not you are officially in an administrative position, your technological expertise will be called upon when your library undertakes a large-scale IT project such as migrating to a new automation system. Specific details will vary depending on your environment and your institution's needs. In any IT venture, however, especially in a large-scale project such as an integrated library system (ILS) migration, the focus needs to remain on completing the project with minimum disruption and with maximum benefit to the library's users and staff. Here, it might be useful to shore up on the basics of IT project management.

So far in this book, we've talked about technology planning and IT project planning; this chapter specifically discusses planning and implementing an ILS migration. The same principles, however, apply to any large-scale IT project in libraries.

Most libraries are now automated, so you will probably be planning the migration of your data to a new automation system instead of automating from scratch (although much of this discussion will also be applicable to setting up a new ILS as well). Many automation systems are nearing the end of their usable life. In part, this is because they were intended largely to handle print resources and now need to manage access to resources and databases in a number of formats. In addition, we also need to meet the rising expectations of users who may be comparing your systems to graphical, customized websites such as Amazon.com. Unfortunately, data migration presents its own set of pitfalls. Systems staff will need to work with technical and circulation services librarians to clean up data prior to the migration. Some data will inevitably be lost or corrupted in the changeover. The change in interface and functionality will be disruptive to library staff and users who have been accustomed to the old system. Computer hardware, networking, and operating systems may need to be upgraded prior to the migration.

You may also be asked to work with your administration to set a timetable for migration. When doing so, consider all of the aspects in the following sections and create a realistic timeframe for changing your system over—then add several months. Realize that the only given in migrating your automation system is that it will never go entirely as planned. There is no way around it: An automation migration will be time-consuming, disruptive, frustrating, and costly. Your job will be to plan carefully so that the changeover occurs with the minimum possible cost, disruption, and frustration. You may also be working with an automation consultant, if your institution/consortium chooses to use one. This is another instance in which your technical communication skills will come in handy.

A successful ILS migration calls for different skills than those required in its day-to-day operation. The day-to-day understanding that you have of your particular automation environment, however, will serve you well as you plan the migration of your data and the post-migration environment.

Your level of direct involvement in your library's ILS migration project will vary, depending on your institutional needs and situation. If your library is part of a larger system or consortium, for example, many of the tasks detailed in this chapter may be handled by staff at your system headquarters. In this case, however, you will likely be asked to serve as your library's liaison to the larger system and to handle or coordinate details such as training and hardware upgrades within your own institution. You will also be required to attend vendor demos and to give input on the new system's desired capabilities and services.

Selecting a Vendor and/or Product

There are two different models for choosing your ILS vendor. When choosing a proprietary ILS (a closed source system that is managed by one company), your institution first selects the product that best fits its needs, and the vendor comes along with it. When choosing an open source ILS, though, you have a bit more flexibility. First, you choose the product you're interested in, and *then* you interview support vendors. With open source, since the software is available for free on the internet, vendors are selling services, not software. This means that if you like a product, but not a vendor, you can keep the product and find another vendor. With the proprietary systems, the vendor and product come hand in hand, leaving you no choice but to migrate again if you're unhappy with the support that the vendor provided.

Open Source Automation Systems

A number of libraries are no longer satisfied simply with relying on outside vendors and on expensive, proprietary systems. This has resulted in the open source movement in libraries, which has begun to produce usable automation systems as an alternative to the large library vendors. (For more on open source software, see Chapter 2.)

Open source automation systems have been around for more than a decade now, but they have only recently started to take off.

After years of fighting with systems that are too slow to change and never quite meet libraries' needs, librarians have taken control into their own hands. They are not only choosing open source automation systems, but they are also helping in their development. With librarians working beside developers, we're seeing products being released that not only meet the needs of the libraries, but that also allow for future growth and change.

In 2005, for example, library news sources were all abuzz over the fact that the Georgia Library PINES system decided to write an open source ILS to meet their consortium's exact needs. Their Evergreen project has continued to grow and has been adopted by libraries of all sizes and types. This rapid adoption has led to a more stable and more impressive project than the original developers ever imagined.

Only 5 years before that, Horowhenua Library Trust, a small library in New Zealand, realized that its ILS might not survive the dreaded Y2K bug. Librarians contracted an outside developer to write a custom automation system (which would later be named Koha, a word meaning gift in Māori), with the plan to release the code on the web so other libraries can benefit from it as well. Who knew that such a small gift would grow to be such an amazing solution for so many libraries worldwide?

Both of these systems have grown by leaps and bounds. When the first edition of this book came out, choosing an open source automation system was a risky venture only pursued by those with a dedicated IT staff. Today, there are more than 30 companies worldwide that are providing support for products such as Koha and Evergreen. This means that libraries no longer have to go it alone; they can choose from many support, training, and development options—and they should always do some comparison shopping. While opting for an open source ILS means that you aren't tied to any one vendor, you still don't want to end up hopping from support provider to support provider. Employ the same tips I've been repeating throughout this book: Ask your network of colleagues and research what options are available and what the various companies can provide for your library.

To keep an eye on new developments in these and similar projects, you can visit:

- BiblioteQ (www.biblioteq.sourceforge.net)
- Evergreen (www.open-ils.org)
- Koha (www.koha-community.org)
- Lib$_2$o (lib2o.info)
- OPALs (www.mediaflex.net)
- OpenOPAC (www.openopac.sourceforge.net)

If you'd like to go a step further, you can sign up for the mailing lists or jump into the chat rooms where the developers and librarians meet to discuss current issues with the software, as well as the direction the software should go next. You don't have to be in a library that's using one of these applications to be involved in the communities around them. As someone who started out that way, I can tell you that the people using these products will welcome you with open arms and encourage you to participate and communicate on a regular basis.

If your library isn't ready for a complete ILS migration, you can also take a look at open source discovery layers. These applications can be used on top of your existing ILS to improve the OPAC without requiring you to migrate to a new system. You can visit the following official websites to explore these projects and contribute to them:

- Blacklight (www.projectblacklight.org)
- Scriblio (www.scriblio.net)

- The Social OPAC (SOPAC) (www.thesocialopac.net)
- VuFind (www.vufind.org)

Lastly, if you wish to investigate open source alternatives to proprietary automation systems, be prepared to counter arguments about your library's experience with "homegrown" solutions or fears about the security of open source. These types of comments are what are known as FUD, or Fear, Uncertainty, and Doubt. It's important to note that not all homegrown systems are open source and not all open source products start out as homegrown. Koha, for example, was developed for one library by an outside firm who then shared the code. Evergreen was developed in-house by the Georgia Library PINES system and then released for other librarians' participation and contributions.

As for security, if you are confronted with this particular flavor of FUD, there are plenty of resources to show you that open source is not only secure, but it can often be more secure than proprietary options. Be sure to amass current information and examples to counteract your administration's memories of the costs and stresses involved in the past. Remember: Institutions have long memories.

Requests for Proposals
Depending on the rules set forth by your library's governing body, the first step in choosing a vendor might be to prepare a request for proposal (RFP). The basic purpose of an RFP is to outline your institution's automation needs and solicit vendor proposals that describe how their products and services can fulfill those needs. Writing an RFP has the added benefit of helping to clarify your library's automation requirements; you will need to create a detailed analysis of such requirements in order to provide clear instructions to the responding vendors.

A number of sample RFPs and guides to creating an effective RFP are available online at TechSoup (www.techsoup.org/tool

kits/rfp). When examining RFPs from other libraries, try to find samples that are similar to your own institution in terms of scope and the type of community served. Also consult the resources in Appendix B to find more on the beginning stages of planning an ILS migration.

Your department may be tempted to choose an automation system by fiat, since one maxim of ILS selection is that you will never have complete agreement among library staff. Departments and individuals may tend to focus on a particular aspect or function—which may be purely cosmetic—and favor a system based solely on that aspect. However, you will need to work with library staff members to ascertain the true needs of their department and to see how both the products and the vendors can meet those needs.

Systems librarians are responsible for looking at the entire picture and must work with their administration (and/or system/ consortium) to select the product and vendor that will best meet the overall needs of the institution. This includes your need for affordable and useful vendor support and training, which is not always apparent from a demonstration. Vendor selection is often discussed on mailing lists such as SYSLIB-L; search its archives to find information on others' experience with the technology and the migration and technical support available from various vendors, and, as with all other areas of systems librarianship, ask your colleagues using various different networking tools.

When researching an ILS, also consider the needs of your library's patrons. The public access catalog is the library's online face to its users and needs to contain sufficient functionality and usability to satisfy your patron base. Realize that patron expectations are higher and ever-growing. Users accustomed to using the web as a common graphical interface to a huge variety of information can be less than patient with text- and menu-based systems; with slowdowns and perceptible lag times; with the need to come to the library to use the OPAC, request an item, or read an article;

and with the use of different databases for different purposes. Since OPACs are largely web-based, the vendors you are evaluating should be able to point you to publicly accessible sites that are using the latest versions of their products. Be sure to test the usability and usefulness of the public interface in a live environment. It might even be helpful to visit a local institution that is using the system you're considering and see how their staff members and patrons interact with the system.

Try to plan ahead. Since technology changes so rapidly, this is often easier said than done, but take some time to try to foresee your library's future needs by considering the following questions:

- Will you be cataloging ebooks?

- Do you want to add the capability to simultaneously search multiple electronic databases and/or other libraries' systems through your ILS?

- Are you looking to add the ability to browse the OPAC through mobile devices such as smartphones and tablets?

- Do you need to add book jacket images, patron reviews and tags, tables of contents, and personalization features to the OPAC?

- Do you need to allow for patron-placed reserves and other self-service features?

- Do you need to send messages to patrons about their accounts using SMS (text messaging) technology?

- Are you moving to thin client technology?

- Will your system be undertaking large new building projects and dramatically expanding collections?

- Will your consortium be adding new members?

- What operating systems do you intend to support?

- Will you be looking for internet or PC time-management software integration with your patron database?

- Do you want to access local history resources or other local databases through the OPAC, provide remote authentication, or add news and local information?

The answers to such questions can dramatically impact your choice of ILS. (There is insufficient space to address these questions thoroughly here, but see Appendix B for reading suggestions that include thoughts on how these elements can be integrated into an RFP.) If you are a smaller institution with less technical support, you might also wish to investigate cloud hosting options where your ILS is outsourced and hosted at the vendor's site.

Keep all of these factors in mind when composing your RFP, which must accurately reflect both your library's current automation environment and, as far as possible, its future needs. Your systems inventory will be useful here in describing your current technological environment, as will statistics on your circulation, number of volumes, number of patrons, and so on. (This is a major reason for accurate recordkeeping.) Also consult your technology plan and try to integrate its goals with those of your automation RFP. Since an ILS is such a major part of library technology, choosing the right vendor is an important step in reaching those goals.

Once you have received responses to your RFP, you will need to select the top bids. This is a decision that will involve you, your administration, your consortium (if applicable), and possibly your library's department heads. Decide on two or three products and vendors that best meet the requirements outlined in your RFP. Then, invite the vendors to demonstrate their systems (when looking at open source systems, you can find public demos online that you and your staff can test-drive beforehand). Be sure at least to have systems staff, administrators, and all department heads attend these demos (nontechnical department heads may wish to attend just a general overview and the demo of the module they will be working with directly). Allow everyone to have direct input into selecting the best product and vendor, and encourage everyone to ask questions of the vendor's representatives or those in the open source communities to help determine how these products can best meet their needs.

After you have selected a product and vendor, you will need to contract with that vendor for the migration of your data and for continuing support post-migration. Your contract should at the minimum include a system implementation plan (with target dates), describe system and operating costs, describe precisely what will be provided by the vendor, and provide for ongoing service, technical support, and security. If you wish the vendor to provide staff training, include this in the contract as well. Involve your institution's lawyer in this stage.

Data Cleanup

Once you have selected and contracted with a vendor, you will need to begin the migration process. The first step is to undertake a massive cleanup of your existing databases. "Clean" data will migrate much more smoothly than data that is "dirty," and if your institution has been using a particular system for some time, it is likely that you will have quite a bit of data to clean up. If you do not have the time or resources in your institution to undertake this task on your own, there are companies that can help you with record and authority cleanup, but this does mean interviewing more vendors and an added cost to your migration, of course.

This will also be a good time to undertake that large-scale weeding or inventory project you may have been putting off. Why pay to migrate records for missing items or those you are going to withdraw? By the same token, this will also be a good time to undertake a similar cleanup of patron records. Why migrate patrons who have not owned a card or used your library in the past 10 years? You may also wish to upgrade locally created or quick catalog records to full versions. This is also the time to consider changing old practices that were put in place due to your previous system's inadequacies, such as creating more item or patron categories than are really necessary. Use this time to reevaluate some of these previous decisions and merge together repetitive types and categories.

Although in most institutions the cataloging department will be doing the actual records cleanup, systems personnel will likely be called upon to create reports for catalogers to work from and to be the liaison to the new vendor. This is another instance in which those library school cataloging classes will come in handy. An understanding of the MARC format will be useful here. As one survey respondent noted, "Knowledge of cataloging and MARC coding has been very helpful."

Types of database records that need to be deleted and/or upgraded in the cleanup include:

- Unlinked item records (with no attached bibliographic records or holdings)
- Bibliographic records with no holdings or items
- Records with a "withdrawn" (or similar) status that need to be fixed/deleted before migration
- 856 links that don't go anywhere
- Unlinked and duplicate authority records
- Unauthorized headings (e.g., subject, name, title, name/title)
- Duplicate bibliographic records
- "See" references with linked bibliographic records

You may also need to replace nonstandard bar codes and will probably wish to upgrade older records that may not be in full MARC format.

Staff Training

Automation vendors generally provide some staff training as part of their migration packages. However, especially in larger institutions or consortia, not all staff will be able to attend vendor-sponsored training, which, depending on the vendor, can be prohibitively expensive and limited in the number of people who can attend. So it is essential to include training in your migration plan. (For more tips on technology training in general, see Chapter 8.) If you have a staff of existing trainers, deploy them to each department to provide individualized training on the appropriate modules. If you do not, you may wish to conduct some "train the trainer" sessions, or have your vendor do so, and send people back to do the initial training of others in their departments. This is also a great time to generate tutorial videos, using your technology skills and training to create short (5- to 10-minute) videos that show your staff how to perform the daily actions they need to do. This way, if the staff member missed a training session, he or she can still have a virtual trainer when learning how to catalog or check out a book in the new system.

An Interview With Librarians
Managing Systems in a Consortium

Jim Minges, Sharon Moreland, Liz Rea, Heather Braum, and Mickey Coalwell of the Northeast Kansas Library System (NEKLS; www.nekls.org) and the NExpress Regional Library Catalog (www.nexpresslibrary.org) talked to us about managing systems in a consortial environment. They collaborated on their answers for this interview.

Please give some background on your consortium.

NEKLS is a regional multitype system with 120 member libraries. However, technology systems services are targeted toward the 48 member public libraries.

The NExpress-shared Koha system currently includes 34 public libraries and one professional library. However, all system member libraries are eligible for participation. NExpress includes:

- 1,530,357 circulation in FY2011 (counts checkout, renewals and local use)

- 921,402 item records

- 123,429 patron records

Tell me a little bit about your consortium and how systems are managed for your libraries. Do your libraries have internal systems librarians, or is all of the work done by the "home office"?

NEKLS includes a broad range of libraries, from large urban public libraries and academic research libraries to very small public and school libraries. A number of the larger member libraries have substantial systems staff. However, the NEKLS technology-based systems, which are primarily used by small- and medium-size libraries, are supported centrally, and do not depend upon internal systems staff in participating libraries. In addition to direct management of systems, NEKLS provides technical support both onsite and remotely to libraries that do not have internal systems staff. Although development and training of internal systems staff is actively encouraged,

NEKLS has found that it needs to directly provide technical support services to many member libraries.

What is your current automation environment? Include information on your ILS and any other digital content management systems (journal databases, digital libraries, etc.).

The NExpress Regional Library Catalog is an arrangement of cooperating libraries sharing a single patron and bibliographic database. NExpress is a service of the Northeast Kansas Library System and is utilizing an open source software platform called Koha. It is remotely hosted as a cloud computing service. Currently, we only have public libraries and the system's professional collection, but we anticipate adding school or small academic libraries in the future. The system is centrally managed by the Northeast Kansas Library System, with hosting and support from ByWater Solutions. Generally libraries do not have internal systems librarians.

NEKLS also manages a statewide web hosting service for public libraries based on the WordPress open source content management/blogging platform. My Kansas Library on the Web (KLOW; www.mykansaslibrary.org) hosts websites for approximately 190 public libraries, the seven regional library systems, and special library projects. KLOW is sponsored by the Kansas Regional Library Systems and the State Library of Kansas, and managed by the Northeast Kansas Library System. KLOW websites are hosted on the Amazon cloud.

NEKLS managed a statewide internet filtering service called Kanguard, based on the SquidGuard open source proxy server software. However, NEKLS recently moved from Kanguard to the Open DNS service and is no longer actively involved in management of that service. In addition, licensing of and access to online databases is approached on a statewide basis in Kansas, and NEKLS has limited involvement in provision of that service.

What have you found to be the most important questions to ask a potential systems vendor?

- What does your support look like? How will you work with us? (preferred communication channels; formal/informal structures in place for help, problem-solving; response time; escalation of support; accountability)

- What is the approach to communication and problem solving? ([The vendor should] not simply process support issues but address them in a meaningful fashion and provide rapid and useful progress reports.)

- What is your product upgrade schedule, past track record, and process?

- How many staff members support the system, and how many of them are product experts?

- Who are your satisfied customers?

- What is your business model, and [what is] your business plan for the next 10 years?

What role do member libraries play in the systems decision-making process?

NEKLS member libraries play a significant role in identifying and prioritizing product development;

forming operational policy; and supporting each other with information-sharing, best practices, and training support.

There is a productive balance and tension between initiation of systems that are often generated by the system staff and board, and modification of systems is based on the consensus of member libraries.

What are the most important things to look for in choosing new systems?

Libraries should be asking these questions:

- Does the new system offer comparable levels of capability? (Features and performance should at least equal the old system, and preferably surpass it.)

- Is the new system stable and sophisticated enough to remain viable in the library environment over the next 10 years?

- Does the new system have forward-looking and appealing innovations?

- Is the system competitively priced (looking at all cost components, including hosting, support, development, and training)?

What kind of training do you offer members of your consortia when implementing new systems?

Local administrators provide initial and continuing training and support to new members. Local administrators provide help-desk-level response to problems, bugs, and questions, which are escalated to our support vendor as necessary.

What one piece of advice would you give to systems librarians involved in planning a system migration/ implementation?

Look at the new system from the outside in, rather than the inside out. In other words, adopt a user-centric approach in evaluating the system's strengths and appeal. Do not attempt to have the new system replicate the existing system but take a fresh look at needs and solutions.

Remember that changing from one ILS to another will be nearly as traumatic for many staff members as the library's initial automation was because they have had years to develop a workflow and perfect their command of the old interface. Keeping staff involved throughout the planning process will help ease the trauma; informed and involved individuals are less likely to fear change when it is not seemingly imposed randomly from above. Focus on the positives that the new system will bring and on any anticipated relief to workload, and on built-in solutions to the often-clunky workarounds staff members have developed to bypass the idiosyncrasies of older automation systems.

Be sure to provide several rounds of training so that all staff members have a chance to attend. Formal training needs to occur as close as possible to the actual changeover date to minimize the chance of staff forgetting all they have learned without an opportunity for hands-on practice. Allow sufficient time to practice on the training days as well, as staff will only learn by doing. It will also be useful to close for a day or two post-migration to allow training in a live environment without the pressure of serving library patrons with the new software. Make sure that trainers are available during these days to answer questions and to provide refresher training as needed.

It may be useful to revisit the staff competencies you created in Chapter 1 and update them to reflect the library's new automation environment. Specific tasks and techniques will change, and providing staff with a list of competencies and the opportunity for self-assessment will allow you to see where additional training may be needed post-migration.

Computer Upgrades

When migrating to a new ILS, especially when moving from an older automation system, you first may need to upgrade computer hardware and operating systems to handle the new modules. If you have been using Windows XP for your staff machines, for example, you may be required to upgrade to Windows 7 (with consequent requirements for upgrading your hardware to support a more demanding operating system). If you are housing the databases at your own institution or system, you will likely need to invest in a newer, more powerful server.

You may also need to examine your networking infrastructure to see if it can handle the demands of your new system. If you have been making do with a patched-together network, now is the time to measure your throughput and ensure that you have the bandwidth and network quality to support your requirements. The quality of the underlying network and its capacity to pass through a great deal of data becomes important.

Your support vendor should be able to help you in making these decisions by specifying what the system requirements are for your system on both the desktop and the server level.

Patron Training

After any migration that affects the public face of your automation system, you will be required to provide training for your library's patrons on using the new system. This is especially important in any situation where the patron interface changes dramatically.

Since it can be difficult to get patrons to attend training sessions, be sure to provide detailed cheat sheets on using the new system. Have these available as handouts next to each patron terminal and consider posting instructions on your website. Although your OPAC may have built-in help files, these can be lengthy and confusing for users who just want to get started. You might also make your own online instructions available via the catalog. As Sandy Schulman suggests in *Information Today*: "If you know that the instructions provided by the system vendor are unclear, rewrite them as soon as possible. I know you don't have the time, but believe me, it will take less time to write clear instructions than to have to help each individual user who runs smack into a riddle of instructions or tutorials from your vendor."[2] Also make sure that public service staff, assistants, and/or student workers in public areas are prepared to do informal patron training on system features.

Usability Testing

Although the underlying functionality of the public access catalog is out of your control, many aspects of the patron's interaction with the catalog will be changeable. Most modern OPACs now use a web-based interface; do not be afraid to tweak its settings. Change any colors, appearance of buttons, layouts, or defaults to create the best and most usable interface for your patrons and staff. Before launching the new OPAC, install it on a test server and allow staff to have input into its usability and appearance, including that of the online help screens. You can also set up patron focus groups to give input on the new system from a typical user's perspective.

Changing Over

The actual changeover process can stretch out over months because all of the tasks need to be completed prior to migration. Before migrating, you will also need to create policy files and work out security settings so that your cataloging and circulation departments can function effectively post-changeover. This is another time when a library background, especially in cataloging, will be useful.

The actual changeover needs to be scheduled and planned months beforehand. If you have a large amount of data to migrate, or if you wish to provide staff training on a live system, you may wish to close your library for one or two days during the changeover to provide sufficient time for transition and training. As hard as the process will be, remember that this experience will come in handy as you progress through your career. As one survey respondent noted, "Get as much experience as you can—especially when a library is migrating from one system to another. Volunteer if you have to. The lessons learned during a migration are worth their weight in gold."

Endnotes

1. Michael Rogers, "ILS Vendors and Librarians Grapple With Their Relationship," *Library Journal* 133, no. 2 (2008), 24.

2. Sandy Schulman, "Applying a Proactive Ounce of Prevention," *Information Today* (August 1998): 46.

Chapter 12

Life Lessons

The first step is recognizing that you are not in control—your customers, employees, and partners are. This is a fad that will not fade, but will only grow stronger, with or without you.

—Charlene Li[1]

Classwork provides a necessary foundation, but only real-life experience can actually create a successful systems librarian and prepare you to be an effective negotiator for yourself and your career. The true pluses and minuses of systems librarianship become apparent as you settle into your profession, and each technology librarian must make a personal decision as to whether the rewards and opportunities outweigh the inherent frustrations. Many universities give credit for related work experience—and for good reason. All of your experiences and interactions with library staff, patrons, and colleagues go into forming the foundation of your philosophy of systems librarianship, as well as the framework for your day-to-day activities.

Getting advice from other professionals (such as a mentor) and cultivating an awareness of the potential pitfalls (and opportunities) will also help you prepare to make the most out of your experience with systems-related work in libraries. In the following sections, you'll find information about dealing with some real-world situations not covered in any class, including finding a job, moving into careers in related fields, negotiating a promotion, dealing with technostress, and the ethics of systems librarianship.

Included are comments from working systems librarians who have been there themselves.

Finding a Job

Although many systems librarians initially enter their careers unintentionally, they often choose to stay in the field because they find the challenges and opportunities of systems work personally rewarding. If you've built up your technology skills in one library, you may wish to seek a new systems position at another library at some point. You will be in a better position to locate opportunities and negotiate terms if you have first done your research on the types of positions available and if you are cognizant of the potential pitfalls of starting a new library systems position. Having the facts will also be useful if you are considering becoming a systems librarian or if you currently work in a nonsystems position in a library but are considering changing specialties.

Finding a rewarding new position as a computer services librarian has its pros and cons. Systems-related jobs in libraries are relatively abundant. Libraries are always in need of people with technical aptitude and a willingness to help manage technology, so it may be easier to find a job with this focus than one in another subfield of librarianship.

While many systems librarians originally grew into their responsibilities at the time technical skills were first needed at their library, when they leave their institutions, they leave a hole that may take some time to fill. Incumbents will have had years to develop expertise with their library's particular technological environment and to build its complexity. Most will be leaving behind an environment that has evolved over the past few years to require consistent systems support. And sometimes these librarians will leave little or less than detailed documentation to help those who come after them. This makes it difficult for an institution that has previously had a systems librarian in place to take the time to "grow" a replacement candidate from inside; a library that has never had someone to manage its systems usually builds such complexity gradually.

If you have built or learned technical skills in your past library jobs (or in library school), you will be ready to start working in a position where a previous systems person has blazed the way. Robert R. Holzmann, systems librarian at Tulsa Community College, recommended just that in his survey response: "Find a degree program with adequate technology education as part of the requirements or available for electives or supplementary classes. Also get at least a part-time position working a systems or technology job, or preferably a library job that deals with systems and technology. Seek out an internship in a library technology role. Volunteer if necessary, as that is just as valuable. Augment your library education with real experience."

Systems-related jobs in libraries tend to start with somewhat higher salaries than other positions in libraries. This, however, is relative; since systems jobs often also include responsibility for other library duties in departments from reference to technical services and since they come with attendant stresses, systems librarians also earn their money. Many library administrations do, however, recognize the importance of compensating and retaining technically skilled staff, and salaries often reflect that understanding. This is particularly true if a position requires certifications or programming experience.

Academic libraries may prefer to hire librarians over non-MLS computer administrators for technical positions; at some institutions, librarians with faculty status can start at a higher pay scale than IT personnel in nonfaculty positions, increasing the odds of retention. This is one reason for the diversity of job titles mentioned in Chapter 1; individuals in similar positions may be classified quite differently, depending on the policies and pay scales of their parent institutions.

Systems-related jobs in libraries, however, tend to have a lower compensation rate than technology-related positions outside of libraries; the lower salaries endemic to librarianship carry through to technology positions. While computer-related work is generally more lucrative relative to other subfields of librarianship, salaries are still lower than those in many equivalent private sector IT jobs. We are all familiar with the tendency of female-dominated professions such as librarianship to have historically lower salaries than others requiring equivalent education and experience, and women in IT in general earn 9 percent less than men in comparable positions.[2]

Additionally, while librarianship has traditionally been seen as a lower-stress field, managing the systems that are essential to the library's operation and dealing with constant change can produce private sector stresses without an equivalent level of compensation. Since most library operations are now dependent on the smooth functioning of computer technology, you may not view your position as having a lower stress level when perhaps the network goes down and all eyes turn to you to resolve the situation. (Read more about technostress later in this chapter.)

But for many, the library field offers opportunities that more than offset these difficulties. One survey respondent accurately sums up the job as "Challenging and frustrating, yet fun." Systems jobs in public and academic libraries, furthermore, are sometimes more stable in uncertain economic times than are private sector IT jobs.

While you are absorbing this mixed news about the systems librarian job market, note that those writing the job ads for systems librarians may have only the vaguest idea of their library's true technology needs. Unfortunately, this can make it difficult for you to create an effective application for the position, discourage applicants who have the qualifications actually needed (rather than those listed in the ad), and lead to surprises when you start working. During your interview, it's a good idea to try to ascertain the technological savvy of your immediate superior and the library's administration. See if you can speak with those who have worked with technology in the library in order to get an accurate overview of the existing computing environment. Some administrators may have an unfortunate tendency to pepper their job ads with buzzwords because they have heard that "X" product (or programming language, or software package) represents the latest and greatest in technology. Whether "X" serves the library's needs or actually represents its current technological environment remains to be seen.

Untangling the Job Ad

Deciphering job advertisements for technology librarians can be an art in itself. Some ads are unfortunately brief or vague, forcing you to make assumptions about an institution's technological environment and providing little help to show how your qualifications match that library's needs. Other ads may seem to err on the side of verbosity, listing every possible qualification, software package, and skill. In academic environments, ads may have been written by committee, sometimes becoming an unfortunate amalgamation of personal preferences and institutional requirements.

When reading an ad, look first for any specific required or preferred technical qualifications. These usually take the form of statements like:

- Minimum of 5 years' experience managing and implementing integrated library systems

- Knowledge of web programming and scripting languages

- Demonstrated knowledge of computers, networks, library automated systems, emerging technologies, and Windows operating systems

- Knowledge of networking, internet, and software applications

Your own best defense against vague requirements such as these is specificity. If the ad asks for "knowledge of networking," clarify in your cover letter and resume the type and size of networks you have administered. If it asks for "knowledge of web scripting languages," provide the URL of a library website you have created and explain how you have used CSS, AJAX, Perl, PHP, and/or other scripting tools to enhance its performance. Also check the organization's website to get a better sense of its computing environment—you should at least be able to ascertain which ILS vendor the library has and the types of computing facilities available for patron use.

Ads that tend toward the overly specific will list requirements such as:

Knowledge of Windows 2008 Server, Exchange mail server, Ubuntu for workstations, Windows 7, Mac OS, Office 2010, OCLC Connexion, Koha, LINK+ interlibrary loan, Drupal, AACR2/RDA, MARC, NCIP, FRBR, Z39.50, Endnote, McAfee Antivirus, Deep Freeze, Syndetics, Dell Inspiron troubleshooting, Moodle, Unix, HTML, XML, Perl, PHP, Ruby, Java, Javascript …

You can respond to such kitchen-sink ads by focusing on the major points and on your major strengths. Explain your skills and background in network administration, point to the URL of a website you have worked on, and describe your ILS and cataloging support activities. Emphasize your willingness to extend these skills to encompass the specific software packages used in the particular library's environment.

Job descriptions—especially technical job descriptions—often contain a "wish list" that describes the qualifications of the institution's ideal candidate. In the real world, administrators and search committees do not necessarily expect to find someone with every skill and qualification listed in a particular ad. If you have some of the skills mentioned and believe you could reasonably acquire the rest, or if you have related skills that could meet the library's needs, a lengthy list of qualifications in a posting shouldn't dissuade you from applying. Be prepared, however, to describe in your cover letter and in an interview how your existing skills can apply and how you intend to acquire additional knowledge in any desired areas.

Forewarned is forearmed. You should be aware of potential pitfalls before applying. In many institutions, you will have broader responsibilities than those specific to maintaining library technology; you may also be required to work the reference desk, catalog materials, help develop the library's collection, and/or manage a circulation department. Scrutinize such split positions carefully to ensure that you will be willing and able to undertake all of the duties and that the compensation is relatively fair for the activities required.

To maximize your chances of finding a position that is a "good fit," be sure to examine your potential working environment and not only your potential salary. Remember that in dealing with your supervisor and co-workers, you will be dealing with them not only as a colleague but also as a representative of the library's computing environment. Consider carefully whether you wish to work in an institution where the staff seems fearful of or resistant to technology and change. Be sure to talk directly with your future supervisor and/or administrator during your interview; these are the people whose support you will need later when it comes to arguing for important decisions regarding the library's computing environment. One systems librarian who responded to the survey listed the most frustrating part of the job as "Dealing with colleagues who are opposed to any new technology because they will have to learn something new and it will mean more work for them." Make sure that you are working with people who understand that systems change, which means you have to make changes from time to time in order to do your job effectively.

Beyond ascertaining the technological environment, level of support, and computing expertise at your new institution, you'll also need to be aware of the opportunities your new position may (or may not) offer for professional development. While all librarians require professional development opportunities and support, this is doubly true for systems librarians who need to keep current both in the library field and with new technological developments that will affect the computing environment in their institutions. Ask if the library provides funding to attend conferences, classes, and workshops; ask what former systems personnel have done to keep up with their skills. While there are a number of low-cost alternatives available (see Chapter 9), sometimes there is no substitute for a formal class or conference.

Also carefully consider the size and type of library you are willing to work in. If you are comfortable with the thought of working independently and serving as a solo systems librarian, a smaller public library may be right for you. If you want the chance to be on the cutting edge of technology or prefer to work as part of a larger systems staff, you may instead investigate options in larger, better-funded research institutions or large public library systems. If you do not wish to work with the public and prefer a more specialized environment, look at corporate and special library opportunities. Think about whether you would prefer to specialize in one area of systems work, such as web design, training, or network administration, or if you prefer to have responsibilities in a variety of areas. Your answers to these questions have a big influence on the types of positions you should be applying for.

If you are considering systems librarianship as a new career, it will also be useful to familiarize yourself with the field's ups and downs by speaking with working systems personnel in libraries before committing yourself to a job or a path of study. Follow the discussions on a mailing list such as SYSLIB-L; see if your library school has a mentoring or job shadowing program; follow other systems librarians on Twitter, Facebook, and LinkedIn; and try to set up informational interviews with systems librarians at nearby libraries or using social networks. (Note that an informational interview differs from a job interview. You are not necessarily seeking a position at that particular library; you are merely trying to get an inside look at the daily responsibilities of the job.) You will find that most librarians are eager to share their experiences and will be honest about the pitfalls and the promise of dealing with technology in libraries. If you are currently enrolled or are planning to enroll in library school, try to locate an internship in the field. Real-world experience will provide the best indication of the true advantages and disadvantages of the specialty.

Once you are convinced that you want to pursue a systems position, note that job opportunities can be found in a number of ways. Library technology associations such as LITA and ASIST hold free placement centers at their annual meetings; this can be a great way to focus your search for technology-related positions in libraries and to attend in-person interviews with out-of-state institutions.

Even if you cannot attend the meeting, you may be able to submit your resume for scrutiny by potential employers. Both associations also maintain online job lists (LITA's at www.ala.org/lita/professional/jobs and ASIST's at www.asis.org/jobline.html), which are good sources for information technology positions in libraries. Job ads are also often posted to SYSLIB-L and other email lists for systems librarians (see Chapter 7). Lastly, remember to consult employment resources that are less specifically focused on technology, such as general library journals (both print and online), local library schools, and major library career-related websites, such as LISjobs.com (www.lisjobs.com), I Need a Library Job (www.inalj.com), and Library Job Postings on the Internet (www.libraryjobpostings.org). Also watch local library pages on Facebook and Twitter.

Branching Out

Working as a systems librarian will also prepare you for jobs in a number of other related fields. Many systems librarians move in and out of libraries or go on to work for related industries, such as library automation vendors and database companies. The skills learned on the job as a computer services librarian provide a useful background for positions as trainers, support representatives, metadata specialists, and product managers, each of which requires a unique mix of library and technical knowledge.

You might also consider contributing to the profession by writing on technical topics for library journals or publishers. Recognizing the impact of technology and the need for librarians to learn about technological issues, many library-related publishing outlets are on the lookout for writers who can address computer-related topics from a library perspective. Information Today, Inc., for example, publishes a number of relevant journals (www.infotoday.com/periodicals.shtml), and LITA and ASIST's member publications are always looking for content. You might also look into writing for the open access journals such as *Code4Lib Journal* (journal.code4lib.org/call-for-submissions) and *D-Lib Magazine* (www.dlib.org). If you have an idea for a monograph, Neal-Schuman, now part of ALA, and Information Today, Inc. tend to publish large numbers of technology-related titles for librarians, while more general library publishing houses sometimes include technical topics among their offerings.

General library journals often include technology-related articles. These journals may be a good outlet if you have a knack for clearly explaining technical issues to a general audience. Library publications often look for "how I did it in my institution" articles, which provide you with an opportunity to describe an innovative or particularly useful deployment of technology at your library. In any of these cases, both your library and your technical skills will be useful as you research and work on your manuscript. If you are in an academic institution, you may instead wish to submit work to peer-reviewed journals to help secure tenure or a promotion. Applicable outlets here include publications such as LITA's *Information Technology and Libraries*, *Journal of Web Librarianship*, and *LIBRES*, as well as more general academic library journals.

Technology book reviewers are also in demand. Although library publications generally do not pay for book reviews, you get to keep a copy of the book and will gain the advantage of having your name listed as a technical expert. FreePint (www.free pint.com) reviews web-related titles, while general library journals often include technology titles in their review sections. Lastly, consider serving as a referee for one of the technology-related peer-reviewed library journals, which occasionally will post calls for applicants on technology lists or in the journals themselves. Watch for calls for contributors, referees, and reviewers on your mailing lists and in journals you follow.

Negotiating a Promotion (or a Raise)

If you are willing and flexible enough to take on systems responsibilities as well as traditional library duties, or if multitasking appeals to you, adding systems duties to your normal tasks can be a good starting point for asking for increased compensation and/or a promotion. You should especially consider brushing up on your negotiating and self-promotion skills if you are an accidental systems librarian who has already taken on these additional responsibilities without a concomitant increase in salary and change in job title. Research the job market to see what other professionals in similar positions are being offered and be prepared to defend your request.

Be sure to enumerate the benefits your work as a systems librarian brings to your institution. This will be most effective if you cite the specifics: "The new ILS has enabled staff to ..." "We have taught __ Web 2.0 classes in 2012." "Bringing support in-house has saved the library __ dollars this year." Unfortunately, if you have been doing your job effectively, your contributions may seem invisible—as long as computer systems are running smoothly, your administration may not realize the potential for disaster without someone continually making the necessary adjustments to ensure they remain stable.

If you have taken advantage of opportunities to improve your technological skills through attending classes, earning certifications, or participating in self-study, this can be another tool in your promotion arsenal. Traditionally, libraries provide pay increases and promotions for those who take charge of their own education and improve the service they are able to give the library by attending library school, earning an LTA certificate, and so on. Taking computer classes and earning certifications should be similarly rewarded, since you are learning practical skills in order to carry out the duties of your position more effectively.

If your attempts to gain increased compensation or recognition go unrewarded, be prepared to back up your arguments with action. Start looking for another job. You are responsible for managing your own career, and the market for experienced systems librarians is strong enough that you should have no problem making a move. The threat of losing you to another institution may shake your administration out of its complacency as it faces the possibility of having to attract and train a new systems person. Do not be surprised if your employer makes a counteroffer. If not, you will likely be able to increase your salary by taking the time to find an appropriate position elsewhere; but don't try this tactic if you are not ready to walk. The more plentiful nature of systems jobs in libraries gives you a stronger bargaining position; your institution will realize that you can easily go elsewhere. As Barbara Arnold states, "Knowledge is power. If you put your knowledge to work, we can all achieve better salary equity."[3] Go into your annual review or interview with information about salary standards in the industry and in your area.

Realize also that merely being willing to fight for fair compensation, promotion, and recognition can have an impact on how you are perceived within your institution. Since much of effective systems librarianship involves being able to argue for the resources to do your job properly, you need to lay the foundation of respect that will make your administration take you seriously in future discussions. As Deborah Kolb and Ann Schaffner note: "Getting what you are worth is not just about money. It is about perceptions of your worth and your contribution. Your perception—and that of others—will affect your ability to command the resources and respect you need to do your job effectively. Each time you successfully negotiate the salary you deserve, you lay the groundwork to get the resources you need and you pave the way for others in the profession to do the same."[4]

Technostress

Although most people who gravitate to systems work in libraries tend to be more flexible and enthusiastic about change than the norm, technostress still takes its toll. This is partially due to the additional level of responsibility library systems personnel assume in keeping themselves up-to-date with the latest technologies and partially due to the frustrations inherent in trying to maintain computer systems and placate computer users when inevitable outages occur. A number of respondents to the accidental systems librarians' survey mentioned inadequate time and resources as the most frustrating aspect of their jobs, and many also emphasized the difficulty in keeping up with new opportunities and technologies while continuing to keep current equipment and software running. While systems librarians tend to enter the field accidentally and their beginning successes are lauded, these initial technological successes only raise the bar and increase their administration's expectations of future performance—even though future and additional systems may be more difficult and time-consuming to manage. Although systems increase in complexity and systems librarians' tasks increase over the years, this increased complexity will likely not be appreciated by library staff and administrators who just see either that things are humming along or they are not.

Technostress (especially when combined with the lower compensation endemic to library work) can also be a major factor in driving library systems people out of the field. As one survey respondent noted: "I doubt I have ever worked as hard as I do now, and that includes when I had seven staff with their 100 manufacturing operatives. The days are long, the pace relentless, but I love it (usually). I miss the money and the travel of the vendor world though."

Technostress often also stems from physical causes. Many libraries, especially smaller institutions, have added technology incrementally and ad hoc rather than planning it out, such as when setting up a new building or lab. Such libraries often give short shrift to ergonomics issues and comfort factors, shoehorning equipment into existing furniture and fitting it where possible throughout the library. This affects all staff, but systems librarians are particularly vulnerable to problems such as carpal tunnel, eyestrain, and backache, due to the amount of time spent working with technology. Argue for attention to ergonomics, and do what you can to adjust your own environment. If you find yourself aching or developing tension headaches, take a break, stretch, walk around—get out from behind the monitor. Just paying attention to your own physical well-being can have a dramatic impact on how you feel about supporting library technology.

This discussion is not intended to sway you from library systems work but rather to raise your awareness of the stresses inherent in these types of positions. The lack of time to keep up with current technology or to provide an optimum level of support for library staff and users was mentioned by a large number of survey respondents. To be an effective systems librarian, you must be willing to commit to a path of lifelong learning, as well as to fight for the time and resources to back up that commitment. You must learn to value constructive change and to thrive on its presence.

Be prepared to work with library staff members and users who refuse to take responsibility for learning about technology. You can create training opportunities for such individuals (see Chapter 8), but you will find that a number are resistant to change. They may refuse to learn and will call on you for every difficulty involving computers, even those problems that are easily resolved by an action as simple as rebooting the machine. This requires you to learn to manage and prioritize your own time. Most libraries lack the luxury of excess systems staff to hold users' hands, so try not to enable dependent behavior. One of the more frustrating aspects of systems work can be the constant interruptions from staff and users wanting an immediate resolution to an annoying (to them) yet minor problem, while you are attempting to find the time to work on a major project such as an ILS migration or technology plan. While you wish to encourage an open-door policy, you also need to maintain the ability to prioritize, and you must refrain from taking up all of your time solving problems that staff could easily resolve on their own.

This is a situation in which it will be helpful to plan for the education of your co-workers. Go back to the computer competencies you created in Chapter 1 and ensure that all library employees have the training and resources they need to achieve these competencies. If you are repeatedly interrupted with the same issue, create a cheat sheet for all relevant staff members that provides step-by-step instructions for resolving the situation. Insist that staff complete the steps on these handouts before you help them with these common problems and establish early on the tasks that you and other systems staff will not be responsible for (such as changing printer toner, removing paper jams, or rebooting a frozen terminal). Also remember that some learners prefer to see the steps. When relevant, include screenshots on your handouts or even create a screencast and post it to the intranet where your entire staff can view it as needed. While this may lead to grumbling on the part of some staff members who don't want to spend time reading or watching a tutorial, the inevitable savings to your time and sanity will more than balance out the impact of any dissension.

Any computer skills you can teach your co-workers or that they acquire on their own will go a long way toward helping technology in your library run more smoothly. Have no fear about educating yourself out of a job; remember, there is as much for you to learn as for them and your skill set is very different. As Kathryn Bergeron, systems librarian for Baldwin Public Library, explained in her survey response: "Find excellent mentors and friends who can help you. You can't keep up with all of the technology trends at once, but if you know the right people, you can all share your information and benefit together."

Useful basic troubleshooting skills to teach your library's staff include:

- Rebooting a malfunctioning machine before calling technical support: Be sure to teach staff that, if neither a proper shutdown nor restart hotkeys will work, they can use the reset button, the off switch, or the power plug to power down the machine manually when needed. When someone calls you for technical support, always ask whether they have rebooted before taking the time to go and investigate the problem in person.

- Using restart hotkeys: At least on staff machines—this combination may be blocked by security software or network policies on patron systems—these keys can shut down a frozen application (for example Control+Alt+Delete on Windows machines or Command+Option+Esc on Mac OS).

- Trying to access a nonresponding website on a second machine before concluding that the problem is with a particular PC (rather than with the particular site)

- Clearing paper jams from, adding paper to, and changing the toner in laser printers

- Checking to see if monitors, computers, and printers are securely plugged into a powerstrip that is turned on—and connected to each other—before concluding that a system has died or will not boot

Additional skills may be appropriate for your library's specific technological environment. Make sure that staff members have enough basic knowledge to report a problem accurately to systems personnel and to fill out the report sheets you created in Chapter 6.

These skills are especially important for public service staff members, who will generally be the first to encounter problems with public access workstations. It needs to be clear what public service staff will be expected to support. Are they responsible, for example, for showing patrons how to use the features of your word-processing software? Helping them send email? Assisting them in pasting a resume into a form on the internet? Signing up for social networks such as Facebook or Google+? You will likely wish to emphasize supporting library-related functions such as the OPAC and subscription databases over helping users with incidental computer issues with features such as email or chat. Ensure that nonsystems staff members know what they will be responsible for helping patrons with and what falls outside the scope of their duties. This will also help ensure a consistent environment for users, so they do not find that one day one staff member can help them and the next day a different staff member refuses to do so or does not know the software well enough.

It may be more acceptable if you make incremental changes to what library staff are expected to do. Allow them to build their skills and feel confident in each step before demanding more. Dramatically changing expectations all at once will trigger staff members' fear of change and resentment at being handed additional tasks that may have been taken care of for them in the past, but empowering your colleagues bit by bit will increase their confidence in their own skills and result in their wanting to accomplish more on their own. Think of this as an evolutionary process of creating change; taking incremental steps over time can lead to dramatic results. As the change agent within your library, it is incumbent upon you to work to conquer your colleagues' fear of change. As Seth Godin writes: "We start by bypassing our fear of change by training people to make small, effortless changes all the time."[5] Dramatic, sudden change gives people something to talk about and to fear, while consciously making change a gradual process allows them to build their confidence with each step.

Staff members will also be less resistant to change if they are kept informed of the changes before they happen and of the reasoning behind any changes. Always keep the lines of communication open and be aware of the potential for staff to see technology shifts as being imposed from "on high" with little rhyme or reason. Involve appropriate staff members in technology decisions as much as possible and show them how any change will positively impact the way they do their day-to-day tasks. Clark and Kalin note that: "What many regard as technostress is really resistance to change. Resistance is certainly not new, nor is it limited to computerization."[6] Make it your task to gradually reduce this resistance.

Sharing knowledge and building incremental change allows you to reduce the technostress level in other library staff members and yourself. The more others are able to do, the less basic technical support you will have to provide, freeing you up for other duties. The more they are able to do, the more they will feel empowered by technology rather than overwhelmed by it. Realize that neither stress nor technostress is a new phenomenon in libraries—although this may seem to provide little comfort to librarians who are overwhelmed by the perception of constant change. Realizing the constancy of change can help you keep some perspective.

Ethics

Systems librarians tend to encounter stresses in other forms as well. While patron privacy and confidentiality have been cornerstones of the philosophy of librarianship, privacy concerns and other ethical issues are compounded by the power of technology. Technological advances make it possible to collect information on the activities of patrons and library staff members that was previously unavailable, and much of this information may be automatically generated without any specific effort on the part of library systems personnel. For example, some personalized website and catalog services can have the side effect of allowing libraries to track individual usage patterns. When patrons demand social network integration into library services, this opens them and their libraries up to sharing personal information. Automated catalogs can keep transaction logs on library items and the patrons using them. Web server logs can track visitors by IP address. You may be involved in deciding whether and how long to keep and whether to use or view this information or in creating and posting privacy policies for your internet services.

Given these technical possibilities, libraries should create policies on the collection and usage of electronic information. For example, staff members should be aware if the institution is collecting information on their email usage and/or websites visited. Packages that have been implemented as filtering solutions in a number of libraries also have the ability to track where users have been by user name or by department. You and your administration need to decide whether such reporting will be implemented and how it will be used. This is an especially tricky issue for librarians who are part of a larger institution such as a university or a corporation, where the rules and philosophy might differ considerably from the library's perspective. For patrons, we have a responsibility to let our users know whether they have the same expectations to privacy of their electronic resource usage as they have had in the past for items such as circulation records.

These privacy issues also extend to internal technologies such as your local area network. If you have administrative privileges on the network, you also likely have the ability to view network-stored files and documents that are normally accessible only by the HR department or your administration. This can be very tempting and requires you to develop the ability to refrain from accessing private areas without good reason. You may accidentally encounter confidential information when you are helping someone in one of these departments resolve a computer issue; this will require you to develop an attitude of discretion.

You will need to decide how you will react if your administration or outside entities ask you to reveal information about your patrons' or your colleagues' usage of electronic resources, especially if your institution does not have a specific policy protecting such information. You may also be confronted with other ethical issues. What will you do if you find out that a staff member has "borrowed" a library-purchased DVD in order to install software on his home computer? If a member of your systems staff is using a large chunk of server storage for copyrighted MP3 files she has downloaded from the internet? If you start a new position and find that the previous systems librarian purchased a single copy of a software package at some point and installed it on multiple machines? What if a patron using a public-access internet PC leaves a site promoting violence or child pornography prominently displayed on the monitor when he leaves the station?

You will encounter less clear-cut ethical challenges as well. As a technological decision maker in a wired institution, you hold a great deal of power over people's computing environment. Avoid the temptation to allocate computing resources more heavily toward individuals you like or departments/functions you personally prefer. Answer questions and resolve issues equally quickly; this shouldn't depend on who is asking. One piece of advice often given to newer employees is to make friends with the janitor and the secretary, who each wield a great deal of power over your ability to work effectively—this extends also to the "systems person." Foster good relations with your co-workers but never at the expense of others' needs.

These are issues for both libraries and individual systems librarians to grapple with. You will need to balance the good of your institution, the legality of users' actions, privacy considerations, and your personal ethical outlook in making tough decisions. Realize that, as in other areas of systems librarianship, there are often no simple answers, but you can draw on your library background to provide an ethical foundation for your technological outlook.

Endnotes

1. Charlene Li, *Open Leadership: How Social Technology Can Transform the Way You Lead* (San Francisco: Jossey-Bass, 2010), 24.
2. Don Tennant, "Dice: Gender Pay Gap Nonexistent in Apples-to-Apples Comparison," ITBusinessEdge, January 24, 2011, accessed May 31, 2012, www.itbusinessedge.com/cm/blogs/tennant/dice-gender-pay-gap-nonexistent-in-apples-to-apples-comparison/?cs=45244.
3. Barbara J. Arnold, "Knowledge Is Power for Salary Equity," Info Career Trends, July 1, 2005, accessed May 31, 2012, www.lisjobs.com/career_trends/?p=337.
4. Deborah M. Kolb and Ann C. Schaffner, "Negotiating What You're Worth," *Library Journal* (October 15, 2001): 52–53.
5. Seth Godin, *Survival Is Not Enough: Zooming, Evolution, and the Future of Your Company* (New York: Free Press, 2002), 30.
6. Katie Clark and Sally Kalin, "Technostressed Out?" *Library Journal* (August 1996).

Conclusion

Most of us view change as a threat, and survival as the goal. Change is not a threat, it's an opportunity, and survival is not the goal, transformative success is. It's thrilling if you give it a chance.

—Seth Godin[1]

A repeated theme among both survey respondents and people I have met in my travels is that fear of change makes their jobs as systems librarians difficult and sometimes frustrating. Even with the constant battles, the technostress, and the lack of funding for professional development, systems librarians love their jobs. If you've learned one thing from this book, I hope it's that this job can be challenging, but it is very rewarding and well worth sticking with—or starting.

While the librarians who answered the survey expressed their frustrations, many also shared how much they love their jobs:

- "I love systems work but find the job especially challenging because I am the only person managing it. I wish more reference librarians would 'explore' and expand their understanding of basic web technology. Directors need to encourage librarians to go out of their comfort zones so they try to solve technological issues before transferring the call to the systems person because almost everything a librarian does involves automation."

- "LOVE my job. LOVE it. Get to still be a librarian, but stay current with technology and trends."

- "I adore working in systems. I wish my job was solely systems now so I could concentrate on my systems projects. The other librarians see systems as very much a specialty and are often in awe of how issues are resolved so there is a lot of job satisfaction."

- "I love it. I love the intersection of people, technology, and information. It's finally coming into its own, and that's good for the profession."

- "I love it and never want to stop doing it. I get to avoid corporate and government environments, I get to play with systems, and I get to learn all sorts of interesting things."

- "I would not wish to work in any other department. It is always interesting and constantly challenging."

Working in systems in the library puts you in a unique position to learn about new technologies before your colleagues. It allows you to take the initiative and foster change within your organization, and it gives you the unique opportunity to educate those around you about these new tools. When librarians were asked what their favorite part of systems work was, one of their top answers was the joy involved in solving problems. This was said in many different ways, but the theme was constant: You get to learn new things, change the way your library operates, and solve puzzles on a daily basis.

Many libraries have been brought to our attention purely because of the technologies they're using. In 2007, my library at the time (Jenkins Law Library) was known by libraries all over the country simply because they had read about our homegrown intranet content management system and research links management system. That exciting use of technology set us apart, and as the one spearheading many of those projects, I was sharing our successes in journals and online. This recognition makes all the stress and all the battling for change worth it to the systems librarian.

If you remember that to succeed as a systems librarian you just need the desire to learn, the will to enforce change, and the love of solving puzzles, you'll do just fine.

Endnote

1. Seth Godin, *Survival Is Not Enough: Zooming, Evolution, and the Future of Your Company* (New York: Free Press, 2002), 4.

Appendix A

Accidental Systems Librarian Survey

This survey was available online on the book's companion website, sent out to several library-specific mailing lists, and posted on social networking sites such as Twitter, LinkedIn, and Facebook. Answers were collected from late 2010 through early 2011.

Respondents are self-described systems librarians. This is not a scientific survey, and no attempt was made to qualify respondents as systems personnel prior to their answering these questions.

The Accidental Systems Librarian Survey

The following survey will be used in writing the second edition of *The Accidental Systems Librarian*. The more detail you provide, the better your answers will help us improve upon this resource. Your answers may be quoted in the book, but your name will not be included unless you give us express permission to do so. We also ask if we're allowed to contact you for more information and maybe a more in-depth interview, so please answer this question. Providing us with examples whenever possible will give us real life stories to share with our readers. Since this survey could potentially take you a long time, you are free to save your progress and come back at a later date to finish things up; we just ask that you do return.

Full Name:

Organization:

Job Title:

Country:

Email:

Would you like your answers to remain anonymous?

Can we contact you to expand upon your answers?

Do you have a library degree?

What year did you graduate?

Do you have additional degrees or certificates?

If so, please specify:

What type of formal training, if any, have you attended to help you keep up with new technological developments?

What other resources do you use to help keep yourself up-to-date?

What library positions have you held prior to your current job (if any)?

What technical positions have you held prior to your current job (if any)?

Please describe the path you took to systems librarianship:

What do you most wish you'd learned in library school that you instead have had to learn "on the job"?

What did you learn in library school that has proven especially useful on the job?

How do you use your skills as a librarian to perform systems duties effectively? (Provide examples if any spring to mind.)

Approximately what percentage of your time is devoted to "systems" responsibilities, including automation support, help desk, computer training, troubleshooting, web development, etc.?

What one piece of advice would you give to an aspiring systems librarian?

What is your favorite tech support resource?

What is your favorite part of systems work?

What is the most frustrating part of systems work?

Do you have any additional comments about your experience with systems work in libraries?

Did you read the first edition of *The Accidental Systems Librarian*?

What would you like to see in the second edition that wasn't covered in the first edition?

Appendix B

Recommended Reading

Throughout this book, I reference various titles of interest to systems librarians. This list includes those references, as well as additional resources. If you have a recommendation that you think other systems librarians will benefit from, please feel free to share it with me (nengard@gmail.com) for potential inclusion on the book's website.

Abubakar, B. M. "Availability and Use of Information and Communication Technology (ICT) in Six Nigerian University Library Schools." *Library Philosophy and Practice* (June 2010).

Adams, J. "What Is a Systems Librarian?" The Systems Librarians' Blog. May 16, 2007. Accessed May 18, 2012. www.systlib.blog spot.com/2007/05/what-is-systems-librarian.html.

Akins, M. L., and J. R. Griffin. "Keys to Successful Systems Administration." *Computers in Libraries* 19, no. 3 (March 1999): 66.

Alcorn, L. "Create a Smart Wireless Network for Your Library." WebJunction. January 10, 2012. Accessed July 9, 2012. www.webjunction.org/content/webjunction/documents/web junction/Create_a_Smart_Wireless_Network_for_Your_Library. html.

Anderson, J. "Wireless Success Stories From the WJ Community." WebJunction. April 12, 2006. Accessed June 29, 2012. resource sharing.webjunction.org/wireless-success/-/articles/content/ 437671?_OCLC_ARTICLES_getContentFromWJ=true.

Arnold, B. J. "Knowledge Is Power for Salary Equity." Info Career Trends. July 1, 2005. Accessed May 18, 2012. www.lisjobs.com/career_trends/?p=337.

Back, G., and A. Bailey. "Web Services and Widgets for Library Information Systems." *Information Technology and Libraries* 29, no. 2 (June 2010): 76.

Balas, J. "Close the Gate, Lock the Windows, Bolt the Doors: Securing Library Computers. Online Treasures." *Computers in Libraries* 25, no. 3 (March 1, 2005): 28–30.

———. "Does Technology Define Librarians' Roles?" *Computers in Libraries* 21, no. 10 (December 2001): 58–60.

———. "Information Literacy and Technology: They Work Best When They Work Together." *Computers in Libraries* 26, no. 5 (May 2006): 26–29.

———. "Systems Administration: How to Avoid Reinventing the Wheel." *Computers in Libraries* 20, no. 9 (October 2000): 64.

Ballard, T. "Zen in the Art of Troubleshooting." *American Libraries* 25, no. 1 (January 1994): 108–110.

Bane, K. "Making Technology More Manageable." *American Libraries Magazine*, March 9, 2011. Accessed May 18, 2012. www.americanlibrariesmagazine.org/solutions-and-services/making-technology-more-manageable.

Barclay, D. *Managing Public-Access Computers: A How-To-Do-It Manual for Librarians*. New York: Neal-Schuman, 2000.

Bates, M. E. "The Newly Minted MLS: What Do We Need to Know Today?" *Searcher* 6, no. 5 (1998): 30–33.

Beck, M. A. "Technology Competencies in the Continuous Quality Improvement Environment: A Framework for Appraising the Performance of Library Public Services Staff." *Library Administration & Management* 16, no. 2 (Spring 2002): 69–72.

Becker, B. W. "Web Development Simplified." *Behavioral & Social Sciences Librarian* 29, no. 4 (December 2010): 301–303.

Benson, A. "Building a Secure Library System." *Computers in Libraries* 18, no. 3 (March 1998): 24.

———. *Securing PCs and Data in Libraries and Schools: A Handbook With Menuing, Anti-Virus, and Other Protective Software.* New York: Neal-Schuman, 1997.

Bissels, G. "Implementation of an Open Source Library Management System: Experiences With Koha 3.0 at the Royal London Homoeopathic Hospital." *Program: Electronic Library & Information Systems* 42, no. 3 (July 2008): 303–314.

Block, C. "In Search of System Stability." netConnect *Library Journal* 126, no.1 (Winter 2001): 22–25.

Block, M. "Mapping the Information Landscape." *Searcher* 10, no. 4 (April 2002). Accessed May 18, 2012. www.infotoday.com/searcher/apr02/block.htm.

Booth, C. "VoIP in Professional Communication, Collaboration, and Development." *Library Technology Reports* 46, no. 5 (July 2010): 20.

———. "VoIP in Reference, User Services, and Instruction." *Library Technology Reports* 46, no. 5 (July 2010): 25.

Boule, M. "Quick Tips for Technology Training." ALA TechSource. May 17, 2011. Accessed May 18, 2012. www.alatechsource.org/blog/2011/05/quick-tips-for-technology-training.html.

Brandt, D. S. "Email Makes the World Go Round." *Computers in Libraries* 21, no. 10 (December 2001). Accessed May 18, 2012. www.infotoday.com/cilmag/nov00/brandt.htm.

Breeding, M. "Analyzing Web Server Logs to Improve a Site's Usage. The Systems Librarian." *Computers in Libraries* 25, no. 9 (October 1, 2005): 26.

————. "Automation Marketplace 2012: Agents of Change." The Digital Shift. March 29, 2012. Accessed July 9, 2012. www.thedigital shift.com/2012/03/ils/automation-marketplace-2012-agents-of-change.

————. "Defending Your Library Network." *Information Today* 18, no. 8 (September 2001): 46–47.

————. "Offering Remote Access to Restricted Resources." *Information Today* 18, no. 4 (May 2001): 52–53.

————. "Professional Development for the Library Technologist." *Computers in Libraries* 30, no. 4 (May 2010): 30–32.

————. "The Open Source ILS: Only a Distant Possibility." *Information Technology and Libraries* 21, no. 1 (2002): 16–18.

————. "The Systems Librarian: Implementing Wireless Networks Without Compromising Security." *Computers in Libraries* 25, no. 3 (March 1, 2005): 31–33.

Brettle, A. "Information Skills Training: A Systematic Review of the Literature." *Health Information & Libraries Journal* 20, no. 1 (2003): 3–9.

Bridges, L., H. G. Rempel, and K. Griggs. "Making the Case for a Fully Mobile Library Web Site: From Floor Maps to the Catalog." *Reference Services Review* 38, no. 2 (2010): 309–320.

Brogan, C., and J. Smith. *Trust Agents*. Rev Upd. Hoboken, NJ: John Wiley & Sons, 2010.

Brown-Syed, C. "Computers in Libraries." valinor.ca, 1995. Accessed May 18, 2012. www.valinor.ca/computing/siframes. htm.

Browning, P., and M. Lowndes. "Content Management Systems: Who Needs Them?" Ariadne, no. 30 (December 2001). Accessed May 18, 2012. www.ariadne.ac.uk/issue30/techwatch.

Burke, J. *Neal-Schuman Library Technology Companion: A Basic Guide for Library Staff*. New York: Neal-Schuman, 2001.

"Buying and Deploying Technology." TechSoup for Libraries. Accessed May 18, 2012. www.techsoupforlibraries.org/Cook books/Planning%20for%20Success/buying-and-deploying-technology.

Cargile, C. "Open Source ILS for the Non-Systems Librarian: A Reality?" *PNLA Quarterly* 69, no. 3 (Spring 2005): 15–17.

Choy, F. C. "From Library Stacks to Library-in-a-Pocket: Will Users Be Around?" *Library Management* 32, no. 1/2 (2011): 62–72.

Chudnov, D. "Open Source Software: The Future of Library Systems?" *Library Journal* 124, no. 13 (August 1, 1999): 40.

Clark, K., and S. Kalin. "Technostressed Out?" *Library Journal* (August 1996).

Clark, S. "IT Training Rip-Offs." *Network World* (March 25, 2002): 44–48.

Cohen, S. "RSS for Non-Techie Librarians." LLRX.com. June 3, 2002. Accessed May 18, 2012. www.llrx.com/features/rssfor librarians.htm.

Cohn, J. M., and A. L. Kelsey. *The Complete Library Technology Planner: A Guidebook With Sample Technology Plans and RFPs on CD-ROM.* New York: Neal-Schuman, 2010.

Cohn, J., A. L. Kelsey, and K. M. Fiels. *Planning for Integrated Systems and Technologies: A How-To-Do-It Manual for Librarians.* New York: Neal-Schuman, 2001.

Collins, M., and A. J. Rathemacher. "Open Forum: The Future of Library Systems." *The Serials Librarian* 58, no. 1 (April 2010): 167–173.

"Core Technical Competencies for Library Staff." Eastern Shore Regional Library of Maryland. Accessed May 18, 2012. www.esrl. org/Core_Competencies.pdf.

Corrall, S. "Educating the Academic Librarian as a Blended Professional: A Review and Case Study." Hong Kong: Pao

Yue-kong Library, The Hong Kong Polytechnic University, 2010. Accessed May 18, 2012. repository.lib.polyu.edu.hk/jspui/handle/10397/1731.

Cortez, E. M., S. K. Dutta, and E. J. Kazlauskas. "What the Library and Information Professional Can Learn From the Information Technology and Project Management Knowledge Areas." *portal: Libraries and the Academy* 4, no. 1 (2004): 131–144.

Crawford, W. "Talking 'Bout My Library." *American Libraries* (April 2002). Accessed May 18, 2012. www.ala.org/ala/alonline/the crawfordfiles/2002columns/april2002talking.cfm.

———. "Talking About Public Access: PACS-L's First Decade." *Information Technology and Libraries* 19, no. 3 (2000). Accessed May 18, 2012. www.waltcrawford.name/pacsl.htm.

"Criteria for Evaluation of Library Software Packages." LISWiki. June 8, 2011. Accessed May 18, 2012. www.liswiki.org/wiki/Criteria_for_evaluation_of_library_software_packages.

Curran, K., and M. Porter. "A Primer on Radio Frequency Identification for Libraries." *Library Hi Tech* 25, no. 4 (2007): 595–611.

De Stricker, U., and J. Hurst-Wahl. *Information and Knowledge Professional's Career Handbook: Define and Create Your Success.* Oxford: Chandos, 2011.

Dhiman, A. K. "Librarian to Cybrarian: Changing Roles and Responsibilities of Library Professionals (wiki)." Tezpur University, Assam. 2010. 435–441. Accessed May 18, 2012. www.ir.inflibnet.ac.in/dxml/bitstream/handle/1944/984/44.pdf.

Dixson, L. E. "YAZ Proxy Installation to Enhance Z39.50 Server Performance." *Library Hi Tech* 27, no. 2 (2009): 277–285.

Doering, W. "Managing the Transition to a New Library Catalog: Tips for Smooth Sailing." *Computers in Libraries* 20, no. 7

(August 2000). Accessed May 18, 2012. www.infotoday.com/cilmag/jul00/doering.htm.

Donohue, M. "The Autobiography of a Modern Community College Librarian." *Computers in Libraries* 21, no. 10 (December 2001): 44–46.

Dougherty, W. C. "Managing Technology During Times of Economic Downturns: Challenges and Opportunities." *Journal of Academic Librarianship* 35, no. 4 (July 2009): 373–376.

Dougherty, W. C., and A. Schadt. "Linux Is for Everyone; Librarians Included!" *Journal of Academic Librarianship* 36, no. 2. (March 2010): 173–175.

Eastmond, G. "Technical Training: From 'Eeek!' to 'Oooh!'" *Library Administration & Management* 16 (Spring 2002): 73–78.

Engard, N. C. "Evaluating New Technologies in Libraries." METRO LibGuides. June 6, 2011. Accessed May 18, 2012. libguides.metro.org/evaltech.

———. *Library Mashups: Exploring New Ways to Deliver Library Data.* Medford, NJ: Information Today, Inc., 2009.

———. *Practical Open Source Software for Libraries.* Oxford [England]: Chandos, 2010.

Ennis, L. A. "Talking the Talk: Communicating With IT." *Computers in Libraries* 28, no. 8 (2008): 14–18.

Fagan, J. C., and J. A. Keach. "Build, Buy, Open Source, or Web 2.0?" *Computers in Libraries* 30, no. 6 (July 2010): 9.

Farmer, T. "Making the Most of Technology: Linux as an Alternative Solution." *Arkansas Libraries* 61, no. 3 (Fall 2004): 14–15.

Feher, J., and T. Sondag. "Administering an Open-Source Wireless Network." *Information Technology & Libraries* (September 2008): 44–54.

Fessler, V. "The Future of Technical Services (It's Not the Technical Services It Was)." *Library Leadership and Management* 21, no. 3 (July 1, 2007): 139–144.

Fiehn, B. "Social Networking Through Your Library Automation System: What Librarians and Vendors Have to Say." *MultiMedia & Internet@Schools* 16, no. 5 (October 2009): 28–31.

Foster, A. "Strains and Joys Color Mergers Between Libraries and Tech Units." *The Chronicle of Higher Education* 54, no. 19 (January 18, 2008): A1–A13.

Gerding, S. "Fabulous Free Public Technology Training Materials." TechSoup for Libraries. January 28, 2011. Accessed May 18, 2012. www.techsoupforlibraries.org/blog/fabulous-free-public-technology-training-materials.

Ghasri, A. N., and M. Dehghani. "Chat Reference: Training and Competencies for Librarians." *Library Philosophy and Practice* (April 2009).

Goddard, L. "The Integrated Librarian: IT in the Systems Office." *Library Hi Tech* 21, no. 3 (2003): 280–288.

Godin, S. *Survival Is Not Enough: Zooming, Evolution, and the Future of Your Company.* New York: Free Press, 2002.

———. *Tribes: We Need You to Lead Us.* New York: Portfolio, 2008.

Goh, D. H. L., A. Chua, D. A. Khoo, E. B. Khoo, E. B. Mak, and M. W. Ng. "A Checklist for Evaluating Open Source Digital Library Software." *Online Information Review* 30, no. 4 (2006): 360–379.

Gordon, R. S. "A Course in Accidental Systems Librarianship." *Computers in Libraries* 21, no. 10 (December 2001): 24–28.

———. *Teaching the Internet in Libraries.* Chicago: American Library Association, 2001.

———. *The Accidental Systems Librarian.* Medford, NJ: Information Today, Inc., 2003.

Gorman, M. "Human Values in a Technological Age." *Information Technology and Libraries* 20, no. 1 (April 30, 2002). Accessed May 18, 2012. www.ala.org/lita/ital/20/1/gorman.

Gregory, V. L. *Selecting and Managing Electronic Resources: A How-To-Do-It Manual.* New York: Neal-Schuman, 2000.

Gu, F. "The Campus-Wide Laptop Loan Service and the Library's Role." *Library Management* 32, no. 1/2 (2011): 6–21.

Guinea, J. "Building Bridges: The Role of the Systems Librarian in a University Library." *Library Hi Tech* 21, no. 3 (2003): 325–332.

Guy, M. "Staying Connected: Technologies Supporting Remote Workers." *Ariadne* no. 57 (October 2008). Accessed May 18, 2012. www.ariadne.ac.uk/issue57/guy.

Haas, L. M., and A. Stillwell. "The Library-Information Technology Partnership: Challenges and Solutions." *Journal of Library Administration* 50, no. 1 (January 2010): 51–66.

Hahn, J., L. Mestre, D. Ward, and S. Avery. "Technology on Demand: Implementing Loanable Technology Services at the University of Illinois at Urbana-Champaign." *Library Hi Tech* 29, no. 1 (2011): 34–50.

Halder, S. N. "Multimodal Roles of Library and Information Science Professionals in Present Era." *International Journal of Library and Information Science* 1, no. 6 (November 2009): 92–99.

Hansen, C. "Issues for Information Access on the Mobile Web." *Library Technology Reports* 47, no. 2 (March 2011): 32.

———. *Libraries and the Mobile Web.* Vol. 2. Library Technology Reports 47. ALA TechSource. Accessed May 18, 2012. www.ala techsource.org/taxonomy/term/106/libraries-and-the-mobile-web.

———. "Mobile Devices in 2011." *Library Technology Reports* 47, no. 2 (March 2011): 11.

———. "Mobile Solutions for Your Library." *Library Technology Reports* 47, no. 2 (March 2011): 24.

———. "Why Worry About Mobile?" *Library Technology Reports* 47, no. 2 (March 2011): 5.

"Hartford Public Library Chief Executive Officer's Report." March 2010. Accessed May 22, 2012. www.hplct.org/assets/uploads/files/about/CEOReportMarch2010.pdf.

Heiberger, M. M., and J. M. Vick. "Networking for Dummies." *The Chronicle of Higher Education* (May 17, 2002). Accessed May 18, 2012. www.chronicle.com/article/Networking-for-Dummies/46091.

Heinrichs, J. H., and N. Czech. "Training Cybrarians: The New Skill Requirements." In *Thinking Outside the Book: Essays for Innovative Librarians*, edited by C. Smallwood, 259. Jefferson, NC: McFarland, 2008.

Heinrichs, J. H., and J. Lim. "Emerging Requirements of Computer Related Competencies for Librarians." *Library & Information Science Research* 31, no. 2 (April 2009): 101–106.

Herzog, B. "Using Firefox on Our Public Computers." Swiss Army Librarian (blog). May 8, 2008. Accessed May 18, 2012. www.swissarmylibrarian.net/2008/05/08/using-firefox-on-our-public-computers.

Hollands, W. *Teaching the Internet to Library Staff and Users: 10 Ready-to-Go Workshops That Work*. New York: Neal-Schuman, 1999.

Horner, P. C. "Linux for Public Workstations." *LITA National Forum*. St. Louis, MO, 2004.

Horrigan, J. *Use of Cloud Computing Applications and Services*. Washington, DC: Pew Internet & American Life Project, September 12, 2008. Accessed May 18, 2012. www.pewinternet.

org/Reports/2008/Use-of-Cloud-Computing-Applications-and-Services.aspx.

Houghton-Jan, S. *Technology Competencies and Training for Libraries*. Vol. 43. Library Technology Reports 2. Chicago: ALA TechSource, 2007.

Howden, N. *Buying and Maintaining Personal Computers: A How-To-Do-It Manual for Librarians*. New York: Neal-Schuman Publishers, 2000.

Huang, P. "How You Can Protect Public Access Computers and Their Users." *Computers in Libraries* 27, no. 5 (May 2007): 16–20.

Hunter, G. *Preserving Digital Information: A How-To-Do-It Manual*. New York: Neal-Schuman, 2000.

Huwe, T. K. "Focusing the Library Web: Library Web Design in 2011 Is No Less of a Priority Than It Was 15 Years Ago." *Computers in Libraries* 31, no. 2 (March 2011): 27.

Ingersoll, P. *Managing Information Technology: A Handbook for Systems Librarians*. Westport, CT: Libraries Unlimited, 2004.

Institute of Museum and Library Services. *Status of Technology and Digitization in the Nation's Museums and Libraries 2006 Report*. January 2006. Accessed May 18, 2012. www.imls.gov/assets/1/AssetManager/Technology_Digitization.pdf.

Jantz, R. "E-Books and New Library Service Models: An Analysis of the Impact of E-Book Technology on Academic Libraries." *Information Technology and Libraries* 20, no. 2 (2001): 104–115.

Joint, N. "Evaluating Library Software and Its Fitness for Purpose." *Library Review* 55, no. 7 (August 1, 2006): 393–402.

Jones, D. E. "Ten Years Later: Support Staff Perceptions and Opinions on Technology in the Workplace." *Library Trends* 47, no. 4 (1999): 711–741.

Jones, K., and P. Farrington. *Using WordPress as a Library Content Management System*. Vol. 47. Library Technology Reports 3.

Chicago: ALA TechSource, 2011. Accessed May 18, 2012. www.alatechsource.org/taxonomy/term/106/using-wordpress-as-a-library-content-management-system.

Jordan, M. "The Self-Education of Systems Librarians." *Library Hi Tech* 21, no. 3 (2003): 273–279.

Keats, D. "Free and Open Source Software for Librarians and Libraries." *Innovation*, no. 36 (June 2008): 1–16.

Kneale, R. "From Static to Dynamic: Choosing and Implementing a Web-Based CMS." *Computers in Libraries* 28, no. 3 (March 1, 2008): 16–20.

Knight, L. A., and K. A. Lyons-Mitchell. "Measure for Measure: Statistics About Statistics." *Information Technology and Libraries* 20, no. 1 (2001): 34–38.

Knox, K. C. *Implementing Technology Solutions in Libraries: Techniques, Tools, and Tips From the Trenches.* Medford, NJ: Information Today, Inc., 2011.

Kolb, D. M., and A. C. Schaffner. "Negotiating What You're Worth." *Library Journal* 126, no. 17 (October 15, 2001): 52–53.

Kozikowski III, C. "Five Steps to Help You Determine If You Need the New 'It' Technology." *Computers in Libraries* 30, no. 6 (August 2010): 6–8.

Kraft, B., and D. Hinderink. "Evaluating Open Source Communities. Why Open Source Is More Than Code—And Why You Should Care." Paper presented at Transformation and Innovation Conference 2006, May 22–24, Washington, DC, 2006.

Krissoff, A., and L. Konrad. "Computer Training for Staff and Patrons: A Comprehensive Academic Model." *Computers in Libraries* 18, no. 1 (January 1998): 28–32.

Krug, S. *Don't Make Me Think!: A Common Sense Approach to Web Usability.* 2nd ed. Berkeley, CA: New Riders, 2006.

"KSAs for Systems Librarian Positions GS 9–12." Federal Library and Information Center Committee. Accessed May 18, 2012. www.loc.gov/flicc/wg/ksa-sys.html.

Kupersmith, J. "Technostress in Libraries." John Kupersmith's Webspace, March 2, 2009. Accessed May 18, 2012. www.jkup.net/tstress.html.

Lankes, R. D., J. Silverstein, and S. Nicholson. "Participatory Networks: The Library as Conversation." *Information Technology and Libraries* 26, no. 4 (December 2007): 17.

Latham, J. "The World Online: IT Skills for the Practical Professional." *American Libraries* (March 2000): 40–42.

Lavagnino, M. B. "Networking and the Role of the Academic Systems Librarian: An Evolutionary Perspective." *College & Research Libraries* 58, no. 3 (May 1997): 217–231.

Lawrence, P. "Access When AND Where They Want It: Using EZproxy to Serve Our Remote Users." *Computers in Libraries* 29, no. 1 (January 2009): 6–43.

Lee, E. *Libraries in the Age of Mediocrity.* Jefferson, NC: McFarland, 1998.

Lewis, G., and L. Wrage. "Library: A Process for Context-Based Technology Evaluation." Integration of Software-Intensive Systems (ISIS) Initiative, June 2005. Accessed May 18, 2012. www.sei.cmu.edu/library/abstracts/reports/05tn025.cfm.

Li, C. *Open Leadership: How Social Technology Can Transform the Way You Lead.* San Francisco: Jossey-Bass, 2010.

Lietzau, Z., and J. Helgren. *U.S. Public Libraries and the Use of Web Technologies, 2010.* Closer Look Report. Denver, CO: Colorado State Library, Library Research Service, April 2011. Accessed May 18, 2012. www.lrs.org/documents/web20/WebTech2010_CloserLookReport_Final.pdf.

Lim, S. "Library Informational Technology Workers: Their Sense of Belonging, Role, Job Autonomy and Job Satisfaction." *Journal of Academic Librarianship* 33, no. 4 (July 2007): 492–500.

Lo, K. "Basic Tips for Evaluating New Technologies for Your Nonprofit." Nonprofit Technology Network. September 21, 2009. Accessed May 18, 2012. www.nten.org/blog/2009/09/21/basic-tips-evaluating-new-technologies-your-nonprofit.

Lowe, M. P. "Evaluating Technology: A Comparative Look at ATM and MPLS." Master's thesis, Michigan State University, 2010. Accessed May 18, 2012. gradworks.umi.com/14/78/1478798.html.

Lundy, M. "Changing Roles of the Systems Librarian at the College of William and Mary: The Explosion of Technology and Position of the Systems Librarian." *Library Hi Tech* 21, no. 3 (2003): 333–339.

Luo, L. "Chat Reference Competencies: Identification From a Literature Review and Librarian Interviews." *Reference Services Review* 35, no. 2 (2007): 195–209.

Manley, W. "The Golden Rule of Supervision." *American Libraries* 33, no. 2 (February 2002): 88.

Marcoux, E. "Being Smart About Technology." *Teacher Librarian* 37, no. 4 (April 2010): 87.

Marmion, D. "Facing the Challenge: Technology Training in Libraries." *Information Technology and Libraries* 17, no. 4 (1998): 216.

Marshall, J. G., V. W. Marshall, J. C. Morgan, D. Barreau, P. Solomon, S. Rathbun-Grub, and C. A. Thompson. "Where Will They Be in the Future? Implementing a Model for Ongoing Career Tracking of Library and Information Science Graduates." *Library Trends* 58, no. 2 (Fall 2009): 301–315.

Martin, M. C. "Managing Your Library's Computer Nerds." *Computers in Libraries* 19, no. 2 (February 1999): 8.

Massis, B. E. "How to Create and Implement a Technology Training." *American Libraries* 32, no. 9 (October 2001): 49–51.

Mathews, J. M., and H. Pardue. "The Presence of IT Skill Sets in Librarian Position Announcements." *College & Research Libraries* 70, no. 3 (May 2009): 250–257.

Mayo, D., and Public Library Association. *Wired for the Future: Developing Your Library Technology Plan.* Chicago: American Library Association, 1999.

McDermott, I. E. "Digital Grease Monkeys: Librarians Who Dare to Repair." *Searcher* 8, no. 9 (October 2000): 10–14.

———. "Solitaire Confinement: The Impact of the Physical Environment on Computer Training." *Computers in Libraries* 18, no. 1 (January 1998): 22, 24–27.

McGeary, T. M. "Applying Lessons From 8 Things We Hate About IT to Libraries." Code4Lib Journal, no. 13 (April 11, 2011). Accessed May 18, 2012. journal.code4lib.org/articles/4944.

Meier, J. J. "Are Today's Science and Technology Librarians Being Overtasked? An Analysis of Job Responsibilities in Recent Advertisements on the ALA JobLIST Website." *Science & Technology Libraries* 29, no. 1 (2010): 165.

Mickey, B. "Open Source and Libraries: An Interview With Dan Chudnov." *ONLINE* 25, no. 1 (January 2001): 23.

Miltenoff, P., S. Parault, and R. Wexelbaum. "Evaluating EReaders for Academic Libraries." *Library Technology Conference* (March 18, 2010). Accessed May 18, 2012. digitalcommons.macalester.edu/libtech_conf/2010/posters/4.

Monson, J. "What to Expect When You're Digitizing: A Primer for the Solo Digital Librarian." *Computers in Libraries* 31, no. 1 (February 2011): 16–20.

Moore, K. L. B., and K. C. Knox. "How Can We Survive in Reality Library?" *Computers in Libraries* 21, no. 10 (December 2001): 34–38.

Morgan, E. L. "Computer Literacy for Librarians." *Computers in Libraries* 18, no. 1 (January 1998): 39–40.

———. "On Being a Systems Librarian." Infomotions, LLC. November 16, 2004. Accessed May 18, 2012. www.infomotions. com/musings/systems-librarianship.

———. "Open Source Software in Libraries." Infomotions, LLC. June 8, 2001. Accessed May 18, 2012. www.infomotions.com/musings/ossnlibraries.

———. "Systems Administration Requires People Skills." *Computers in Libraries* 19, no. 3 (March 1999): 36.

———. "Technical Skills of Librarianship." LITA Blog. August 7, 2005. Accessed May 18, 2012. www.litablog.org/2005/08/technical-skills-of-librarianship.

Müller, T. "How to Choose a Free and Open Source Integrated Library System." *OCLC Systems & Services* 27, no. 1 (2011): 57–78.

Murley, D. "Law Libraries in the Cloud." *Law Library Journal* 101, no. 2 (2009): 249–254.

Neidorf, R. *Teach Beyond Your Reach: An Instructor's Guide to Developing and Running Successful Distance Learning Classes, Workshops, Training Sessions, and More.* Medford, NJ: Information Today, Inc., 2006.

Nesbeitt, S. *The Information Professional's Guide to Career Development Online.* Medford, NJ: Information Today, Inc., 2002.

Noble, C. "Reflecting on Our Future." *Computers in Libraries* 18, no. 2 (February 1998): 50–54.

O'Leary, M. "New Roles Come of Age." *ONLINE* 24, no. 2 (March 2000): 20–22, 24–25.

Osborne, L. N., and M. Nakamura. *Systems Analysis for Librarians and Information Professionals.* 2nd ed. Library and information science text series. Englewood, CO: Libraries Unlimited, 2000.

Oshri, I. "The Rise of Firefox in the Web Browser Industry: The Role of Open Source in Setting Standards." *Business History* 52, no. 5 (2010): 834–856.

Pace, A. K. "Technically Speaking." *American Libraries* 35, no. 4 (April 2004): 92–93.

———. "Technically Speaking: The Next 100 Years." *American Libraries* 38, no. 1 (January 2007): 32, 34.

Padgett, L. "Give and Take." *Information Today* 25, no. 8 (2008): 46–47.

Partridge, H., J. Lee, and C. Munro. "Becoming 'Librarian 2.0': The Skills, Knowledge, and Attributes Required By Library and Information Science Professionals in a Web 2.0 World (and Beyond)." *Library Trends* 59, no. 1–2 (Summer/Fall 2010): 315–335.

Partridge, H., V. Menzies, J. Lee, and C. Munro. "The Contemporary Librarian: Skills, Knowledge and Attributes Required in a World of Emerging Technologies." *Library & Information Science Research* 32, no. 4 (October 2010): 265–271.

Patton, S. "The Deliberate Systems Librarian." Info Career Trends, November 3, 2008. Accessed May 18, 2012. www.lisjobs.com/career_trends/?p=486.

Pearce, A., S. Collard, and K. Whatley. "SMS Reference: Myths, Markers, and Modalities." *Reference Services Review* 38, no. 2 (2010): 250–263.

Peters, C. "The Joy of Computing: Recipes for a 5-Star Library." TechSoup for Libraries. Accessed May 18, 2012. www.techsoup forlibraries.org/cookbooks/recipes-for-a-5-star-library.

Pfohl, D., and S. Hayes. "Today's Systems Librarians Have a Lot to Juggle." *Computers in Libraries* 21, no. 10 (December 2001): 30–33.

Porter, M., and D. L. King. "101 Resources & Things to Know (RTK)." Library 101. 2009. Accessed May 18, 2012. www.libraryman. com/blog/101rtk.

———. "Library 101: Why, How, and Lessons Learned." *Computers in Libraries* 30, no. 2 (March 2010): 35–38.

Ralston, R., M. A. Rioux, and K. D. Ellis. "With Feet Planted Firmly in Mid-Air: Staff Training for Automation System Migration." *The Serials Librarian* 36, no. 3/4 (1999): 407–413.

Ramkumar, M. "8 Best Sources to Follow Computer Virus News and Alerts." MakeUseOf. July 5, 2010. Accessed May 18, 2012. www.makeuseof.com/tag/8-sources-follow-computer-virus-news-alerts.

Randolph, S. E. "Are Ebooks in Your Future?" *Information Outlook* 5, no. 2 (February 2001): 22.

Raymond, E. S. "The Cathedral and the Bazaar." September 2000. Accessed May 18, 2012. www.catb.org/~esr/writings/cathedral-bazaar/cathedral-bazaar.

Resnick, T., A. Ugaz, and N. Burford. "E-Resource Helpdesk Into Virtual Reference: Identifying Core Competencies." *Reference Services Review* 38, no. 3 (2010): 347–359.

Rhyno, A. "From Library Systems to Mainstream Software: How Web Technologies are Changing the Role of the Systems Librarian." *Library Hi Tech* 21, no. 3 (2003): 289–296.

Roberts, G. "Network Security Is Manageable." *Computers in Libraries* 26, no. 1 (January 1, 2006): 28–30.

Rogers, M. "ILS Vendors and Librarians Grapple With Their Relationship." *Library Journal* 133, no. 2 (2008): 23–24.

Ross, J. B., and D. L. Bosseau. "Defining the Divide: Causes of Fiction Between Librarians and Computer Support Staff." *Journal of Academic Librarianship* 23, no. 2 (1997): 132–133.

Rossman, D. "Twenty Tips for Becoming More Computer Savvy: Or, How to Think Like a Systems Librarian." *PNLA Quarterly* 68, no. 1 (Fall 2003): 21–22.

Rossmann, B., and D. Rossmann. "Communication With Library Systems Support Personnel: Models for Success." *Library Philosophy & Practice* 7, no. 2 (Spring 2005): 1–8.

Saffady, W. *Introduction to Automation for Librarians.* 4th ed. Chicago: American Library Association, 1999.

Sauers, M. *Blogging and RSS: A Librarian's Guide.* 2nd ed. Medford, NJ: Information Today, Inc., 2010.

———. "Firefox Search Plugins: Searching Your Library in the Browser." *Journal of Web Librarianship* 1, no. 1 (January 1, 2007): 65–75.

Saunders, L. "Systems Administrators: The Unsung Library Heroes." *Computers in Libraries* 19, no. 3 (March 1999): 47.

———. *The Evolving Virtual Library II: Practical and Philosophical Perspectives.* Medford, NJ: Information Today, Inc., 1999.

Schneider, K. "The Old Guard and the New Technology." *Library Journal* 119 (March 1, 1994): 64.

Schulman, S. "Applying a Proactive Ounce of Prevention." *Information Today* (August 1998): 46.

Schuyler, M. "Cutting-Edge Statistics." *Computers in Libraries* 21, no. 3 (March 2001): 51–53.

———. "View From the Top Left Corner: Turnkey Systems Solutions." *Computers in Libraries* 20, no. 10 (December 2000).

Accessed May 18, 2012. www.infotoday.com/cilmag/oct00/schuyler.htm.

Schwartz, M. "Features—Librarians and Technology: An Interview With Julie Bozzell." LLRX.com. February 15, 2002. Accessed May 18, 2012. www.llrx.com/features/bozzell.htm.

Seadle, M. "The Status of Systems Librarians." *Library Hi Tech* 21, no. 3 (2003): 267–269.

Sharma, P. L. "Changing Role of Librarians in Digital Library Era and Need of Professional Skills, Efficiency and Competency." December 2005. Accessed May 18, 2012. www.drtc.isibang.ac.in/xmlui/handle/1849/407.

Shoemaker, K. "Libraries and Linux: The Strange Parallels of Stacks and Software." LISNews. August 13, 2009. Accessed May 18, 2012. www.lisnews.org/libraries_and_linux_strange_parallels_stacks_and_software.

Sisler, E. "Linux in Your Library?" netConnect *Library Journal* (Fall 2001): 12–14.

Smith, A. *Mobile Access 2010*. Washington, DC: Pew Internet & American Life Project, July 7, 2010. Accessed May 18, 2012. www.pewinternet.org/Reports/2010/Mobile-Access-2010.aspx.

Stahl, B. "IT-Library Mergers Require Good Leaders." *The Chronicle of Higher Education* 54, no. 23 (February 15, 2008): A39.

"Steal This Idea: Helene Blowers." LibraryJournal.com. March 15, 2007. Accessed May 18, 2012. www.libraryjournal.com/article/CA6423431.html.

Stephens, M. "Steal This Idea: Learning 2.0 at PLCMC." ALA TechSource. August 15, 2006. Accessed May 18, 2012. www.alatechsource.org/blog/2006/08/steal-this-idea-learning-20-at-plcmc.html.

Stover, M. *Leading the Wired Organization: The Information Professional's Guide to Managing Technological Change.* New York: Neal-Schuman, 1999.

Sweat, J. "Staying Put." *InformationWeek* (January 21, 2002): 36–42.

Tebbetts, D. R. "The Costs of Information Technology and the Electronic Library." *The Electonic Library* 18, no. 2 (2000): 127–136.

"Technology Competencies for Libraries in North Carolina." State Library of North Carolina. May 2007. Accessed May 18, 2012. www.statelibrary.ncdcr.gov/ce/images/Competencies.pdf.

"Technology Competencies for Staff." University of Minnesota Duluth. September 1, 2010. Accessed May 18, 2012. www.d. umn.edu/itss/policies/techplan/staff.html.

"Technology Core Competencies for California Library Workers." California Library Association. 2005. Accessed May 18, 2012. www.infopeople.org/sites/all/files/past/2006/managing/Hand out-CLA_Core_Competencies.pdf.

"Technology Planning for Public Libraries." SOS Missouri. Accessed May 18, 2012. www.sos.mo.gov/library/certifications/ tech_planning.asp.

techxplorer. "What Exactly Makes a Systems Librarian?" *Libraries Interact*, October 9, 2006. Accessed May 18, 2012. www.librariesinteract.info/2006/10/09/what-exactly-makes-a-systems-librarian.

Tennant, D. "Dice: Gender Pay Gap Nonexistent in Apples-to-Apples Comparison." ITBusinessEdge. January 24, 2011. Accessed May 18, 2012. www.itbusinessedge.com/cm/blogs/ tennant/dice-gender-pay-gap-nonexistent-in-apples-to-apples-comparison/?cs=45244.

Tennant, R. "Honoring Technical Staff." *Library Journal* (May 15, 2001).

———. "The Digital Librarian Shortage." *Library Journal* (March 15, 2002): 32.

———. "The Most Important Management Decision: Hiring Staff for the New Millennium." *Library Journal* 123 (February 15, 1998): 102.

Thompson, S. "Riding Into Uncharted Territory: The New Systems Librarian." *Computers in Libraries* 19, no. 3 (March 1999): 14–18.

Tovell, C. "Whippersnappers vs. the Old Guard? Making E-Resources Training a Collaborative Experience." Info Career Trends. September 2001. Accessed May 18, 2012. www.lisjobs. com/career_trends/?p=124.

Turner, L. "20 Technology Skills Every Educator Should Have." THE Journal. June 2005. Accessed May 18, 2012. www.thejournal. com/articles/2005/06/01/20-technology-skills-every-educator-should-have.aspx.

Tyson, L. "Library Systems Teams—More Than Just Peripherals." *Library Hi Tech* 21, no. 3 (2003): 317–324.

Walsh, A. "Quick Response Codes and Libraries." *Library Hi Tech News* 26, no. 5/6 (2009): 7–9.

Warnken, P. "A Reflective History of Gophers, Mice, and Missions." *Journal of Academic Librarianship* 30, no. 1 (January 2004): 73–76.

Weber, L., and P. Lawrence. "Authentication and Access: Accommodating Public Users in an Academic World." *Information Technology & Libraries* 29, no. 3 (2010): 128–140.

Webster, M. R. "Let Your Fingers Do the Training." *Library Software Review* 18, no. 1/2 (1999): 4–12.

Webster, P. *Managing Electronic Resources: New and Changing Roles for Libraries.* Oxford: Chandos, 2008.

Weiss, E. *The Accidental Trainer: You Know Computers, So They Want You to Teach Everyone Else.* San Francisco: Jossey-Bass, 1996.

Weissman, S. "Shoptalk Answers to Real-World Problems." netConnect *Library Journal* 124, no. 17 (October 15, 1999): 20.

"What to Consider When Evaluating and Implementing Web 2.0 Tools in Your Library." TechSoup for Libraries. Accessed May 18, 2012. www.techsoupforlibraries.org/cookbook-3/innovation/what-to-consider-when-evaluating-and-implementing-web-2-0-tools-in-your-librar.

White, H. S. *Librarianship—Quo Vadis? Opportunities and Dangers as We Face the New Millennium.* Englewood, CO: Libraries Unlimited, 2000.

Williams, R. L. "Thick or Thin? Evaluating Thin Clients in Sustaining Library Technology." *Library Hi Tech News* 22, no. 7 (2005): 9–14.

Wilson, T. *The Systems Librarian: Designing Roles, Defining Skills.* Chicago: American Library Association, 1998.

Wolfe, J. A. "Managing Electronic Resources: New and Changing Roles for Libraries." *Collection Building* 29, no. 2 (2010): 79–80.

Wurman, R., L. Leifer, D. Sume, and K. Whitehouse. *Information Anxiety 2.* Indianapolis, IN: Que, 2001.

Xu, H. "Global Access and Its Implications: The Use of Mailing Lists by Systems Librarians." In *Proceedings of the American Society for Information Science Annual Meeting: Information Access in the Global Information Economy*, 501–515. Pittsburgh, PA, 1998.

Xu, H., and H. Chen. "What Do Employers Expect? The Educating Systems Librarians Research Project Report 1." *The Electronic Library* 17, no. 3 (1999): 171–179.

———. "Whom Do Employers Actually Hire? The Educating Systems Librarians Research Project Report 2." *The Electronic Library* 18, no. 3 (2000): 171–182.

Youngman, D. C. "Library Staffing Considerations in the Age of Technology: Basic Elements for Managing Change." *Issues in Science and Technology Librarianship* (Fall 1999). Accessed May 18, 2012. www.istl.org/99-fall/article5.html.

Zimerman, M. "E-Readers in an Academic Library Setting." *Library Hi Tech* 29, no. 1 (2011): 91–108.

———. "Oh No, I Lost All of My Work!" *Computers in Libraries* 29, no. 8 (September 2009): 36–40.

———. "The Dangers of Malware in a Library Computing Environment." *The Electronic Library* 29, no. 1 (February 15, 2011): 5–19.

Appendix C

Websites

Websites are listed in alphabetical order by chapter. All of these can also be found online at tasl.web2learning.net, where they will be kept up-to-date.

Chapter 1

Eastern Shore Regional Library of Maryland Core Technical Competencies, www.esrl.org/Core_Competencies.pdf

KSAs for Systems Librarian Positions GS 9–12, www.loc.gov/flicc/wg/ksa-sys.html

Library 101, www.libraryman.com/blog/101rtk

On being a systems librarian, www.infomotions.com/musings/systems-librarianship

State Library of North Carolina Competencies, www.statelibrary.ncdcr.gov/ce/images/Competencies.pdf

UMD: Technology Competencies for Staff, www.d.umn.edu/itss/policies/techplan/staff.html

Chapter 2

Annoyances.org, www.annoyances.org

Apple Support, www.apple.com/support

Computer and Internet Security, Microsoft Safety & Security Center, www.microsoft.com/security

Drupal, www.drupal.org

Evergreen open source library system, www.open-ils.org

Firefox (Mozilla Firefox web browser), www.firefox.com

Flashblock :: Add-ons for Firefox, addons.mozilla.org/en-US/
firefox/addon/flashblock

FOSS4LIB, www.foss4lib.org

Free/Libre and Open Source Software and Libraries Bibliography,
www.zotero.org/groups/freelibre_and_open_source_
software_and_libraries_bibliography

GIMP, www.gimp.org

GNU General Public License, www.opensource.org/licenses/
gpl-license

Google Apps for Business, apps.google.com

Google Chrome, www.google.com/chrome

Google Docs, docs.google.com

Greenstone Digital Library Software, www.greenstone.org

Hartford Public Library CEO Report, www.hplct.org/assets/
uploads/files/about/CEOReportMarch2010.pdf

Internet Explorer Administration Kit, technet.microsoft.com/
en-us/ie/bb219517

kbAlertz.com: Knowledge Base Alerts, www.kbalertz.com

Koha Open Source Integrated Library System, www.koha-
community.org

LibraryFind, www.libraryfind.org

LibreOffice, www.libreoffice.org

Linux Distributions, www.linux.com/directory/Distributions

LISNews, www.lisnews.org

MacFixIt, reviews.cnet.com/macfixit

Macworld, www.macworld.com

Microsoft Support, www.support.microsoft.com

Microsoft Support (@microsofthelps) on Twitter, www.twitter. com/microsofthelps

Nicole C. Engard Open Source Zotero Library, www.zotero.org/ nengard/items/collection/MB5S62ZP

NoScript :: Add-ons for Firefox, addons.mozilla.org/en-US/ firefox/addon/noscript

Office Watch, news.office-watch.com

Open Source Initiative, www.opensource.org

Open Source Licenses, www.opensource.org/licenses

Open Source Living, www.osliving.com

Open source software in libraries, www.infomotions.com/ musings/ossnlibraries

Planet Ubuntu, planet.ubuntu.com

Practical Open Source Software for Libraries, opensource. web2learning.net

Private Browsing, www.support.mozilla.com/en-US/kb/Private %20Browsing

Public Web Browser, www.teamsoftwaresolutions.com/projects. html

Songbird, www.getsongbird.com

Swiss Army Librarian on using Firefox, www.swissarmylibrarian. net/2008/05/08/using-firefox-on-our-public-computers

The Apache Software Foundation, www.apache.org

The Cathedral and the Bazaar, www.catb.org/~esr/writings/ cathedral-bazaar/cathedral-bazaar

TidBITS, www.tidbits.com

Ubuntu, www.ubuntu.com

Ubuntu Geek, www.ubuntugeek.com

Ubuntu Support, www.ubuntu.com/support

U.S. Impact Study, www.tascha.washington.edu/usimpact/
us-public-library-study.html

WordPress, www.wordpress.org

Zoho, www.zoho.com

Chapter 3

A List Apart, www.alistapart.com

Blogger, www.blogger.com

Code4Lib, www.code4lib.org

Code4Lib Journal, journal.code4lib.org

David Lee King (blog), davidleeking.com/face2face

DokuWiki, www.dokuwiki.org

Drupal, www.drupal.org

Drupalib, drupalib.interoperating.info

Drupal4Lib mailing list, drupalib.interoperating.info/node/88

Facebook, www.facebook.com

Google+, plus.google.com

Joomla, www.joomla.org

Journal of Web Librarianship, www.lib.jmu.edu/org/jwl

Library Mashups, mashups.web2learning.net

Library Success: A Best Practices Wiki, www.libsuccess.org

Lynda.com, www.lynda.com

MediaWiki, www.mediawiki.org

PBworks, www.pbworks.com

Pew Research Center's Internet & American Life Project: Mobile
Access 2010, www.pewinternet.org/Reports/2010/Mobile-
Access-2010.aspx

Pew Research Center's Internet & American Life Project: Use of Cloud Computing Applications and Services, www.pew internet.org/Reports/2008/Use-of-Cloud-Computing-Applications-and-Services.aspx

Pinterest, www.pinterest.com

Twitter, www.twitter.com

W3Schools Online Web Tutorials, www.w3schools.com

Web4Lib Electronic Discussion, www.web4lib.org

Wetpaint Central, www.wetpaintcentral.com

WordPress, www.wordpress.org

WordPress and Librarians Facebook group, www.facebook.com/groups/214139591937761

WordPress.com, www.wordpress.com

Wp4Lib—WordPress for Libraries Wiki, www.wp4lib.bluwiki.com

Chapter 4

Ad-Aware, www.lavasoft.com/products/ad_aware.php

Bill the Librarian blog, www.billthelibrarian.com/category/wireless-libraries-blog

Building Mobile Web Apps the Right Way, www.sixrevisions.com/web-applications/building-mobile-web-apps-the-right-way-tips-and-techniques

Clonezilla, www.clonezilla.org

Code4Lib Journal ("iRoam"), journal.code4lib.org/articles/5038

"Create a Smart Wireless Network for Your Library," www.web junction.org/content/webjunction/documents/webjunction/Create-a-Smart-Wireless-Network-for-Your-Library.html

DC Public Library App Store, dclibrary.org/appstore

Drupal, www.drupal.com

EZproxy, www.oclc.org/ezproxy

Faronics Deep Freeze, www.faronics.com/enterprise/deep-freeze/

Fortres Grand: Clean Slate, www.fortresgrand.com/products/cls/cls.htm

Hennepin County Library Mobile App, www.hclib.org/pub/info/mobileapp.cfm

Libraries and the Mobile Web, www.alatechsource.org/taxonomy/term/106/libraries-and-the-mobile-web

Lifehacker, www.lifehacker.com

"Look Ma, No Wires! or The 10 Steps of Wireless Networking," www.infotoday.com/cilmag/mar01/glover.htm

MaintainIT, www.techsoupforlibraries.org/cookbook-3/maintaining-and-sustaining-technology/remote-desktop-software

Mashable, www.mashable.com

Mashable tools for creating mobile websites, www.mashable.com/2010/12/16/create-mobile-site-tools

M-Libraries, www.libsuccess.org/index.php?title=M-Libraries

Mobile Technologies for Libraries, crln.acrl.org/content/72/4/222

Mobile Usability Update, www.useit.com/alertbox/mobile-usability.html

Mobile Web Design: Best Practices, www.sixrevisions.com/web-development/mobile-web-design-best-practices

Norton Ghost, us.norton.com/ghost

pcAnywhere, www.symantec.com/business/pcanywhere

Pew Internet & American Life Project: Americans and Their Cell Phones, www.pewinternet.org/Reports/2011/Cell-Phones.aspx

Recipes for a 5-Star Library at TechSoup for Libraries, www.techsoupforlibraries.org/cookbooks/recipes-for-a-5-star-library

Serials Solutions, www.serialssolutions.com

Six Revisions, www.sixrevisions.com

Smashing Magazine, www.smashingmagazine.com

Smashing Magazine articles on current trends in design, www.smashingmagazine.com/tag/trends

Smashing Magazine articles on mobile web development, www.smashingmagazine.com/guidelines-for-mobile-web-development

Technical skills of librarianship, www.litablog.org/2005/08/technical-skills-of-librarianship

VNC Free Edition, www.realvnc.com/products/free/4.1

Web4Lib, www.web4lib.org

WebJunction, Wireless Networking, www.webjunction.org/content/webjunction/documents/wj/WebJunction_Pathfinder_Wireless_Networking_for_Libraries.html

WebJunction, "Wireless Success Stories," resourcesharing.web junction.org/wireless-success

"Zen in the Art of Troubleshooting," ccbs.ntu.edu.tw/FULLTEXT/JR-EPT/ballard.htm

Chapter 5

AWStats, www.awstats.sourceforge.net

Citrix Online, www.citrixonline.com

Google Analytics, www.google.com/analytics

Implementing Technology Solutions in Libraries, www.karen cknox.com/ITSiL.php

LimeSurvey, www.limesurvey.org

Request Tracker, www.bestpractical.com/rt

Scribus, www.scribus.net

Search Tools for Web Sites and Enterprise, www.searchtools.com

Snagit, www.techsmith.com

SpiceWorks, www.spiceworks.com/free-pc-network-inventory-software

Useful Links from IFLA, www.ifla.org/en/statistics-and-evaluation/useful-links

Webtrends, www.webtrends.com

Chapter 6

Code4Lib, www.code4lib.org

Code4Lib IRC, www.code4lib.org/irc

Engadget, www.engadget.com

Experts Exchange, www.experts-exchange.com

Guide to ILS Marketshare and Migrations, www.library technology.org/web/breeding/ILS-marketshare-migrations

Lifehacker, www.lifehacker.com

LITA Publications List, www.ala.org/lita/publications

Microsoft Support, www.support.microsoft.com

Microsoft TechNet, technet.microsoft.com

O'Reilly Media, www.oreilly.com

Perceptions 2011: An International Survey of Library Automation, www.librarytechnology.org/perceptions2011.pl

Stack Overflow, www.stackoverflow.com

TechRepublic, www.techrepublic.com

TechSoup, www.techsoup.com

Web4Lib, www.web4lib.org

"Zen in the Art of Troubleshooting," ccbs.ntu.edu.tw/FULLTEXT/JR-EPT/ballard.htm

Chapter 7

ASIST 2011 Annual Meeting Proceedings, www.asis.org/asist2011/
proceedings

CataList, www.lsoft.com/catalist.html

Code4Lib conference, www.code4lib.org/conference

Code4Lib Mailing List, dewey.library.nd.edu/mailing-lists/code
4lib

Digital Libraries Research mailing list, infoserv.inist.fr/wwsympa.
fcgi/subrequest/diglib

Drupal4Lib Mailing List, listserv.uic.edu/archives/drupal4lib.html

ERIL-L Mailing List, listserv.binghamton.edu/scripts/wa.exe?A0=
eril-l

Facebook, www.facebook.com

Google+, plus.google.com

LIBNT-L Mailing List, listserv.utk.edu/archives/libnt-l.html

LinkedIn, www.linkedin.com

LinkedIn Answers, www.linkedin.com/answers

LISEvents.com, www.lisevents.com

LITA Regional Institutes, www.ala.org/ala/mgrps/divs/lita/
learning/regional

LITA-L and Other Discussion Lists, lists.ala.org/sympa/arc/lita-l

NETTRAIN Mailing List, www.lsoft.com/scripts/wl.exe?SL1=NET
TRAIN-L&H=UNM.EDU

Networking for Dummies, www.chronicle.com/article/
Networking-for-Dummies/46091

Norton (@nortononline) on Twitter, www.twitter.com/norton
online

PACS-L Mailing List, www.lsoft.com/scripts/wl.exe?SL1=PACS-
L&H=LISTSERV.UH.EDU

Perl4Lib Mailing List, perl4lib.perl.org

SYSLIB-L Mailing List, iulist.indiana.edu/sympa/arc/syslib-1

Twitter, www.twitter.com

Web4Lib: Web Systems in Libraries Mailing List, lists.web
junction. org/web4lib

wp4lib—WordPress for Libraries Wiki, www.wp4lib.bluwiki.com

XML4Lib: XML in Libraries Mailing List, lists.webjunction.org/
xml4lib

Chapter 8

ALA TechSource "Quick Tips for Technology Training," www.ala
techsource.org/blog/2011/05/quick-tips-for-technology-
training.html

ALA TechSource "Steal This Idea: Learning 2.0 at PLCMC,"
www.alatechsource.org/blog/2006/08/steal-this-idea-learning-
20-at-plcmc.html

Ann Arbor District Library Computer Class Handouts, www.aadl.
org/handouts

Bicycle Tutor, www.bicycletutor.com

Blip, www.blip.tv

Boeninger's Business Blog, www.library.ohiou.edu/subjects/
businessblog

ByWater Solutions Tutorial Videos, bywatersolutions.blip.tv

CamStudio, www.camstudio.org

Camtasia, www.techsmith.com/camtasia

iTALC, italc.sourceforge.net

Jing, www.techsmith.com/jing

LanSchool, www.lanschool.com

LimeSurvey, www.limesurvey.org

MediaWiki, www.mediawiki.org

Microsoft Download Center, www.microsoft.com/downloads

Moodle, www.moodle.com

Net-Support School, www.netsupport-inc.com

Prezi, www.prezi.com

Sachem Public Library, www.sachemlibrary.org

Screencast-O-Matic, www.screencast-o-matic.com

ScreenFlow, www.telestream.net/screen-flow

SlideShare, www.slideshare.net

Snagit, www.techsmith.com

TechSoup technology training materials, www.techsoupforlibraries.
org/blog/fabulous-free-public-technology-training-materials

Tech Training for Libraries, Colorado State Library, www.colorado
virtuallibrary.org/techtraining

TILT, The Information Literacy Tutorial, tilt.library.skagit.edu

Vimeo, www.vimeo.com

YouTube, www.youtube.com

Chapter 9

ALA TechSource Blog, www.alatechsource.org/blog

David Lee King (blog), www.davidleeking.com

Information Today NewsBreaks, newsbreaks.infotoday.com

InfoWorld Newsletter Subscriptions, www.infoworld.com/news
letters

Librarian in Black Blog, www.librarianinblack.net

Library Journal Newsletters, www.libraryjournal.com/csp/cms/
sites/LJ/info/newsletterSubscription.csp

LISNews, www.lisnews.org

LockerGnome, www.lockergnome.com

Mashable, www.mashable.com

METRO Calendar and Event Registration Information, metro.org/events/month

MIT OpenCourseWare, www.ocw.mit.edu

NetworkWorld Newsletters, www.networkworld.com/newsletters/subscribe.html

O'Reilly School of Technology, Online Certificate Programs, www.oreillyschool.com/certificates

Simmons GSLIS Continuing Education, alanis.simmons.edu/ceweb

Technology Grant News, www.technologygrantnews.com

TechSoup for Libraries Blog, www.techsoupforlibraries.org/blog

TechSoup for Libraries, www.techsoupforlibraries.org

TechTraining for Libraries, www.coloradovirtuallibrary.org/techtraining

TechTutorials, www.techtutorials.net

University of Wisconsin–Madison School of LIS Continuing Ed, www.slis.wisc.edu/continueed.htm

W3Schools Online, www.w3schools.com

WebJunction Courses, www.webjunction.org/catalog

Windows Secrets Newsletter, www.windowssecrets.com/newsletter

Chapter 10

"Automation Marketplace 2012: Agents of Change," www.thedigitalshift.com/2012/03/ila/automation-marketplace-2012-agents-of-change

Implementing Technology Solutions in Libraries, www.karen
  cknox.com/ITSiL.php

Library Resource Guide, www.libraryresource.com

Library Technology Guides: Automation Companies, www.library
  technology.org/companies.pl

LisVendor.info, www.lisvendor.info

NJ State Library Technology Planning Resources, ldb.njstatelib.
  org/E-Rate/utechpln.php

"Systems Librarian," www.systemslibrarian.co.za

Technology Planning, www.webjunction.org/techplan

TechSoup, www.techsoup.org

"The Most Important Management Decision: Hiring Staff for the
  New Millennium," www.libraryjournal.com/article/CA156490.
  html

Chapter 11

BiblioteQ, www.biblioteq.sourceforge.net

Blacklight, www.projectblacklight.org

Evergreen open source library system, www.open-ils.org

Koha Open Source Integrated Library System, www.koha-
  community. org

Lib$_2$o, lib2o.info

My Kansas Library on the Web, www.mykansaslibrary.org

NExpress Regional Library Catalog, www.nexpresslibrary.org

Northeast Kansas Library System, www.nekls.org

OPALS, www.mediaflex.net

OpenOPAC, www.openopac.sourceforge.net

Scriblio, www.scriblio.net

TechSoup RFP Library, www.techsoup.org/toolkits/rfp

The Social OPAC, www.thesocialopac.net

VuFind, www.vufind.org

Chapter 12

ASIST Jobline, www.asis.org/jobline.html

Code4Lib Journal, journal.code4lib.org/call-for-submissions

D-Lib Magazine, www.dlib.org

"Dice: Gender Pay Gap Nonexistent in Apples-to-Apples
Comparison," www.itbusinessedge.com/cm/blogs/tennant/
dice-gender-pay-gap-nonexistent-in-apples-to-apples-
comparison/?cs=45244

FreePint, www.freepint.com

I Need a Library Job, www.inalj.com

Information Today, Inc. Periodicals, www.infotoday.com/
periodicals.shtml

"Knowledge is Power for Salary Equity," www.lisjobs.com/career_
trends/?p=337

Library Job Postings on the Internet, www.libraryjobpostings.org

LISjobs.com, www.lisjobs.com

LITA Job Site, www.ala.org/lita/professional/jobs

About the Author

Nicole C. Engard is the vice president of education at ByWater Solutions. She directs the company's open source education endeavors and works with systems librarians on a daily basis. In addition to her responsibilities at ByWater, Engard writes about technology, systems, and libraries on her website What I Learned Today … (www.web2learning.net).

Engard's interest in library technology started at the Jenkins Law Library in Philadelphia, where she worked as the web manager, metadata librarian, and librarian trainer. In 2007, she was named one of *Library Journal*'s Movers & Shakers for her innovative uses of technology in libraries.

Engard received her BA in Literary Studies and Computer Programming from Juniata College in Huntingdon, Pennsylvania, and her MLIS from Drexel University in Philadelphia. She is an active member of the Special Libraries Association and is on the committee that is spearheading the switch to WordPress for all chapter and division websites.

Some of Engard's previous publications include articles in *Computers in Libraries, ONLINE Magazine,* and the *Journal of Hospital Librarianship.* She has also written chapters for *Thinking Outside the Book: Essays for Innovative Librarians* (McFarland, 2008) and *Writing and Publishing: The Librarian's Handbook* (American Library Association, 2010), both edited by Carol Smallwood. Most recently, she was the editor of *Library Mashups: Exploring New Ways to Deliver Library Data* (Information Today, Inc., 2009) and *Practical Open Source Software for Libraries* (Chandos, 2010).

She lives in Pennsylvania with her husband, Brian, and her two shelties, Coda and Beau. You can reach her via email at nengard@gmail.com.

Index

R

raises, negotiating for, 232–33
Ranganathan's Rules, 29
Ratledge, David, 95
Raymond, Eric S., 26, 27
Rea, Liz, 212–17
rebooting, 237
Red Hat Linux, 40
reference interview, 96, 107–8,
    108–9
Regional Institutes, 132
registration, software, 83
Rehman, Ata ur, 93–94
remote-access software, 71
replacement cycle, 116
requests for proposals (RFPs),
    206–10
Request Tracker, 94
research
    resources, 97–98
    techniques, 100–104
    and technology purchases,
        112–16
resources, print, 97–98
restart hotkeys, 237
RFPs (requests for proposals),
    206–10
rights and permissions, network,
    72–73
roving reference, 61
RSS feeds, 177, 178–79
Ruby-on-Rails, 53

S

Sachem Public Library, 152–53
Sams "Teach Yourself ..." titles, 176
Sauers, Michael, 50
Schnaffer, Ann, 233
Schneider, Karen, 142
Schulman, Sandy, 219

screen-capture programs, 93
Screencast-O-Matic, 159
screencasts, 162–64
ScreenFlow, 163
Scriblio, 205
Scribus, 93
search engines, 91
Searcher, 180
Search Tools for Web Sites and
    Enterprise, 91
security
    open source software, 206
    physical, 73–74
    public workstation, 71–74
    and social networking, 126
    wireless networks, 64
self-directed learning, 151
self-education, 176–77
self-promotion, 232
self-study materials, 145
Serials Solutions, 75
servers, proxy, 64, 88, 214
Sheehan, Michael G., 168
Simmons Graduate School of
    Library and Information
    Management, 175
Six Revisions, 60
smartphones, 59
Smashing Magazine, 60
Smith, Julien, 119
SnagIt, 93, 156
social networking, 52–53, 98,
    125–27
Social OPAC (SOPAC), 206
software, 23–46
    antivirus, 32, 71–74
    audits, 82
    buying, 191–94
    content management systems,
        48
    demos, 191
    discounts on, 115

More Great Books from Information Today, Inc.

The Cybrarian's Web
An A–Z Guide to 101 Free Web 2.0 Tools and Other Resources

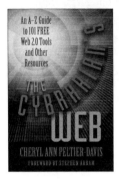

By Cheryl Ann Peltier-Davis

Here is a remarkable field guide to the best free Web 2.0 tools and their practical applications in libraries and information centers. Designed for info pros who want to use the latest tech tools to connect, collaborate, and create, you'll discover dozens of lesser-known resources and learn exciting new ways to use many of the most popular sites and tools. With all this and a supporting webpage, *The Cybrarian's Web* is a winner!

512 pp/softbound/ISBN 978-1-57387-427-4 $49.50

Teach Beyond Your Reach, 2nd Edition
An Instructor's Guide to Developing and Running Successful Distance Learning Classes, Workshops, Training Sessions, and More

By Robin Neidorf

In this expanded new edition, Robin Neidorf takes a practical, curriculum-focused approach designed to help distance educators develop and deliver courses and training sessions. She shares best practices, surveys the tools of the trade, and covers such key issues as instructional design, course craft, adult learning styles, student-teacher interaction, and learning communities.

216 pp/softbound/ISBN 978-1-937290-01-6 $29.95

Implementing Technology Solutions in Libraries
Techniques, Tools, and Tips From the Trenches

By Karen C. Knox

Created for staff who want to ensure success with a technology project that may consume a significant part of the library's budget, Karen Knox deconstructs an entire project implementation, from planning to evaluation, carefully examining each step. She draws on her experience to help readers identify the most critical components of any project while modifying and scaling to meet their library's unique needs. The array of tips, tricks, techniques, and tools she shares here are designed to spell success.

192 pp/softbound/ISBN 978-1-57387-403-8 $35.00

The Intranet Management Handbook

By Martin White

Despite widespread implementation of intranets in recent years, no expert has risen to the challenge of creating a comprehensive guide to intranet management—until now. In *The Intranet Management Handbook*, Martin White fills the gap, drawing on more than 15 years of intranet consulting experience to present a wealth of examples, techniques, and strategies. White's guidance will prove invaluable for any information professional involved in developing and running an organization's intranet.

256 pp/hardbound/ISBN 978-1-57387-426-7 $69.50